JERE CLEMENS KING

GENERALS & POLITICIANS

CONFLICT BETWEEN FRANCE'S HIGH COMMAND, PARLIAMENT AND GOVERNMENT, 1914-1918

GREENWOOD PRESS, PUBLISHERS
WESTPORT, CONNECTICUT

DC
387
K38
1971

Copyright 1951 by
The Regents of the University of California

Originally published in 1951
by University of California Press, Berkeley and Los Angeles

Reprinted with the permission
of University of California Press

First Greenwood Reprinting 1971

Library of Congress Catalogue Card Number 74-112325

SBN 8371-4713-1

Printed in the United States of America

PREFACE

THIS STUDY attempts to fill the need of an English-language account of France's wartime conflict between the formulators of policy and the executants of strategy, a struggle which appears all but inherent in modern industrialized democracy. I wish to acknowledge my indebtedness to Dr. Howard M. Smyth of the Department of the Army and to Professor Franklin C. Palm of the University of California for invaluable advice and criticism in this undertaking.

Without the use of the Hoover Library of War, Revolution, and Peace at Stanford University, I should not have been able to pursue this investigation. The Hoover Library kindly put at my disposal relevant material from what is now one of the world's best collections of war books.

J. C. K.

CONTENTS

1	Background of the Conflict	1
2	Five Months of "Military Dictatorship," August–December, 1914	11
3	The Exercise of Parliamentary Inspection	36
4	L'Affaire Sarrail	67
5	The Verdun Crisis	89
6	Parliament's Ascendancy over the Ministry and Command	115
7	The Tragedy of Chemin des Dames	140
8	The Fabian Policy of Pétain and Painlevé	170
9	Clemenceau's Jacobin Rule	192
10	Foch and Clemenceau	219
	Notes	247
	Bibliography	277
	Index	285

Wars are in reality... only the manifestations of policy itself. The subordination of the political point of view to the military would be unreasonable, for policy has created the war; policy is the intelligent faculty, war only the instrument, and not the reverse. The subordination of the military point of view to the political is, therefore, the only thing which is possible.

CLAUSEWITZ

1
Background of the Conflict

"WAR," WROTE CLAUSEWITZ, "IS NOT MERELY A political act but a real political instrument, a continuation of political intercourse, a carrying out of the same by other means." The successful prosecution of this most complex of all political activities—warfare—presupposes the proper functioning of its three basic agents: the people of a nation, the commander and his army, and lastly, the government. "The passions which are to blaze up in war," declared Clausewitz, "must be already present in the peoples concerned; the scope that the play of courage and talent will get in the realm of the probabilities of chance depends on the character of the commander and the army; the political objects, however, are the concern of the government alone."

Inasmuch as "popular passions" may be considered an imponderable factor, attention can more profitably be focused upon the two agents of warfare which are somewhat responsive to reason and volition: the military themselves and the civilian government. In modern war the military, as the executants of strategy, cannot be separated from the government, the formulator of policy. But since policy, according to Clausewitz, must be construed "as the representative of all the interests of the whole community," it naturally claims primacy over strategy. "Wars are in reality ... only the manifestations of policy itself. The subordination of the political point of view to the military would be unreasonable, for policy has created the war; policy is the intelligent faculty, war only the instrument, and not the reverse. The subordination of the military point of view to the political is, therefore, the only thing which is possible."

GENERALS & POLITICIANS

The paramount claim of policy was recognized by the Third French Republic in a decree of October 28, 1913, which stated: "The government, assuming the responsibility for the vital interests of the nation, has the sole right to determine the political objective of ... war." As a corollary of its control over policy, the government, according to Professor Joseph Barthélemy of the Ecole Libre des Sciences Politiques, could in legal theory "designate the principal enemy; order an offensive at one point and defensive action at another; transport troops to such and such a place. The government would determine the objectives, while leaving to the military technicians the responsibility for taking the measures necessary for their achievement."

Friction between the formulators of policy and the executants of strategy arises from "imperfect knowledge," according to Clausewitz. The framers of policy must not make demands which the strategists cannot fulfill. The strategists, in turn, should recognize that "the main outlines of a war have always been determined by the cabinet, that is ... by a purely political and not a military organ." This interrelationship of policy and strategy takes for granted some knowledge of strategy on the part of the statesmen, and a comprehension by the military of at least the broad principles of statecraft—a degree of mutual understanding which does not always exist in actuality. Since the government appoints the commander of an army, civilian politicians have more legal power than the military. But in the ability to exert physical force, the military, if followed by blindly obedient troops, can effect a *coup d'état* and violently suppress the government. This unpleasant possibility creates a perceptible tension between the military and the politicians, especially in states renowned for past military glories. For, as Joseph Barthélemy points out, "the control of the technician by the non-specialist, by a man who simply possesses intelligence and general culture, is always an infinitely delicate matter...." Even Clausewitz, the honored theorist from the garrison state par excellence—Prussia—insisted that "we do not mean to say that ...

BACKGROUND OF THE CONFLICT

acquaintance with military affairs is the principal qualification for a minister of state; a remarkable, superior mind and strength of character—these are the principal qualifications which he must possess; a knowledge of war may be supplied in one way or another. France was never worse advised in its military and political affairs than by the two brothers Belleisle and the Duke of Choiseul, although all three were good soldiers."

When the functions of policy and strategy coincide in the same individual, as in Caesarism, open conflict does not exist between the military and the civilian element. But the peace of Caesarism is the quiet of the dead, so far as civil liberty is concerned. Clausewitz suggested an alternative to Caesarism: "make the commander in chief a member of the cabinet, that he may take part in its councils and decisions on important occasions." However, the Prussian expert considered "this is only possible when the cabinet, that is, the government itself, is near the theater of war, so that things can be settled without noticeable waste of time."

Proximity to the battlefield may have been necessary in Clausewitz' day for a government to keep itself informed about the unfolding of strategy. With modern methods of communication this is no longer true, since the radio can keep a cabinet instantly informed. But a new form of friction between soldiers and civilians emerged with the evolution of government along democratic lines. When Clausewitz wrote, most cabinets were responsible to kings, but with the rise of parliamentary government they were responsible to elected legislatures. This increased the likelihood of friction between civilian politicians and soldiers, and it had the effect of making the cabinet the confederates of the military in parrying parliamentary enquiry and interpellation. A cabinet answerable only to a monarch could be more independent toward generals than a democratic cabinet responsible to a parliament made up of hundreds of caviling civilians. With the growth of ministerial responsibility, cabinets and commands tended to stand or fall together, except when wily ministries sacked unsuccessful generals to save themselves from parliamentary attack.

Another modern development which led to discord between soldiers and civilians was the mechanization of warfare, which entailed an enormous burden of supply. This devolved primarily upon the civilian government. The Industrial Revolution, according to H. A. De Weerd, "made the workshop as vital a part of the struggle as the battlefield. With the development of railways, internal combustion engines, and communication equipment, with the perfection of weapons through the use of precision machine tools and the adaptation of metallurgical scientific advances, the fundamental interdependence of the military and civilian elements was vastly increased. The changing character of the times required increasing participation by the civilian elements in war, and quarrels between soldiers and statesmen became inevitable."

The specialization of function inherent in modern society merely intensified a latent conflict between the civilians and the military. The increasing size and the diversification of the branches of the armies made it more difficult for statesmen to understand an evermore involved strategy. At the same time, those specialists, the professional soldiers, were vexed by a policy which had to include more and more economic factors in its purview. The problems of commanding and governing increased apace in their difficulty.

Even if there had been no Industrial Revolution, with all its resultant social complexities, generals and politicians would have continued to view one another askance. Especially was this true in France, where the generals and the civilian statesmen were schooled in different traditions. The professional soldiers of France were regarded as the historical allies of their fellow authoritarians, the nobles, prelates, and kings—all imbued with the feudal concepts of order, honor, glory, and *noblesse oblige*. The French politicians, on the contrary, were disciples of the revolution—at least they professed to be—and the ideals to which

BACKGROUND OF THE CONFLICT

they paid allegiance were the bourgeois catchwords of liberty, equality, and fraternity. Herein lay an important ideological difference between the military and the civilians.

French history between the revolution of 1789 and the outbreak of the First World War is replete with instances of open or covert conflict between the civilian statesmen and the professional soldiers. In the great revolution itself, it was suspected that many—not to say most—of the senior army officers were, as beneficiaries of the *ancien régime,* estranged from the leveling policy pursued by the National and Legislative assemblies. After such notables as the Marquis de Lafayette and General Charles Dumouriez quit their posts with the revolutionary armies and went over to the Austrian monarchy, many Jacobins were convinced that a close surveillance would have to be maintained over the military commanders who were supposed to be fending off the coalition armies. Accordingly, in 1793, the civilian government, the Committee of Public Safety, departed from its proper function of framing policy and invaded the jurisdiction of strategy. It appointed representatives on mission, who not only supervised the army's political morals, but even gave military orders to the generals. At only one other time in modern French history (during the Franco-Prussian War) was there such a bold usurpation of the office of the strategist by the policy maker. Needless to say, the representatives on mission improvised make-shift campaign plans, although centrifugal forces operating in the enemy coalition helped save France from disaster.

When it became apparent even to the amateur strategists themselves that warfare called for specialized skill, they were willing to defer to the genius of a "politically reliable" soldier, Lazare Carnot, who was left relatively unmolested in his efforts to raise a great conscript army. Carnot brooked no interference from civilian "meddlers." When two members of the Committee of Public Safety, Maximilien Robespierre and Antoine de Saint-Just, reproached him for using aristocrats in his campaigns, he put them firmly in their place by shouting at them, "You are ridiculous dictators!" Carnot, in his vindication of the freedom of the commander in executing strategy, perhaps unwittingly made possible the swing of the pendulum from the extreme of civilian domination by the representatives on mission to its opposite, militarism incarnate—Caesarism—or Bonapartism.

In Napoleon, the functions of policy and strategy coincided in the same person, thereby permitting quick military decisions and prompt execution. The short-term result was a succession of victories which made the Corsican general the idol of later generations of professional soldiers. The essential irresponsibility of autocratic power permitted Napoleon to identify his own pathological ambition with national interest, with the result that France was bled white on one battlefield after another. Georges Clemenceau's famous observation that "war is too serious a business to be entrusted to generals" might well be applied to the lesson of Napoleon Bonaparte.

After Waterloo, there was little immediate prospect of a revival of Caesarism, the victorious allied powers tolerating under Louis XVIII only a small professional army as a sort of police force. The myth of Bonapartism refused to die, however, and the passage of time merely served to dim the recollection of its bloody reality and refurbish the "glory" of its victories. Under Napoleon III, Caesarism came forth again in full bloom. Once again, France was turned into a garrison state. Once more, policy and strategy were controlled by the same person. As before, the absence of checks and balances so characteristic of Caesarism brought the nation to a new disaster at Sedan.

Militarism created its own antithesis. Napoleon III and such paladins as the Marshals Bazaine and MacMahon and General Trochu demonstrated their complete incapacity to save France from ruin, permitting Paris to be invested by the Germans. At this juncture, the control of the remnant of the French army still in the field fell into the untried hands of two civilian ministers of the provisional Government of National Defense.

BACKGROUND OF THE CONFLICT

Léon Gambetta, minister of interior, and Charles de Freycinet, minister of war, intervened in strategy with the same amateurish gusto which the revolutionary representatives on mission had shown. These two civilians set about ordering a *levée en masse* in the vain hope of throwing back the Germans. The titular commander of the French army, General Louis d'Aurelle de Paladines, was treated with arrogance and irascibility as Gambetta and de Freycinet tried to prod him to go to the relief of Paris. This highhandedness may have represented a degree of poetic justice for the military, but it did not raise the siege of the capital, nor win the war.

The prestige of the professional soldiers, having reached its nadir, was miraculously restored by the success of Marshal MacMahon in subduing the Communard uprising. The military sins of Sedan were atoned by the sacrificing of the *canaille* at "The Wall of the Federals" in Père Lachaise cemetery, where the workers' bid for power was at last suppressed, to the grateful relief of the property owners, the monarchists, and the clericalists. France's generals may not have succeeded in defeating the Prussians, but at least they served as a bulwark of law, order, authority, and property. Radicalism was discredited for a generation, and the ideological alliance between the military, the monarchists, the church, and the *grande bourgeoisie* remained cemented as firmly as ever. The unforeseen inability of the Legitimist and Orleanist pretenders to agree upon the proper flag for France produced a deadlock over the question of the monarchy. While the followers of the Count of Chambord tried to persuade him to accept the tricolor, Marshal MacMahon occupied what was considered to be a temporary presidency of a "makeshift" republic.

The willfulness of the Count of Chambord prejudiced the royalists' chances of success (and, conversely, strengthened the hopes of the republicans), but the failure to restore either a king or an emperor did not chasten the conservatives in France. In August, 1876, a Bonapartist deputy challenged the primacy of the civilian power by declaring to the Chamber: "The army is above existing institutions." This presumptuousness was corrected by the republican president of the Chamber, Jules Grévy, who retorted: "Nothing is above institutions, nothing is above the law of the nation, and nothing is more revolutionary... more factious, than putting the military force above the law."

This was a view accepted—not merely by a Clausewitz—but by a steadily increasing majority of Frenchmen who were not so much interested in *revanche* as in continued peace. Consequently, there was deep concern in 1886 over a new threat of Caesarism. War Minister General Georges Boulanger, a dashing demagogue, won the admiration of the boulevard crowds by his horsemanship; he commanded the support of troops by improving their living conditions; the League of Patriots idolized him for his *revanchard* speeches. However, when the time came for him either to risk a *coup d'état* or be tried for treason by the Senate, he ingloriously fled to Brussels. There, several years later, he shot himself on the grave of his mistress, eliciting the comment from Caroline Remy that Boulanger "had begun as Caesar, continued as Cataline, and ended as Romeo."

The fiasco of Boulangism scarcely strengthened the position of the military in France. But in *l'affaire* Dreyfus—in which a court-martial judged the Alsatian Jewish captain "guilty" of selling military documents to the Germans—the army command seemed to have been given a windfall whereby the Israelites, republicans, and Socialists (who largely made up the ranks of the Dreyfusards) could be exposed as the subversive rabble which the military, the royalists, and the clericalists privately considered them to be. Proclaiming to the world the guilt of Dreyfus (and of his followers) would have the effect of restoring respect for the old feudal virtues of order, hierarchy, and authority. But the proof of Dreyfus' innocence through the testimony of Colonel Georges Picquart, the investigations undertaken by Dreyfus' brother, Mathieu, and Emile Zola's *J'Accuse*, dealt the prestige of the French High Command a blow from

BACKGROUND OF THE CONFLICT

which it never fully recovered. Naturally, a fringe of reactionaries retained a faith in the infallibility of the army which was based more on the substance of things hoped for than the evidence of things seen.

More and more Frenchmen were disenchanted by the cumulative evidence that generals were quite as prone to error as politicians. Furthermore, the disciples of the revolution did not like the associates of many of the generals. The practice of receiving recommendations from Jesuits or Dominicans for officer candidates seeking promotion may not have appeared questionable to a royalist war minister like General Gaston Gallifet, but it seemed so to his republican successor in 1900, General Louis André. War Minister André fought chicanery with chicanery, however, merely substituting the files of the Grand Orient Order of Freemasons as a source of information about officer candidates. When an exposé resulted, André lamely protested that he was only trying to safeguard the republic, even as others sought to destroy it. The scandal of "Andréism" demonstrated that both friends and opponents of the Third Republic were willing to use the army for partisan purposes.

Undue interference of civilians in strictly military matters can be as disastrous for a nation as the refusal of its generals to accept unhesitatingly the authority of the policy-making government. On the eve of the First World War, after more than a century of friction between the military and the politicians, there was cause for concern as to how France would meet the impending test. Would policy and strategy be kept in proper equilibrium? Would a new Committee of Public Safety attempt to dictate military decisions to the generals? Would there be another "man on horseback," militarizing every aspect of life, and trying to resolve the conflict by controlling both policy and strategy? These were some of the problems confronting the nation in August, 1914. Never before had statecraft been such a complicated art. Would the generals, as well as the politicians, grasp its intricacies? Or, could the civilian government, vested with the right of appointing and removing the army commanders, be expected to understand the refinements of a strategy which was to deploy armies many times the size of Napoleon's? These and related questions bearing upon the French war experience from August, 1914, to November 11, 1918, this study proposes to investigate.

2

Five Months of "Military Dictatorship," August-December, 1914

WARFARE IS A SEVERE TEST OF THE STRENGTH AND adequacy of a governmental system, as France was rudely reminded in 1914. France of the Third Republic fell a fairly easy victim to military ascendancy, for her democratic machinery (as set forth in the Constitution of 1875) was too makeshift, too recent, too subject to recurrent attacks from within, and her traditions of military glory too effulgent for the nation not to be doubly imperiled by a foreign invasion. An indefinite prolongation of peace would doubtless have allowed France to continue the consolidation of her hard-won democratic gains, but the exigencies of war affected the nation atavistically—at least for the first five months—throwing her back into a mild form of the military rule which the country had already experienced virulently under the two Napoleons. For a rephrasing of the problem of the conduct of war by a democracy, the French could thank Germany which posed the question for the Viviani government in the summer of 1914.

On August 4, President of the Council René Viviani, the Algerian-born Republican Socialist, performed the unhappy duty of reading to the Chamber Poincaré's war message: "France will be heroically defended by all of her sons, whose *sacred union* in the face of the enemy nothing will break, and who are today fraternally assembled in a common indignation against the aggressor and in a common patriotic faith."[1]

The Sarajevo assassination had precipitated the conflict after a series of crises dating from the war scare of 1875, including the Congress of Berlin, Boulangism, the Schnaebelé affair, the

---

[1] For notes to chap. 2, see pages 247-251.

GENERALS & POLITICIANS

Tangier incident, the annexation of Bosnia and Herzegovina, the Casablanca affair, Agadir, and the Balkan Wars. Now the issue was joined, and France's destiny was very soon to devolve from Parliament upon General Joseph Jacques Césaire Joffre, a portly savior indeed.

That so unspectacular a soldier as Joffre should have been in command of the French army during its greatest trial was attributable to a new minister of war, Adolphe Messimy, Radical Socialist deputy from Ain,[2] who in 1911 was searching for a successor to the cautious, defensive General Michel. After rejecting as candidates General Pau (who wanted to nominate generals and take part in Cabinet meetings)[3] and General Gallieni (who was too old, and too narrowly colonial in experience),[4] the war minister turned to Joffre, reputed a staunch republican and former Freemason[5] and at that time a fifty-nine-year-old member of the Supreme Council of War, whose "equipment was the experience of a single little colonial expedition in early life and a technical knowledge of fortifications and railway construction." Despite these modest qualifications, Joffre greatly appealed to Messimy, since the general was an advocate of the attack.[6] Messimy declared to a group of journalists: "With General Joffre...I shall strive to develop the doctrine of the offensive with which our army is impregnated."[7] Fortunately, the theory of the *offensive à outrance,* which had been the General Staff's fetish for two decades, did not call for great experience in a leader, "for directly an enemy was sighted he had merely to give the order 'Forward!' "[8] This stratagem certainly did not exceed Joffre's capacities.

Joffre had made an orthodox ascent of the hierarchical ladder. Born at Rivesaltes in the Pyrénées-Orientales on January 12, 1852, Joffre, the cooper's son, was sufficiently talented in mathematics to qualify for admission to the Ecole Polytechnique. After his graduation, he served with distinction in China and Indo-China, and in 1893 led an expedition to Timbuctoo, a Tuareg stronghold. Further colonial experience was gained in

MILITARY DICTATORSHIP

Madagascar before he reached the rank of general at the early age of forty-nine. Ten years later, in 1910, as commander of the 2d Army Corps at Amiens, he was appointed to the Supreme Council of War,[9] and the following year replaced General Michel in the newly unified role of vice-president of the Supreme Council of War and commander in chief of *Grand Quartier Général*.

The rise of this unexceptional officer to the command of the French army was described by Joffre's critics as a triumph for the "high priest" of the doctrine of the offensive, Colonel de Grandmaison, chief of the operations branch of the General Staff.[10] According to this hostile school of thought, the newly appointed Joffre was to prove "merely a solid shield behind which subtler brains could direct French military policy...."[11] But whatever his limitations, "Papa Joffre" appealed to the civilian public, who saw in his corpulent frame and his amiable, florid face the embodiment of the *bon bourgeois* whom they instinctively identified with themselves.[12] Such was the nature of the person destined to command one of the greatest of armies, and to gain a political ascendancy as well which, for a season, eclipsed Parliament and subordinated the executive power to a minor role of his apologist and advocate.

Even had Joffre been a person of angelic abnegation, circumstances would have tempted him to extend his nebulously defined powers to the utmost. The heightening diplomatic crisis of the latter part of July, 1914, occurred at a time when France's heads of government, President Poincaré and Premier Viviani, were absent from the country on a state visit to Russia, and consequently the remaining Cabinet ministers in Paris experienced "nervousness" over the course to be followed.[13] No timorousness or uncertainty was felt by Joffre when, as early as July 24, War Minister Messimy informed him of German Ambassador von Schoen's note to the French government to the effect that Germany had given its entire approval to the Austrian ultimatum to Serbia. Sensing the imminence of hostilities,[14]

Joffre lost no time in revealing the scope of his intentions, beginning with a determination to prevent his legal superior, the war minister, from exceeding his authority: supervising the smooth functioning of the army, while leaving its actual operation to the military technicians.[15] On July 25, Adolphe Messimy sent telegrams to all absent general officers and unit commanders, ordering them to return to their garrisons.[16] Joffre immediately called the war minister's attention to the existence of a "document fixing in chronological order the various measures to be taken in case of political tension"—Annexes II and IIA of the "Instructions on the Preparation of Mobilization" (drawn up February 15, 1909, and revised April 4, 1914).[17] Thus admonished, Messimy docilely agreed henceforth "to follow the order" set down in the document. Already Joffre was able to state with satisfaction: "I may say that from this moment, the minister did nothing without consulting me."[18]

The government's submission to the general in chief was to be more gradual than Messimy's capitulation, for it refused to grant Joffre's urgent request that covering troops be sent to the frontier until Poincaré and Viviani had returned from Russia.[19] Messimy, serving as Joffre's spokesman at a Cabinet meeting on July 30, won only a reluctant consent from Viviani and his fellow Cabinet members to station covering troops ten kilometers behind the frontier. But no reservists were to be called up as yet, and only those troops who could march to their station were to be moved.[20] This restrained policy was designed to proclaim to the world the French government's peaceful intentions, but Joffre feared that the Germans might attack by surprise, omitting the formality of a declaration of war.[21]

Joffre strongly protested against the Cabinet's "half-measures" in regard to reservists and moving troops by foot (although he conceded the wisdom of the ten kilometers policy), but he had to admit ruefully that his "objections were without effect; the decision had been taken by the Council of Ministers; M. Messimy could not alter it on his own authority."[22] Joffre felt so

MILITARY DICTATORSHIP

convinced that war was probable by July 30 that he formed the nucleus of his future *Grand Quartier Général,* appointing General Henri Berthelot as assistant chief of staff charged with operations.[23]

When Joffre learned of the German ultimatum of July 29 addressed to Russia, he sent a note to the Council of Ministers, wherein he declared that "the commander in chief would not be able to accept responsibility" for further delay in calling up the reserves.[24] This implicit threat of Joffre's resignation forced the hand of the Cabinet which agreed to the order of general mobilization on August 1.[25] The government maintained its independent position only one day more, for on August 2 it learned that the French frontier had been violated by German patrols at Delle near Belfort, as well as at Joncherey and Baron, north of Delle.[26] At 2:00 P.M. on August 2, the War Ministry telephoned Joffre's headquarters to say that the government "gave to the commander in chief *absolute liberty* of action for the execution of his plans, even if these should lead to crossing the German frontier."[27] Policy thus stood aside for strategy, and Joffre, accordingly, ordered all his commanders in the field "to drive any attacking forces back across the frontier, but without pursuing them further" in order to leave to the Germans the entire responsibility for hostilities.[28] On August 3, France was left no choice when German Ambassador von Schoen delivered to M. Viviani the German declaration of war against France for alleged aerial reconnaissance violations of Belgian and German territory at Wesel and Eiffel, and bombardment of the railway near Karlsruhe and Nuremberg by French planes.[29]

With the outbreak of hostilities, problems were raised which should have been settled long before, had France's halting political evolution permitted.

Her armament was incomplete and she was not supplied with the political organization which might be necessary for the public safety. She had to improvise.... Would the republic survive the war with its constitution? In the face of the enemy, would Parliament meet, debate, govern, or would it abdicate momentarily? Would it hand over the burden of its duties and powers to some dictatorship, presidential, ministerial, or military? Would the omnipotent legislative power be delegated to a commission in permanence; or would its exercise be left to the great commissions of finance, foreign affairs, army; or would it concentrate itself in the electorate of the assembly? Would the legislators subject to mobilization remain on their benches or rejoin their regiments?[30]

That such questions could be asked during actual hostilities indicated clearly that the nation which had once typified the Caesarian or Bonapartist solution of the strategist–policy-maker problem had failed utterly to provide a ready-made alternative formula. Consequently, France at war was to grope by trial and error from the military rule of Joffre to the ministerial firmness of Clemenceau. Though the problem does not admit of any facile or automatic solution, it was unfortunate that the only basis of understanding between strategist Joffre and policy-maker Messimy was to the effect that:

The political direction of the war belongs properly to the government.

The conduct of operations is the exclusive purview of the commander in chief.

The state of siege...confers upon the chief the most extensive powers over all the territory, this authority in the zone of the armies being delegated *ipso facto* to the general in chief.[31]

As expected, Parliament convened on the afternoon of August 4 only to abdicate. No one in France, not even the martyred Jean Jaurès, the peace-loving Socialist whose funeral was to be held that very day, would have dreamed of criticizing this decision at the time, so great was the indignation over German aggression, and so widespread the confusion over the proper role of the government during a military death struggle.

The absence of adequate legislation setting forth the functions of Parliament during war[32] had its origins in past genera-

MILITARY DICTATORSHIP

tions of French history. In conservative circles the military enjoyed a vast prestige extending back to the Middle Ages; among the sons of the revolution most generals were regarded as bulwarks of reaction. Consequently, the army in France had become enmeshed in the complex struggle between revolutionaries and counterrevolutionaries. In so far as the Constitution of 1875 represented a truce in this deep-seated conflict between Left and Right, it had to exhibit marked caution in the delicate question of Parliament's relations with the military, especially during a war. In the interest of preserving this truce, the Chamber had never taken the step of exempting its members from military service. To have done so would have invited the derision of the conservatives and their military allies, who in the best of circumstances had a thinly veiled contempt for "bourgeois politicians." Deputies, therefore, were tacitly expected to serve in the army, although the jurist Eugène Pierre, secretary general of the Chamber, had cautioned the country a quarter of a century before that if no provision were made for the exemption of legislators from mobilization, the legislative power would be paralyzed by the abrupt departure of at least 150 delegates responding to a call to arms.[33] Various halfhearted efforts had been made to confer upon the mobilizable deputies a dual role of combatant and honorary legislator, but neither War Minister Georges Boulanger nor such successors as Maurice Berteaux and Louis L. Klotz succeeded in giving definite status to the wartime duties of the deputies.[34] The only attempted clarification was the decision of Premier Paul Doumer and War Minister Eugène Etienne, stated in a ministerial circular of February, 1906, to grant to mobilized deputies, in event of war, a period of eight days within which to join their regiments.[35] Messimy was able to cite this precedent when he notified the Chamber on August 1, 1914, that their 200 or so members (a third of the roster) subject to war service would have until August 9 to join their regiments.[36]

The members of Parliament apparently shared the generally

accepted opinion that it was their primary duty in a war crisis to defer to the executive power and to the strategists. The belief prevailed that if the legislative branch exercised its constitutional rights of interpellation and enquiry while the country was being overrun by the enemy, only confusion, delay, and disaster would result. The legislators were expected to help create a "strong government," and then abdicate for the duration of the fighting. Especially were the parliamentarians to give a free hand to "an independent high command," which would be "guided only by military considerations." Abstention from the technical affairs of strategy, it was assumed, would safeguard the generals from civilian officiousness such as the "orders from Paris" which were thought to have hampered MacMahon at Sedan in 1870.[37] The legislators, then, were expected to yield temporarily to the executive, and the ministry, in turn, would display its full confidence in the strategists by leaving them undisturbed in their technical operations. The ministry would merely keep itself informed, exercising a passive, discreet surveillance of the army.

Had the war been brief and victory sure and swift, this tacitly accepted plan for the abdication of Parliament and the self-effacement of the ministry before the High Command might have worked without friction. It was generally expected that the war would be short, which would necessitate only a momentary eclipse of the civilian power. The legislators were scarcely more prescient than the military experts, and as General Jean Marie Pédoya testified ruefully, the "General Staff remembered too much the campaigns of 1859 which had ended in two months, and that of 1870 which had lasted only six months; it had envisaged only a war of short duration, only a struggle between two armies terminated by the avowed defeat of one of them. The war administration, of the same opinion, had not anticipated a war between two nations struggling until the complete exhaustion of their military, economic, and financial resources...."[38] Quite unforeseen was what actually came to pass in 1914: a heroic but inconclusive victory on the Marne, a stra-

MILITARY DICTATORSHIP

tegic stalemate, and the tendency of the military to profit from the continuing vacuum so patriotically created in governmental machinery by civilian self-effacement.

President Poincaré's proclamation of the "sacred union" was dramatic in its plea for a political truce but it was somewhat of an anticlimax, since on the morning of August 4 the "fraternal alliance of all Frenchmen" had already been manifested at Jean Jaurès' funeral. The famed Socialist leader who had long been known as a proponent of the citizens' militia, as a critic of the three-year period of compulsory military service, and as a fervent advocate of peace, had been shot on July 31 by an unbalanced young reactionary, Raoul Villain,[39] who apparently thought he was rendering France a service by ridding it of a dangerous "pro-German."

The murder of Jaurès caused a tremor of apprehension to run through the capital. Paris was already fearful of a possible civil war because of the resolution passed at the International Socialist Congress at Stuttgart in August, 1907, which had exhorted the workers to revolt in the event of a declaration of international war by a capitalistic government.[40] But Jaurès had put aside doctrinaire commitments in his speech of July 29, 1914, delivered at a great meeting at the Royal Circus in Brussels: "I have the right to say that at the present moment the French government desires peace and [it] works for the maintenance of peace." The Socialist support of the government was not ruptured by the assassination, for Gustave Hervé spoke for the working class when he wrote in his paper, *La Guerre Sociale:* "They have assassinated Jaurès; we shall not assassinate France."[41] Because of labor's loyalty, the minister of interior, Radical Socialist Louis Jean Malvy, rejected the demand of the *Sûreté générale* which sought the arrest of all the "Socialist-pacifist suspects" whose names were listed in a special police file, *Carnet B.* One can easily imagine the fervor with which eulogistic orations were delivered beside Jaurès' bier on the morning of August 4. These sentiments of the need for "unity," "national appeasement," and "harmony" were repeated in the opening address delivered to the Chamber by its president, Paul Deschanel.[42]

The parliamentarians settled down briefly to the passage of some fundamental laws bearing upon national defense, the first measure confirming the state of siege which had been decreed by Poincaré on August 2. Parliament declared that the state of siege governing eighty-six departments, as well as the territory of Belfort and three departments of Algeria, would be maintained for the entire duration of the war, although it could be revoked by the decree of the president of the republic, acting upon the advice of the Council of Ministers.[43] The state of siege was to be superseded by a state of war, decreed for a part of the territory by the government on August 10.[44] A law was passed authorizing the government to suspend the time limit upon commercial and civil obligations to protect citizens in the army from foreclosures or dunning by creditors;[45] another extended modest aid to needy families of members of the armed forces.[46] Two more fiscal laws authorized the president of the republic, upon the advice of the Council of State and the Cabinet, to decree an increase in the amount of bank notes which the Bank of France could issue and to order the opening of supplementary credits for war financing, even in the absence of Parliament.[47] Thus, until the next regular legislative session scheduled for December 22, 1914, Parliament "renounced temporarily its most ancient and incontestable prerogative, abandoning to the [executive] in fact, if not in legal [theory], the essentials of the legislative power."[48]

Significant politically was the controversial "Law Repressing Indiscretions of the Press in Time of War." This measure prohibited the publication of news, "other than that which would be issued by the government or the High Command," on such matters as troop movements, the size or composition of forces, casualties, fleet operations—in general, any information "concerning military operations or diplomatic affairs which might favor the enemy or exert a harmful influence on the morale of

MILITARY DICTATORSHIP

the army and the population."[49] The effect of this law upon the freedom of the press was ironically expressed in a paraphrase of Beaumarchais by M. Alfred Capus, editor of *Le Figaro:* "Provided journalists do not refer in their writings to the authorities, or to the government, or to politics, or to credit societies, or to the wounded, or to German atrocities, or to the postal service, they are able to print freely everything—under the inspection of two or three censors."[50]

Strict press censorship met with Joffre's full approval, since he was anxious to avoid a repetition of the journalistic indiscretions of 1870 when the Germans had been informed of French troop movements by no less a source than a Parisian newspaper. The declaration of the state of siege already gave the military authorities the right to forbid the publication of "dangerous journals,"[51] but because Parliament feared this power might lend itself to arbitrary usage,[52] the press law of August 4 allowed the government, as well as the High Command, to authorize the issuance of news.

Although this regime of press control did not propose an antecedent restraint upon publications, in actual practice a preventive censorship was established,[53] for journalists found it expedient to rely upon previous examination of their copy by the Press Bureau.[54] The minister of war showed his confidence in the press by appointing on August 12 a commission of forty-five journalists representing all parties and the principal papers. While undertaken in the spirit of the "sacred union" the honeymoon of press and censor was to prove of short duration.[55]

The historic parliamentary session of August 4 closed with a resounding cry of "Vive la France! Vive la république! Vive l'Alsace!" There was a general embracing of one another by the deputies, while the spectators stood and applauded.[56] The chambers adjourned sine die and two hundred members left for military service "with the fasces of the legislature in their knapsacks."[57] France's welfare now lay entirely in the hands of the ministry and the army.

GENERALS & POLITICIANS

The "action" so urgently demanded by the logic of events was begun magnificently, albeit mistakenly, when the French army lunged heroically at the aggressor—but in the wrong direction. Joffre's plan of campaign, known as "Plan XVII," almost brought about a repetition of the catastrophe of 1870, the defect lying in the fact that it simply failed to take into account where the enemy would deploy his forces. Joffre and his advisers, the "Young Turks,"[58] refused "as if on principle" to credit the purpose of the Schlieffen plan, which called for the massing of 36 corps of regulars and reserves on the German extreme right wing to penetrate France through Belgium and along the two banks of the Meuse, while only a few corps would remain in Lorraine.[59] Joffre and his staff rested their case upon Wilhelm II's assurance that "no fathers of families would be in the armies of the first line." From this statement, Joffre deduced the comforting thought that, without reservists, the Germans would lack sufficient forces to extend their front from Mulhouse to Brussels. The French General Staff (except for Gallieni, Sarrail, and Lanrezac) held to the opinion that the Germans would not attack north of the Meuse;[60] they thought an invasion of Switzerland quite as probable.

Obstinately convinced that the Schlieffen plan was a bluff, Joffre felt reassured about his own Plan XVII, according to which he was to deploy five French armies in a lozenge-shaped formation for an attack between Belfort and Mézières, ready to cut the Germans in two if they should be so mad as to attempt a diversion in the direction of Lille.[61] A flanking effort by the Germans might even be desirable, it was thought, for it would avoid a stalemate at the center and thus lead to a fluid battle and a quick decision.

As late as August 15, Joffre still dreamed of executing his plan. To carry out his strategy, Joffre set up his general headquarters at Vitry-le-François, conveniently situated for the anticipated French advance between Lorraine and the Ardennes. No sooner was the general in chief settled at *Grand Quartier Général* than

MILITARY DICTATORSHIP

he showed that he would brook no interference in strategy—however well-intentioned—from the apprehensive government. On July 31, War Minister Messimy had notified General Gallieni that he was being recalled from retirement and would be retained under the orders of the War Ministry, that he would serve as deputy to the commander in chief, Joffre, and as his successor if the need arose.[62] Gallieni hastened to Paris, but Joffre—sensing a ministerial "spy" or a rival—refused to attach him to G.Q.G. However, as a courtesy, General Gallieni was provided by Messimy with a room in the War Ministry, where he remained for a week or two studying maps and the reports telephoned by Joffre at the end of each day to the minister of war.[63]

The government was worried over the presence of Alexander von Kluck's army north of the Meuse (contrary to the anticipation of Plan XVII), and their anxiety was shared by General Charles Lanrezac who averred afterward that it was impossible not to see that the German maneuver would develop chiefly in that sector.[64] Even Joffre's imperturbable calm might reasonably have been upset by the news of August 13-14 that columns of German infantry reservists had been seen north of beleaguered Liége;[65] but with unshakable optimism, Joffre consoled himself with the thought that "the presence of the Belgian army north of the Meuse, in the region of Louvain, was enough to explain the action of the German forces."[66] Joffre did propose to M. Messimy that three French territorial divisions might be placed as a barrier between Maubeuge and the Channel.[67] Three divisions against an avalanche!

Gallieni was by no means so confident as Joffre that the German halt at besieged Liége was a final check.[68] The war minister, likewise, was disturbed—so much so that he sent General Gallieni on August 14 to Vitry-le-François to see Joffre. Joffre gave him short shrift, as he recorded in his *Mémoires:* "I sensed that [Gallieni] was trying to broach the question of operations, and that M. Messimy must have charged him with presenting to me the manner in which he thought they ought to be conducted. One can easily imagine how disagreeable this suggestion was to me, if one considers the responsibility which I was bearing. Accordingly, I broke off the conversation abruptly enough."[69]

Not merely was Joffre complete master of strategy, but he also exercised sweeping administrative authority in the departments threatened with invasion. On December 2, 1913, War Minister Eugène Etienne had issued a new "Field Service Regulation" which gave the war minister the power to fix at "the beginning of war the limits separating the territory placed under the authority of the commander in chief, taking the name of 'zone of the armies,' and the territory remaining under his [the minister's] authority ... the 'zone of the interior.' These limits could be changed, according to the course of events, upon the demand of the commander in chief."[70]

The decree of August 2, 1914, declaring a state of siege, had placed in Joffre's zone of the armies eight entire departments. In these departments the commander in chief exercised extraordinary powers, being authorized by the laws of siege passed August 9, 1849, and April 3, 1878, to serve as the "prefect of police, the great judge, the censor of writings."[71] The "state of war," decreed August 10, 1914, "applied to all the territory the rules of procedure foreseen for courts-martial in the army.... Henceforth, courts-martial in Toulouse or Lyons [for example] were to use the same summary methods.... An individual who had been arrested for seditious libel could be brought before the courts-martial twenty-four hours after being cited; he was defended by a lawyer who had scarcely the time to open the dossier."[72] Fortunately for civil liberties, this drastic course was not always strictly followed, but, nevertheless, this procedure was discretionary with the commander.

Joffre asked for still more control in the zone of the armies, and on September 6, 1914, special courts-martial were established so that the military authority could appoint three judges to try summarily and sentence on the spot a soldier caught loot-

MILITARY DICTATORSHIP

ing, deserting, or mutilating himself.[73] These special courts-martial remained in effect until abolished by the Chamber of Deputies on December 10, 1915.

The right to requisition in the zone of the armies all the commodities needed for the "supplying of the armies" added control over property to the arbitrary powers over persons. The military were given direct control of all means of transport and communication.[74] The military administrator thus "had an immense authority which soon came into conflict with the pretensions of the members of the parliamentary commissions.... The inhabitants of the zone of the army were not able to move about... outside their place of residence without a permit from the local military authority, and no one was able to cross the boundary of this zone without an authorization from G.Q.G."[75]

The territorial limit of the military administrator's jurisdiction proved as fluid as the battle line. As the Germans crossed the northern frontier of France, more and more of the national territory was placed in the zone of the armies, until by the time of the Battle of the Marne, thirty-three departments had come under the rule of Joffre, if not of the Germans.[76] After the victory of the Marne and the stabilization of the front into trench warfare, civilians were to recover control of eight of these departments.[77] This exercise of brusque military control over the daily lives of civilians was originally intended for foreigners, since the sanguine proponents of the *offensive à outrance* had assumed that a war of movement would carry the French forces at once into foreign territory, where the vigilant precautions and rigors of military rule would have been logical in the midst of a hostile population.[78] The administration of a militarized zone well inside France, threatening to last month after month and year after year, was a state of affairs neither foreseen nor borne supinely by Parliament when it became aware of what was happening.[79]

Paris, meanwhile, remained calm but depressed, since the cafés were ordered to roll down their shutters at eight o'clock

GENERALS & POLITICIANS

each night, no theaters were open, and only a few cinemas offered their flickering attractions.[80] The optimistic communiqués carried accounts of the French reoccupation of Mulhouse and of the advance into Lorraine,[81] but they did not explain that this very advance was desired by the Germans, who hoped thereby to bait the Schlieffen trap. The intelligent French public, which had been buoyed up by Messimy, was shocked to learn on August 20 that the vital industrial basin of Briey was entirely in enemy hands.[82] Word seeped out that certain regiments from the Midi had behaved badly at Morhange—Rightists hinting darkly that these troops had been "gangrened" with Radical-Socialism and pacifism.[83] The men of the Left took a different view of the reverses of the 15th Corps. Significantly enough, they insinuated, it had been commanded by that arch clericalist, that "booted Capuchin," General Edouard de Castelnau. An indignant Rightist described how, the day following the check in Lorraine, a politician of the Left approached a conservative and greeted him with the remark, "Ah! Ha! Your Castelnau!" rubbing his hands and smiling with malicious satisfaction at the thought of the general's disgrace.[84]

These early reverses brought Joffre around to making a minor concession to the government. Premier Viviani had "complained very discreetly that he was informed [of events too] sketchily,"[85] a circumstance which placed him in a difficult position in view of the government's responsibility for "progressively preparing public opinion" for what was happening. Joffre consented to the appointment of two liaison officers, Colonel Jean Pénelon and Lieutenant Colonel Emile Herbillon, who would go back and forth between G.Q.G. and the government, carrying "information on the development of operations."[86]

On August 24, General Lanrezac was defeated at Charleroi, and the Germans took in sickening succession Namur, Longwy, Montmédy, Soissons, Laon, Reims, and Maubeuge. The maneuver bore a distressing likeness to a game of ninepins. Joffre was goaded to drastic action: he summarily dismissed Lanrezac

MILITARY DICTATORSHIP

(who had forewarned G.Q.G. of a German thrust by way of Namur) and several score more generals "during the retreat which was mainly due to the blind folly of Joffre himself and his staff."[87] War Minister Messimy loyally supported Joffre in this action, requesting of him that henceforth he "send officers relieved of their command to G.Q.G. by automobile, and there have them court-martialed...."[88] There were to be only two punishments—dismissal and death.

The approach of the Germans to the capital so seriously upset the government that on August 25 Messimy telegraphed to Joffre that "if victory does not crown our efforts, and if our armies are forced to retreat, an army composed of at least three active corps must be based upon the entrenched camps of Paris in order to assure its protection."[89] The defense of the capital of a nation could reasonably be considered a matter of policy as well as strategy, but the government's concern greatly displeased Joffre, who saw in the telegram "the threat of a governmental intervention which would risk ... impeding considerably his freedom of maneuver at a moment when it seemed more necessary than ever."[90]

The military reverses suffered by the French in the frontier battles prompted Viviani to reshuffle his Cabinet on August 26, calling to the Foreign Affairs Ministry fiery Théophile Delcassé. As final proof of the "sacred union," he induced two Socialists, Jules Guesde and Marcel Sembat, to enter the government for their first time.[91] Adolphe Messimy was succeeded in the War Ministry by Alexandre Millerand, who appeared to Joffre's liaison officer, Lieutenant Colonel Herbillon, as a "gentleman very downright, very decided, authoritative, active, and not liking to lose time."[92]

One of Messimy's last acts before leaving the War Ministry was the appointment of General Joseph-Simon Gallieni as military governor of Paris. Despite a Corsican name, Gallieni was a French meridional like his commander in chief. There the likeness ended, for the contrast in appearance between the tall, spare figure of the bespectacled military governor and the portliness of Joffre was as great as the temperamental differences which separated the two. Gallieni was as alert, insomniac, and restless as Joffre was ponderously placid. Finding Paris' defenses in a sad state of unreadiness, Gallieni set to work with great energy, taking an inventory of its needs[93] and obtaining permission from the government to destroy houses which might be obstacles in the zones of fortifications.[94] Old Gallieni was preparing to defend Paris to its last stone if the battle line should reach the capital.

By August 30, von Kluck's army was sweeping so close to Paris that Joffre sent for his liaison officer, Herbillon. With his usual calm Joffre remarked, "And now, my friend, we must invite the government to leave Paris. Oh, not today, but in three or four days."[95] When Joffre's view was made known, some deputies not subject to military service protested to President Poincaré that according to the law of 1879 the government could not move from the capital without a vote of the chambers, which had adjourned sine die on August 4.[96] Guesde and Sembat remarked to Poincaré that convoking Parliament was out of the question since a "part of their members were under the flag."[97] Poincaré was strongly opposed to quitting Paris, but in the Cabinet meetings Millerand reiterated that, as minister of war, he "would not accept the responsibility of letting the government be invested."[98] The tragic siege of 1870–1871 could not be repeated.

The menace to Paris of Alexander von Kluck's and Karl von Bülow's armies was real, it cannot be denied, but it has been suggested that possibly one reason for the transference of the government to Bordeaux was that it "would favor and develop the omnipotence of G.Q.G."[99] Whatever Joffre's motive in asking for the government's removal, the decision to depart could only play into the hands of those who already scorned "politicians." With sardonic humor, the conservatives dwelt upon the circumstances of the "governmental hegira to Bordeaux"

MILITARY DICTATORSHIP

on September 2. It was a flight, they declared.[100] The departing parliamentarians were given the derisive nickname of *Les francs-fileurs* (free runners), and a parody upon the refrain of *La Marseillaise* was bandied about at their expense:

> To the stations, citizens!
> Mount the railway coaches![101]

The lame rationalization of Gaston Doumergue, minister of colonies, was repeated with gusto: "True courage does not consist of getting oneself killed, but in sheltering the government of the republic from the enemy, at the risk of passing for a coward."[102] Parliament had adjourned sine die, but many unmobilized parliamentarians went with the government to Bordeaux. There, the very choice of buildings for their unofficial gatherings gave rise to ridicule, for the senators met informally at the *Apollo* theater, while those deputies not at the front congregated at the *Alhambra*.[103]

Whether Joffre ever intended to put the government in this unflattering position—or whether the parliamentarians were really poltroons at heart—is scarcely ascertainable, but what could not be escaped was the deadly effectiveness of the satire.[104] It even colored the attitude of General Gallieni, who surely was no foe of the republic as might have been charged against some clericalists. On September 3, Gallieni issued an ironical proclamation as follows:

Army of Paris
Inhabitants of Paris,
The members of the government of the republic have left Paris in order to give a new impulse to national defense. I have received the mandate of defending Paris against the invader. This mandate I shall fulfill to the end.[105]

GALLIENI

At the time of the governmental "hegira" or "banishment" to Bordeaux (depending upon the point of view) there was unfolding one of history's decisive battles, the "Miracle of the

Marne." The Schlieffen plan, as is quite well known, originally called for a sweep through Belgium by a massive German right wing which would swing down behind Paris after wheeling through northeastern France. The real subtlety of the plan lay in its astute weakening of the German left wing, hinged upon Lorraine, for the purpose of luring the French into Germany. Fortunately for France, Schlieffen's successor, General Helmuth von Moltke, quailed at the thought of weakening the German left wing and he thereby frustrated the essential stratagem.

Von Moltke was not the only enemy commander to lose his nerve. After an astonishing series of successes, von Kluck's First Army and von Bülow's Second Army bore down upon Paris, having driven before them the Fourth Army of General Langle de Cary, the Fifth Army commanded at first by Lanrezac and then by Louis Franchet d'Esperey, and the British army of Sir John French. The British and the French fell back toward the Marne. Joffre hastily organized a Sixth Army, assigning it to General Michel Maunoury who was placed under Military Governor Gallieni's orders to assist in the defense of the approaches of Paris.[106]

On August 31, General Maunoury telegraphed to Joffre some astonishing news: von Kluck's army had abandoned its direction toward Paris and was veering to the southeast.[107] This information was also brought to the attention of General Gallieni, who ordered Maunoury to get ready to move eastward against von Kluck's exposed right flank.[108] Von Kluck, it appeared, had become separated from von Bülow and had modified the Schlieffen plan by skirting southeast of Paris to regain the support of the Second German Army. Joffre opposed Gallieni's request for an immediate attack on the German flank, because the general wished to give battle only after his troops had rested.[109] Joffre wanted Maunoury to move to the south bank of the Marne, to give the British army and the Fifth Army time and space to prepare for the counterattack.[110] Gallieni preferred the north bank of the Marne as the place for the most telling blow, for if

MILITARY DICTATORSHIP

the counterstroke had been delivered from the south bank, the enemy's flank could not have been turned.[111] Rather, it would have been a frontal collision.

Gallieni telephoned Joffre at G.Q.G. and, by dint of importunate requests, obtained permission to strike north of the Marne "as part of a general counteroffensive by the left-wing armies."[112] Joffre issued an order to the Allied armies of the extreme left to prepare for a general attack on September 6.[113] Millerand wired Joffre: "No objection to your plan of operations."[114] To whom was due the credit for the Battle of the Marne? That question precipitated an acrid polemic, but it is sufficient to say that Joffre "took the final decision," while "General Gallieni had sought to suggest the opportune moment" and had been "the inspirer of the hour."[115] Joffre, as the general in chief, naturally won the lion's share of fame for the "Miracle of the Marne."

Politics reared its head even as the critical battle was at hand. On September 4, M. Paul Doumer, a Republican Union senator representing Corsica and former president of the Chamber of Deputies, wrote from Bordeaux to General Gallieni, requesting the military governor of Paris "to create in his Cabinet a service or a secretariat of civil affairs"—and to call him to direct it.[116] Gallieni's preoccupation with the defense of the capital left him little time for such administrative duties as attending to the police, provisioning the city of three and a half million inhabitants, meeting with the prefect of the Seine and the prefect of police, issuing passports authorizing the bearers to leave or enter the city, exercising surveillance over foreigners and suspicious characters, and organizing counterespionage. Gallieni was, of course, responsible to the war minister as well as to Joffre. After considering Doumer's petition, he telephoned Millerand in Bordeaux and received permission to appoint as his civilian aide this "man of industry, decision, and knowledge." Doumer was assisted by a staff of civilians whose patriotic motives appealed to Gallieni.[117]

Joffre seems to have been uneasy over the collaboration of politicians and a subordinate commander, since on September 7, the general in chief wrote to the military governor: "I will ask you not to turn over to the government information concerning operations. In the accounts which I send them, I never make known either the aim of the operations under way or my intentions; in any case, in whatever I tell them, I indicate the parts which ought to remain confidential. In doing otherwise, certain operations could come to the knowledge of the enemy at a useful time for him. It is for that [reason] that I consider it indispensable that I alone take up these questions with the government, because I am better able to judge what can be said without inconvenience."[118]

This surprising letter revealed fully Joffre's cavalier attitude toward the government. Joffre, apparently, was determined that the ministry should learn military news too late to make possible any intervention on the part of the politicians. Gallieni accepted Joffre's prohibition in part, although he continued to send confidential reports to War Minister Millerand,[119] his superior as well as Joffre's. With a different war minister Gallieni's despatches might have been turned over to other members of the government as well, but it was soon apparent that Millerand was even more deferential to Joffre, more "accommodating" than his predecessor, Messimy.

The government, groping in the penumbra of remote Bordeaux, wanted a more complete account of what was going on in Paris. Gallieni received from Millerand on September 10 a letter which announced the visit to Paris of Aristide Briand, an Independent deputy from Loire and minister of justice, and Marcel Sembat, a Socialist from Seine and minister of public works. These members of the government "wished to speak with him on certain questions concerning the provisioning and the welfare of the inhabitants of the capital in event of siege."[120] Gallieni graciously received the politicians and set their minds at rest. Only later did he realize what was "the true purpose of

MILITARY DICTATORSHIP

the trip: to verify, it seemed, if the rumors current in Bordeaux on the political role attributed to [the general] were correct." Gallieni felt that a conversation "... of only a few minutes was enough to convince the delegates of the government that [he] had only one preoccupation: the defense of the capital...."[121]

Now that the worst danger seemed averted at the Marne, Joffre, the national savior, moved to reduce his rival, Gallieni. The general in chief decided to remove permanently from the command of the military governor the Sixth Army of General Maunoury, which had been originally assigned to Gallieni to assist in the defense of Paris. Joffre blandly explained in a letter to Gallieni, dated September 11, that henceforth the Sixth Army would receive its orders directly from the commander in chief, "because of the situation which removed the entrenched camp [of Paris] further away each day" from operations.[122] There were to be no competitors who might even momentarily vie with the High Command for a public adulation which bordered on the hysterical.

Following the "Miracle of the Marne" and the scarcely less known "Race to the Sea" in October and November, 1914, the western front had become fairly well stabilized into a war of position. Though both the government and the citizens felt relief at the successful outcome of the Battle of the Marne, the failure to achieve a quick decision in the war brought surprise and disappointment. Joffre's liaison officer, Lieutenant Colonel Herbillon, found President Poincaré anxious about the digging in of the Germans along the heights of the Aisne. Poincaré did not respond to the boundless enthusiasm of Joffre's communiqués. "We are stopped on all fronts," said the president to Herbillon, "and we have let the enemy organize himself.... There will still be a battle to wage; this will not be the last, either."[123]

It would have been natural for Poincaré, not to mention Viviani, to have visited the armies after the victory of the Marne. It was not to be forgotten that "the President [was] head of the

Army and the Fleet, and thanks to a personal intervention of MacMahon's in the constitutional debates, he [had] theoretically the right to command them in person like an emperor."[124] Poincaré would have been mad to attempt to exercise such a theoretical right, for usage would not have tolerated it. But Poincaré had to postpone even a visit in his civilian capacity because of the "formal and oft-repeated desire of the military authority" that he forego visiting the front.[125] Were the civilian statesmen, then, to be "quarantined?" Not quite, since on October 5, 1914, Joffre arranged to receive Poincaré, Viviani, and Millerand at the new location of G.Q.G., Romilly.[126] A pleasant luncheon was arranged for the government delegation by Joffre's staff, but a visit to G.Q.G., far behind the lines, was scarcely the same as an inspection of the front.

Papa Joffre, for all his complacency over halting the enemy, was privately concerned over the great consumption of munitions[127] which had resulted in a dangerous scarcity. Joffre frankly admitted to Herbillon that in supplies "unfortunately the forecasts made in the time of peace [were] quite exceeded.... Nearly all the factory workers [were] mobilized. It would be necessary to take measures...."[128] Joffre knew that Millerand would skillfully parry any questions about shortages, even though the war minister had expressed the opinion to Herbillon that "the military themselves had never believed that such an expenditure of munitions was ever possible or necessary."[129]

G.Q.G. set out to obviate any parliamentary "interference" in replenishing exhausted stocks by putting to work, under army control, skilled specialists who might reasonably have been released from military service to work in the munitions factories of the zone of the interior.[130] In the shops of the artillery, the engineers, and the air forces, mechanics in uniform "engaged in repairs, experimented with inventions, manufactured, made a thousand things which should have been made in the zone of the interior.... The armies took charge of the tasks of the interior and there was as much disorder as there would have

MILITARY DICTATORSHIP

been if the interior had mixed in the affairs of the army."[181] As Military Governor Gallieni expressed it, "The High Command, exceeding its role of director of military operations, encroached upon the political domain...."[182]

On December 7, 1914, Lieutenant Colonel Herbillon carried to Millerand a letter from Joffre in which he magnanimously invited the government to return to Paris.[133] On December 11 the return was made, although three ministries remained in Bordeaux: War, Navy, and Justice.[134] Millerand, who was almost more belligerent than the military in defending the authority of the High Command, was reluctant to see the government return to Paris, since the armies and the latest site of G.Q.G., Chantilly, were close to the capital, and the parliamentarians might be tempted to make inspection trips to the armies without the proper invitation.[185]

The period of "military dictatorship" was already approaching its end. It was almost inevitable that France's civilian element would defer to the military during the actual invasion of the country. The crisis caused by the approach of the Germans was regarded as only temporary, and patriotism enjoined "silence in the presence of the enemy" as the nation set about defending itself. This was considered a technical matter which the military specialists alone knew how to solve. When the Victory of the Marne checked the Germans, but nevertheless allowed them to entrench themselves well inside France, a new set of problems was posed. The French High Command apparently intended to apply indefinitely the rigors of military government to its own citizens, a contingency quite unforeseen. Furthermore, the exhaustion of stocks of matériel necessitated drastic measures of manufacture and purchase, and supply was normally a governmental function. The civilian element, therefore, would have to reconsider its role, and reoccupy a place so patriotically vacated. Parliament would have to reassemble to survey new problems and vote the budget. Thus Joffre and Millerand would undergo supervision, despite their objections.

3

The Exercise of Parliamentary Inspection

THE CONVENING OF PARLIAMENT SUBJECTED THE ministry and command to their first taste of criticism—not through public parliamentary attack or interpellation, but through the secret investigations of the commissions of army, finance, and foreign affairs, it being tacitly understood that the parliamentarians would not serve the enemy by raising in open debate controversial questions on the conduct of the war.[1] The finance commissions of the Chamber and Senate were the oldest agencies of parliamentary investigation of army and navy supplies, having been initiated on August 23, 1876. At that time the budget commissioner instructed the finance commissions of both assemblies to appoint two inspectors each to check annually on the state of matériel "through an investigation on the spot and the study of records." This "verification" of war supplies proving haphazard and ineffective,[2] the *rapporteur* of the war budget in 1906, Louis L. Klotz, declared that the War and Navy ministries would have to furnish the finance commission delegates "with all the documents which could be of use to them in...their mission."[3] Still limiting the effectiveness of this system of inspection was the practice of merely "taking inventory"—checking existing stocks against the credits appropriated for their manufacture; the finance delegates did not venture opinions as to whether "what was on hand corresponded to what was needed."[4] Notwithstanding its inadequacy, such was the principal peacetime procedure of verification.

A more effective parliamentary inspection was undertaken by the army commissions of the Senate and Chamber as war ap-

[1] For notes to chap. 3, see pages 251–254.

PARLIAMENTARY INSPECTION

proached. These agencies, which were to assume an increasing importance, supplemented the "accounting" or "inventory" tasks of the finance commissions by supervising the War Ministry. According to accepted doctrine, the primary function of the war minister was to superintend the services of the army, whereas the army commissions of the Chamber and Senate investigated the manner in which the war minister—"the executor of the government"—fulfilled his task of supervision. Stated in the most rudimentary terms, the army commissions supervised the supervisor. The well-known professor of law at the Ecole Libre des Sciences Politiques, M. Joseph Barthélemy, emphasized this view when he declared that the National Assembly possessed the incontestable right to inquire into all the details of the war services, provided it was understood that its inquiries were to be addressed to the government—in particular to the war minister. The government, for its continuation in office, was responsible to Parliament, and so long as it retained the confidence of the legislative body, the ministry was entitled to "full liberty corresponding to its complete responsibility."[5]

The government alone was accountable for the conduct of the war, and consequently it alone should be in direct contact with the army and its chiefs.[6] "It is not the services of the army which Parliament can control, but only the manner in which the government directs them. If it were otherwise, the government would have no more freedom of action, since it would have no more responsibility; the direction would then pass to Parliament, and since one cannot speak of the responsibility of two assemblies comprising 903 members, no one any longer would be responsible for the war."[7]

The urgent need of a parliamentary investigation of the rumored unpreparedness of the French army had been called to the Senate's attention on July 13, 1914, by M. Charles Humbert,[8] a pinchbeck character who was to be indicted for treason one day, a Republican Union senator from Meuse, and *rapporteur* of the Senate's army commission. Humbert gave the senators an exhaustive catalogue of deficiencies in matériel: artillery inferior to German models; outmoded guns for border fortresses; inadequate aeronautical equipment; insufficient gasoline reserves; shortages in cartridges; continued use of the old-fashioned, garish, crimson trousers as part of the uniform; a shortage of two million pairs of army boots; insufficiencies or defects in such supplies as field tents, pontoon bridges, and wireless equipment.[9] Humbert's exposé was so hair-raising that it prompted old Georges Clemenceau to say to the Senate: "Gentlemen ... since 1870 I have not attended a session of Parliament as moving ... as harrowing as this of today."[10]

Humbert's charges could not be ignored by the army commissioners, although many persons tended to discount the senator's jeremiads as part of his alleged arms-peddling activities in behalf of the *Comité des Forges*.[11] But the army commission of the Chamber (the only one in session) had scarcely begun to hear testimony on the charges from War Minister Messimy and his director of artillery when war was declared, and the commission members were called up for military service.[12] The president of the Chamber's army commission, General Jean Marie Pédoya, a Radical Socialist deputy from Ariège, was placed at the head of an army corps at Grenoble,[13] remaining for several months in this inactive sector. On December 13, 1914, he received a letter from War Minister Millerand, who apparently was trying to make a favorable impression by suggesting that the army commission might wish to reconvene. Millerand had nothing to lose by such a "coöperative" gesture, since Parliament would soon meet and its commissions would be sure to undertake investigations. The general reported that Millerand was helpful in furnishing information about the distressing situation in matériel and provisions, supplying him with documents which he discussed with his colleagues of the commission.[14] Pédoya plunged his listeners into such gloom with his account of unpreparedness that "the next day two ministers ... begged him not to continue his exposure,"[15] for the government was immediately

PARLIAMENTARY INSPECTION

seized with faintheartedness over its rash gesture of helpfulness to the commission. Pédoya agreed to discontinue the painful disclosure, provided the government, with the aid of the commission, would make the most serious efforts to remedy so dangerous a situation.[16]

Pédoya, in effect, had intimated that past negligence and mistakes might be condoned; he had not renounced future inspection. The right of such investigation seemed clear beyond all dispute to the commission, stemming directly from the Chamber's right to interpellate the government. Furthermore, the commissions were the direct delegation of Parliament, which selected their members.[17] The commissions, according to Pédoya, clearly understood that they had no power of judicial inquest nor of sanction (which the Chamber could not delegate), but "solely the right of investigation and verification."[18] The commission felt all the more inclined to exercise its right of investigation since Parliament had waived its prerogative of interpellation while the nation was at war.[19] The government, whatever its impulses, could not afford to be highhanded toward the commissioners in view of the special budgetary session of the Parliament scheduled for December 22, to be followed by the regular session set by the constitution for the second Tuesday of January, and customarily lasting until the month of June. If the government should be so misguided as to try to avoid criticism by ridding itself of the chambers, the deputies could simply refuse to vote it more credits for the war.[20] But even if the government should take an "accommodating" attitude toward the chambers, it could assume that many of the deputies—especially the mobilized parliamentarians who were coming to Paris from the trenches of the Aisne and the Yser—would nevertheless be self-righteous and captious, forgetting their own niggardliness in past military appropriations which had often compelled the War Ministry to reduce the military budget from 50 to 75 per cent, thus preventing construction of heavy artillery and renovation of border fortresses.[21]

The special session of Parliament opened on December 22 with patriotic addresses and tributes to the mobilized deputies. The following day, the Senate and Chamber accepted all the proposals of the ministry, "without debate, with a silent and impressive majority." Provisional credits were voted for the first six months of 1915, and those credits which had been arbitrarily decreed by the government since August 4 were approved ex post facto.[22] Funds were appropriated to indemnify persons whose property had undergone war damage.[23] The problem of holding the approaching senatorial elections, which was complicated by enemy occupation of the northeastern departments, was settled by the decision to postpone all balloting until the end of the war.[24] The extraordinary session was then suspended.

The opening of the regular session of Parliament on January 12, 1915, was relatively uneventful since at this period controversial questions were left to the greater privacy of the commissions.[25] It quickly became apparent, however, that most of the parliamentarians expected the chambers to remain in session for at least the regular five-month period as in peacetime, although some conservatives and reactionaries wanted Parliament to hold no more than two or three sessions of a formal nature and then adjourn in deference to the military leaders. The moderately conservative view was expressed by Dominique Delahaye, Right senator from Maine-et-Loire, who bluntly told his colleagues: "Gentlemen, at the present time we ought to be concerned only with our army and with the enemy who has invaded France. The country is not with us.... (Lively protests on a great number of benches.) ... No, no, silence in Parliament and before the army! I am opposed to all discussions not bearing upon the war and the army."[26] M. Pugliesi-Conti expressed a much more openly authoritarian view by declaring that the cavilings and chafferings inseparable from parliamentary procedure could not be tolerated during a time of war, "when authority and responsibility ought to be more than ever con-

PARLIAMENTARY INSPECTION

centrated and stabilized."[27] The editor of the dyed-in-the-wool royalist *L'Action Française,* Charles Maurras, voiced the opinion that the executive power ought never to "account publicly" to the representatives of the nation for its war policy; it might make a few disclosures, but only "as an act of condescension."[28] To a hard-bitten Rightist such as the journalist Léopold Marcellin, these weekly "phantom sessions" of Parliament were to be a mere "practical joke in order to prevent the mobilized deputies from returning to the firing line."[29]

Rightists greatly feared that the soldier-deputies would be tempted to "meddle in strategy," especially since five months in uniform would make many of them feel qualified to pass judgment upon military questions. Two incidents arose on January 6, 1915, which seemed to lend foundation to conservative presentiments. President Poincaré was visited by the mobilized parliamentarian, Lieutenant Colonel Léonce Rousset, a Mutuality deputy from Verdun, who boldly urged upon the president nothing less than a Balkan offensive against Austro-Hungary as a means of breaking the stalemate on the western front.[30] Almost immediately thereafter, an identical proposal was made to Poincaré by Lieutenant Paul Louis Benazet, a Left Radical deputy from Indre and an aide of General Franchet d'Esperey.[31]

These plans for sending an expeditionary corps against Vienna and Berlin via Belgrade were brought up at a council meeting the following day by Viviani and Briand.[32] Poincaré repeated Lieutenant Benazet's arguments (without revealing the source) that a Balkan offensive would aid Serbia, cut off Turkey from her allies, and open up a connection with Russia by way of Rumania. General Joffre was so outraged by this civilian "officiousness" that he declared he "would throw in his hand" before he would consent to such a dispersion of his forces.[33] To Poincaré's challenge that the government would force him to remain at the head of his troops, Joffre retorted that he would go and have himself killed, "no matter where," but never would he remain the responsible chief if the government doled out the resources and tried to impose unacceptable ideas upon him.[34] It was difficult to draw a line between policy and strategy here, since the government possessed the legal right to order the opening of a distant front, yet in actual practice any such effort which was opposed by the military technicians would have had unhappy results. For all Joffre knew, the idea of a Balkan front had its inception with Viviani, Briand, and Poincaré. A knowledge of the true authorship would have outraged the general all the more, because he would then have been aware of the government's acceptance of a parliamentary "interference in strategy." Joffre had become so pampered through the zeal of War Ministers Messimy and Millerand in "shielding" him that he had grown to regard the War Ministry as a buffer between himself and the government; he now expected the government as a whole to protect the command from Parliament.

There was no doubt that civilians—even devoted ones like Millerand—had to approach Joffre cautiously, for French generals still expected deference from civilians. Nevertheless, the general in chief was popularly regarded as "a soldier-citizen of a democracy."[35] Even critics conceded that Joffre, for all his foibles, did not allow political considerations to govern his actions in breaking or promoting officers.[36] Army commanders were popularly classified as "men of the Right" or "men of the Left," depending on their tepid or ardent republicanism, but if Joffre knew of this nomenclature he ignored it,[37] since he certainly was no General André of Freemasonic memory. Only one thing was likely to provoke Joffre into an abrupt abandonment of his toleration—and that was when his hearty appetite was affected by the clericalists on his staff. Jean de Pierrefeu, for three years the writer of the official "communiqué," related that at Chantilly on Good Friday in 1915, Joffre, the gourmet, came down in jovial expectation to his dinner table. Suddenly, he noticed that the table was set in observance of the Lenten fast. Joffre flew into a violent rage, and then and there ordered that

PARLIAMENTARY INSPECTION

meat be added to the menu. He made one of his rare political avowals during this transport of anger. "I am a republican general," he reminded his officers.[38]

There was at least one notable exception to the prevailing confidence in Joffre's loyalty to the republic: the commander of the Third Army, the archrepublican General Maurice Paul Sarrail, suspected that the general in chief was politically unreliable. Joffre related in his *Mémoires* that he had received a letter written by General Ferdinand Foch on December 3, 1914, wherein Foch informed his commander in chief what General Sarrail had said in a conversation with a mobilized deputy:

> Yes, we are headed straight for a dictatorship. When the Germans give in, General Joffre will be promoted marshal and [he] will hand over the reins to General Foch.... You are going to Paris for the opening of Parliament.... Do not come back. It is essential for the Chamber to remain in session and to see that no *coup d'état* takes place.[39]

That suspicions of political dubiety could have been more properly directed against Joffre's Young Turk entourage at Chantilly was revealed in an anecdote of Jean de Pierrefeu's which threw light on the staff officers' contemptuous attitude toward the parliamentarians. Lieutenant Colonel Edmond Buat, who had been attached to Millerand's civilian staff at rue St. Dominique, returned to G.Q.G. for a few days before assuming the field command of a brigade. Fellow officers twitted Buat about his need of "bracing" contacts with the troops after his "impure" association with the politicians. Lieutenant Colonel Buat "courageously" rallied to the defense of the services rendered by the civilians, going so far as to praise the Socialists for their patriotism.[40] Buat's attitude produced an uproar, "halfserious," according to Pierrefeu. Buat was reconciled with his fellow officers a few days later when he agreed that at last he "breathed purer air," and added that he had regained a "healthy spirit" among his soldier companions. So satisfactory was Buat's recovery from the civilian virus that, after his departure, it was said that Buat's "sojourn at G.Q.G. had made him well again, and had rid him of parliamentary miasmas."[41] To succeed at G.Q.G., according to Pierrefeu, it was best "to show oneself to be a merry fellow during the hours of relaxation—and to raise one's voice in the chorus of antiparliamentary maledictions."[42] Joffre was astute enough not to join in this raillery, for as André Tardieu once said of him, "he was a born deputy and knew perfectly how to maneuver in the lobby of the Chamber."[43] Accordingly, he did not want his staff to jeer at the parliamentarians in his presence."

Suspicion between the military and the parliamentarians was thoroughly reciprocal. Parliament, for its part, supplied on January 14 an earnest of what the General Staff and the government could expect in the future. The Chamber's newly elected president, Paul Deschanel, in an address to his colleagues, drew "lively and repeated applause" by his challenging assertions:

Your wisdom will know how to reconcile [moral unity] with our legislative mandate and our duty of inspection. Not in this assembly will the admirable discipline of the nation be weakened. There have been directed against the Parliament of the republic certain unjust attacks: we shall reply to them in time. If we have assembled to compel ourselves to improve, not by silence, but by deliberation, I believe that one of the principal lessons of this war will be, in the future, the necessity of a more rigorous inspection, more energetic than ever. If Parliament had only dared, if it had understood better, France today would have found herself better off.[45]

Deschanel's statement caused Poincaré to register anxiety in his memoirs. The president of the republic was ready to agree that a strong, energetic inspection of provisions and armament would be a progressive step, but he felt that if such "control" meant the substitution of Parliament for the High Command; if it meant the total subordination of the technicians to the legal sover-

PARLIAMENTARY INSPECTION

eignty, Parliament would be usurping a power which it was not qualified to exercise, and France would lose the war."[46]

Poincaré was not alone in perceiving the complexity of the interrelationship of Parliament, ministry, and command. To try to clarify the problem of inspection, General Pédoya, in behalf of the Chamber's army commission, addressed the following letter to the minister of war on January 12, 1915:

> The army commission, upon examining its duties and responsibilities to the Chamber and nation, has unanimously recognized that in the present circumstances it ought to be informed of the measures concerning national defense which the executive power believes should be adopted.
>
> Just as the finance commission has a right of examination and certification of questions of a financial nature, so the army commission ought to have the right of examination and verification of questions of a military nature, without, however, interfering in any way with the movements and conduct of troops, and without extending its action beyond the zone of the interior....
>
> The commission of the army greatly desires to assist in national defense by collaborating closely with the government. In this [connection], I have the honor to ask your coöperation [in] giving to the different directors of your ministry... the necessary orders to assist the subcommissions [in] the mission which has been confided to them.
>
> The army commission fully recognizes that there are interesting data on national defense which ought to remain absolutely secret; moreover, it assumes the responsibility of making public only those documents and facts which do not seem to you to be of a confidential character."[47]

Pédoya candidly admitted in his book on the work of the army commission that "the members of the commission had desired [to extend] the right of investigation well into the zone of the armies... but [they] wished to avoid collisions [and] conflicts; [they] dreaded to disturb the government and the High Command.... [They] had decided from the first to limit inspection to the zone of the interior.... For the moment, [they] expected to exercise inspection... only in the arsenals, factories, and war plants for the purpose of ascertaining the kinds of matériel... the causes of insufficient production... and the value of manufactured products."[48] They wanted to "discover the faults and to call the attention of the responsible authorities to these various matters. [They] wished, moreover, to assure [themselves] that the supplies sent to the armies approximated what the general in chief declared indispensable."[49]

In writing to Millerand, Pédoya ostentatiously renounced any intention of extending investigation "beyond the zone of the interior," yet in his explanatory statement he readily conceded that only the expedient desire of avoiding conflict with the ministry and command caused the commissioners to suspend for a time their intention of pushing missions "well into the zone of the armies." Pédoya's policy of disingenuousness foreshadowed a prolonged contest with the war minister. In view of the insufficiency of regulations governing the work of the army commissions, it was only natural for them to try to extend their inspections into the very trenches; likewise, the war minister would bend every effort to circumscribe the commissions as closely as possible even in the zone of the interior. Constant probing and pushing by the commissions was as inevitable as Millerand's countervailing efforts to protect Joffre's autonomy in the zone of the army and his own authority at the War Ministry.

The Senate followed the lead of the Chamber in convening its army commission of 36 members to supplement the work of its only permanent commission in peacetime—finances.[50] Public favor was much more attracted toward the Senate's army commission than the Chamber's, since the senatorial commission had among its members such well-known figures as its president, Charles de Freycinet from Seine, secretary general of the Ministry of War with Gambetta in 1870–1871; its vice-president, Paul Doumer, representing Corsica; the redoubtable Georges

PARLIAMENTARY INSPECTION

Clemenceau from Var; Louis Charles Boudenoot from Pas-de-Calais, a graduate of the Ecole Polytechnique; Jules Jeanneney from Haute-Saône, future undersecretary of state in the 1918 Cabinet; and Charles Humbert, the popular but questionable Lorrainer.[51] As compared with these celebrities who for years had shown "patriotic foresight" by demanding more armament, the army commission of the Chamber had such relatively commonplace figures as General Pédoya—not to mention openly "suspect" members like Pierre Renaudel and Maurice Viollette. Renaudel, the successor of Jaurès as director of Socialist *L'Humanité,* was unable to live down the "taint" of pacifist suspicions, for in the 1914 elections he had denounced "the folly of armaments."[52] Viollette, of the Republican Socialist group, had difficulty in explaining away his vote of March 26, 1914, which he had cast against the proposed credits for much-needed heavy artillery.[53]

Millerand wished to make the War Ministry as well as the zone of the armies difficult of access to all except the professional military. So determined was Millerand to convert the War Ministry into something sacrosanct that he even rebuked Poincaré—the titular head of the army and the fleet—when the President visited rue St. Dominique to question the director of aeronautics, General Edouard Hirschauer, concerning reports of greater German efficiency in plane construction. The director of aeronautics acknowledged to Poincaré that general headquarters had been a "little too indifferent" to the need of rapid construction.[54] Millerand, upon learning of Poincaré's visit, immediately protested against the president's act in "going over his head" and interrogating one of the war minister's subordinates. Poincaré was almost pensive in his account of this reproof in his memoirs. "Thus," he wrote, "in the course of hostilities, when I wish to know the condition of our armament, a minister, who is one of my oldest friends, pretends to leave me less power than a senator or a deputy; I must not confer with a chief of the service without his previous consent."[55] Millerand, nominally Joffre's superior, proved a veritable fortress of Verdun for the High Command, deflecting criticism and complaints. Lieutenant Colonel Charles Bugnet, in describing Millerand, observed approvingly that "the minister...unyielding and obstinate, is moved by nothing; he shrugs his shoulders and smiles; everything slides over him without affecting his nerves, without troubling his sangfroid."[56]

General Pédoya, for all his promise of remaining in the interior, was resolved to surmount Millerand's barriers and to push his missions of inspection as far as he could. Pédoya sent a formal request to Millerand on January 25 for authorization to visit Verdun in his capacity as president of the army commission of the Chamber. The war minister supplied Pédoya with a pass containing the inscription: "I authorize you to go to Verdun in military title, with the reservation that you will travel under discipline."[57] Verdun, incontestably, was well within the zone of the armies, but even so, Millerand's proviso was not accepted by Pédoya or his commission,[58] since they were trying to extend the scope of their missions without admitting it openly. Millerand took an even more intractable stand against the president of the health service branch of the subcommission of the army, who wanted to go to the zone of the armies to visit medical units and to "follow the [course of] a casualty from the moment he fell on the battlefield, to his final hospitalization." Millerand refused to authorize such an investigation in the battle zone.[59]

The right to enter the army zone was at least debatable, but the army commission of the Chamber learned that Millerand had imposed an interdict upon all members of Parliament—even upon the members of the duly constituted army commission itself—denying them entrance to the Ministry of War which was, beyond question, in the zone of the interior. Pédoya protested against this obstruction which would have made it impossible for the commission to fulfill the duties which were expected of it.[60] The war minister replied to this protest as follows: "At the present moment the ministry is swamped. If in

PARLIAMENTARY INSPECTION

addition to the manifold tasks incumbent upon it there are to be demands coming from a hundred or so deputies, it will be impossible to fulfill them. The directors will reply only to the presidents of the commissions, or in their stead, to the vice-presidents, to the presidents of the subcommissions, and to the *rapporteurs*."[61] There was no question but what Millerand was partly justified in his desire not to be unduly annoyed by the aggressive parliamentarians. The writer, Léopold Marcellin (who was usually jaundiced in his attitude toward the civilians' role in the war), estimated that between January 1 and March 14, 1915, more than twelve hundred questions were addressed in writing to the War Ministry, either by commissions, or by the parliamentarians. Moreover, some of these questions were stupidly hypothetical, as for example, the one submitted by a commission member who wanted to know the "forecasts concerning the number of wounded by the end of hostilities."[62]

Pédoya reported that his army commission was willing to accept Millerand's limitations upon the persons who would be authorized to enter the War Ministry. But then the commission learned that, in actual practice, only the president of the commission could gain entrance to the closely guarded penetralia of the rue St. Dominique. Even the vice-presidents and the *rapporteurs* were not received by certain of the directors.[63] Pédoya and his colleagues immediately responded to Millerand's challenge by passing a resolution: "The commission of the army declares that the orders concerning admission to the services of the War Ministry do not apply to members of the commission of the army."[64] Millerand had to raise the interdict, since the *rapporteurs* of the commission obviously could not fulfill their functions if they were forbidden to go to the proper quarters for information.[65] Pédoya, proceeding with jaunty confidence, had boldly attempted to push his first mission to Verdun, far in the zone of the armies; the war minister, with equal effrontery, had tried to curtail the legitimate activity of the commission even in the zone of the interior.

Conflict soon broke out anew over inspection missions in the interior. This time the dispute was over parliamentarian visits to factories engaged in war work. When the Chamber's subcommission charged with supervising the army's clothing supply was informed that the troops' shoes and uniforms were of bad quality, it felt the need of an investigation. The necessary authorization was refused it.[66] Millerand insisted that a request for inspection should be addressed to him by the president of the commission, who would indicate which factory was to be visited. Such previous notification would have made unannounced control—"the only kind effective"—quite impossible. The subcommission of clothing offered its collective resignation in protest and passed a resolution of censure: "The fourth subcommission, finding it impossible to fulfill suitably the mission assigned to it, despite the declarations made by the minister before the commission of the army, expresses its regrets upon not being able to continue the work of collaboration and inspection which it had undertaken."[67]

Before confronting Millerand with the *fait accompli* of a collective resignation—a drastic step, which, undoubtedly, would have resulted in a demand for a full-scale investigation before Parliament—Pédoya wanted to remonstrate with the war minister. Millerand was asked for precise information on the rights of the subcommissions. A prolonged discussion ensued, and it was finally conceded by the minister that the subcommissions had the right to visit war plants in the zone of the interior without restrictions.[68] The minister tried further to define the proper limits of the subcommissions' field of action by sending Pédoya a written explanation. "There are two well-marked spheres," he wrote, "the zone of the interior, which depends upon the minister; the zone of the army, which is not in my province. It depends upon General Joffre. General Joffre does not want it invaded by civilians. Always send to me the program of what the commissions wish to see at the front, and I will submit it to the general in chief."[69]

PARLIAMENTARY INSPECTION

The commissioners had their complaints against Joffre and his sentry, Millerand, but the general had his grievances also. Joffre expressed disapproval of the frequency of parliamentary interventions and of the dubious "comings and goings" of the mobilized deputies, who seemed almost to be shuttling between the Chamber and the armies.[70] Joffre wrote a letter to Millerand (who forwarded it to the Council of Ministers), wherein the general in chief expressed the view that the deputies should choose between Parliament and the army, and once the choice was made, that it should be held with no further vacillation. Either they ought to remain at the Palais Bourbon, or they should stay at their military posts,[71] since they could hardly fulfill both tasks at the same time.

One of the first undertakings of the recently convened senatorial army commission revealed the spirit of parliamentary audacity and "aggressiveness" which Joffre found so irritating. Commission President de Freycinet and his colleagues confidently proposed that the 500,000 idle troops which the High Command had been holding as reserves to fill the gaps in "existing formations" might be more profitably employed as a newly organized army of maneuver which could suddenly appear on the battlefield, break the enemy lines, and thereby liberate France.[72] This plan was doubtless conceived as a legitimate senatorial enquiry into the adequate use of military resources—of which man power was a part—but it demonstrated the difficulty of fulfilling parliamentary supervision without encroaching upon the functions of the war minister, or in this case, the commander in chief himself. Millerand simply ignored the proposal when the commission first broached it in a letter of January 22, 1915. Refusing to be so easily balked, the senatorial army commission blandly went over Millerand's head on February 9, 1915, addressing a letter directly to President Poincaré which called his attention to the advisability of organizing an army of maneuver out of the idle reserves.[73]

In view of a possible constitutional irregularity in this novel procedure whereby a parliamentary commission addressed itself—not to the ministry—but to the president of the republic, Poincaré cautiously agreed to discuss the proposed army of maneuver only in the presence of President of the Council Viviani and the war minister.[74] At the meeting held in the Elysée, Millerand appeared adamant in opposing the plan, but Poincaré tried discreetly to make the senatorial delegates understand that, apart from Millerand, the government would probably be receptive.[75]

Poincaré became so interested in the proposal that he visited Commission President de Freycinet on February 14 to tell him that even Millerand privately supported the government and the commission on the question of the army of maneuver.[76] The general in chief opposed it, for Joffre feared that precisely those reserves would go into the new army which were needed to reconstitute badly depleted old units. De Freycinet tried tactfully to suggest that Joffre need have no fears that the new army of maneuver would be assigned to another chief, since the commission was willing for it to remain under Joffre's command. Poincaré explained that the government—with Millerand's tacit concurrence—was determined to form the new units, but that "it was necessary to humor Joffre, who had already spoken of resigning."[77]

President Poincaré, as a student of the political world, was well qualified to pass judgment upon Millerand. The stiff-necked war minister, in Poincaré's opinion, was a woeful politician. Millerand, it seemed, distrusted the discretion of several of the commissioners and he showed his suspicion by a flat refusal to discuss such topics as the total size of the forces with the senatorial army commission, before which he appeared on February 18. Poincaré observed that if Millerand had "informed individually the members of whom he was sure, and had not opposed everyone indiscriminately," he would have avoided much misunderstanding.[78] For Millerand was quite capable of

PARLIAMENTARY INSPECTION

winning a favorable response when he was in the right mood. At the session of February 23, for example, the war minister addressed the senatorial army commission "for more than an hour, speaking with clarity and an admirable logic." He willingly compared the volume of war production in August, 1914, with the output in February, 1915. "Clemenceau ventured some objections," Viviani told Poincaré, "but he was turned to stone."[79] Léopold Marcellin, the Rightist author, was convinced "that the most serious complaint which the deputies had against Millerand was his unsociability. He does not frequent the lobbies, he does not pat the deputies on the back, he does not chat with them...."[80]

General Pédoya contended with more than the "aloofness" of the war minister when he blandly notified Millerand on May 5, 1915, that he intended to make an inspection of the Dunkirk and Yser sectors, where the Germans had launched the first gas attacks.[81] When Pédoya telephoned G.Q.G. to obtain a pass for Dunkirk, he was asked, "Do you wish to go to the front as a general?" His reply to the effect that he wished to make the trip "as the president of the commission of the army" did not satisfy the spokesman of G.Q.G., who told him that the "commander in chief, Joffre, wishes to know what you want to do at Dunkirk." Pédoya's response was curt for one who had renounced the intention to enter the zone of the armies. "I have no explanations to give; the president of the army commission wishes to go to the front because he believes that he ought to go there." This defiance provoked the G.Q.G.'s spokesman to threaten Pédoya with "arrest" if he tried to make the trip without further explanation.[82] Pédoya retorted: "If I am arrested, the commission will know what to do." G.Q.G., anxious to avoid a political squabble, backed down at this point, and Pédoya made the trip in the company of a fellow commissioner without further hindrance. Pédoya's experience (as well as two similar cases) emboldened the Chamber's commissioners of the army to draw up the following strongly worded resolution.

The commission, resolved as always not to interfere in the conduct of operations,

Declares that, notwithstanding its efforts, it is quite impossible to fulfill the mandate which it holds from the Chamber, in the face of the difficulties created by the government for the delegates in carrying out their investigations at the places where inspection is required,

Decides unanimously that its authorized representatives must be allowed henceforth to go wherever it will be judged necessary to make their investigations, whether in the zone of the interior or the zone of the armies.[83]

This, in truth, was a ringing assertion—especially the reference to the alleged right of the parliamentarians to go "wherever ... necessary," even in "the zone of the armies." Upon further reflection it was agreed that it might be more politic for the commission to bring the matter orally before the war minister.

Millerand was summoned before the army commission on May 7 to hear the resolution. His reaction to the commissioners' claims was spirited for a man usually so phlegmatic.

I have, Mr. President, only one thing to say in response. When the day comes that the army commission offers an example of resistance to the orders of the commander in chief (which would astonish me), Parliament will judge the claims which you have communicated to me. I say "claims." I am entirely willing to assist the army commission in the accomplishment of its mission, but one consideration takes priority above all others, the interest of national defense, the interest of the army. When the general in chief says: "I do not judge it possible to grant this permission," while I have confidence in the general in chief it will not be done except as he deems necessary.[84]

General Pédoya replied to the war minister that "the commission had not entered into a discussion with the general in chief, since it recognized only the government." He went on to enumerate all the persons—from photographers to municipal councilors of Paris—who had been granted permits to visit the front, a right denied only to the army commissioners. Even more offensive was the fact that authorizations of visits "had been

PARLIAMENTARY INSPECTION

given to members of Parliament under the reservation that they took no part in the [work of] the army commission."[85] Millerand was reminded that while he had his responsibilities, the commissioners also had theirs. "The commission has decided that its members will go wherever I, the president (who has been entrusted by them with that title) will deem it useful to send them."[86]

Pédoya was no longer making a pretense of avoiding conflict by remaining in the zone of the interior. His new claim of the right to send commissioners wherever he wished would have meant the virtual erasure of the demarcation line between the zone of the interior and the zone of the armies,[87] and no one was more aware of this than Millerand, who delivered a sharp riposte. He called Pédoya's attention to the fact that the minister of war was answerable to Parliament—not to the army commission. "This responsibility I assume entirely. The trial to which you are subjecting me (in the best faith in the world, I do not doubt) is a tendentious one." The war minister acknowledged that persons had been allowed to go to the front who ought not to have been permitted to pass, but it was "through the faults of subordinates rather than of G.Q.G."[88] He repeated that he had taken measures to prevent a repetition of the abuse. Millerand expressed "deference" for the commission and denied that prejudice had been shown against either the army commission of the Senate or the Chamber. But the war minister, he declared, was bound to observe the regulations, and that he was going to do "solely in consideration of the interests of France."[89]

Pédoya denied that the army commission was holding a "tendentious trial" either of Millerand or of the government, but it "wanted [its] rights and those of Parliament respected." Millerand could not ignore such a case as that of two commissioners who were recently sent on a mission to a town "near the zone of the armies," only to be arrested on the order of a general.[90]

It is inadmissible [Pédoya asserted] that we are not allowed to make certain investigations, that we are prevented from rendering an account of how the service for transporting the wounded is organized. We know that on the front 40,000 rifles are lost each month and it is our responsibility to seek the cause of this loss. It is not a question of our meddling in concerns of a purely military nature, still less in the [matter of] leading the troops, but it is our duty to perform investigations. The army commission has its rights and it wishes to have them respected. The question is grave. It has decided unanimously to bring its resolution (if it is not accepted) before Parliament and, if necessary, to resign and to make the nation judge. You would be wise, Mr. Minister, to accept my proposition. I repeat, it is not a question of our intervening in any fashion or degree in the conduct of operations. It is I who, as president, will designate the missions under my responsibility; it is I alone who will deliver the authorizations to go to the front and who will sign them.[91]

Millerand's retort to this declaration was brief and pointed: "I have nothing to reply; I am ready to collaborate with the commission, but I cannot allow it to substitute itself for me."[92] With this Parthian shot, the war minister withdrew. The next day Pédoya went to rue St. Dominique "to demand a reply" to his definition of the commissioners' rights in the zone of the armies. The president of the Chamber's army commission had a "long discussion" with Millerand, who proved conciliatory to the point of promising support of Pédoya's proposition in transmitting it to Joffre,[93] if each time a mission to the front was ordered its purpose and itinerary would be furnished. Pédoya readily agreed (thinking the matter settled), and suggested afterward to his colleagues that they should go to the zone of the armies "only for a serious military purpose, upon real necessity, and with the desire to avoid conflict."[94]

According to Colonel Emile Herbillon, Joffre was understandably suspicious of the motives of Pédoya. The members of the commission of the army, said the general in chief, "have the presumption of going wherever they might wish, simply with an order... signed by the president of the commission. It is Pédoya who would become the grand inspector of everything

PARLIAMENTARY INSPECTION

which takes place in my armies. That is not to be tolerated; I have told M. Millerand that I would never accept it."[95]

The unremitting efforts of the commissioners to inspect matériel at the front and the reluctance of the War Ministry and command to admit them posed a dilemma which was succinctly expressed by Poincaré. "The minister is right," wrote Poincaré, "in wishing to govern. The commission, elected by the Chamber, is right in wishing to inspect. Is it impossible to reconcile their respective rights and to separate inspection from execution?"[96] In the opinion of Colonel Herbillon, G.Q.G. did not deny the theoretical right of parliamentary inspection, but it was apprehensive especially over the unauthorized "side trips" of the commissioners in the zone of the armies. "The parliamentarian departs on a well-defined mission wherein he is given assistance, but sometimes he forgets the goal in order to see something which interests him more. It is oftentimes in regions and places which to enter would be to endanger the secrecy of operations."[97]

There was a kind of irony in what befell the war minister when he decided to visit the front for himself barely a week after his skirmish with Pédoya over the question of parliamentary inspections in the zone of the armies. Millerand asked Colonel Herbillon to prepare for him an itinerary of a visit on May 15 to the armies in the Artois sector, with a return trip via Chantilly for the purpose of seeing Joffre. When Joffre learned of this, he said to his liaison officer: "Tell M. Millerand that he may come to see me, if that pleases him, but I request him not to go where there is fighting. That would trouble people."[98] Herbillon tried to remonstrate with Joffre by assuring him that Millerand "would disturb no one," and by pointing out that the war minister merely wished to go to G.Q.G. "to give an account of events." Herbillon thought that Millerand—"as jealous of [Joffre's] authority as [Joffre] could be himself"[99]—should be allowed to visit the front, since he could then "reply to those who accused him of letting the general in chief put him under a bushel, [thereby] denying all action to the government." When Millerand was told of Joffre's attitude, he burst out laughing good-naturedly, saying to Herbillon that "of course he would go to the front."[100] Joffre's secretiveness may have aroused only the amusement of his indulgent war minister, but in the opinion of many of the parliamentarians it was no matter for jesting. Even Joffre's own liaison officer conceded that the attitude of the entourage of the general in chief played into the hands of "the adversaries of the general in Parliament," since Joffre's staff seemed "to consider the zone of the armies as their own domain where no one, except the initiated, was entitled to cast a glance. It might be well and good to forbid access to the indiscreet, but it is unthinkable to try to prevent the *government* from going there...."[101]

Especially irritating to Joffre and his staff were the "shuttle trips" between Paris and the front of such a soldier-parliamentarian as Abel Ferry, a Radical Left deputy from Vosges, and a nephew of the renowned Jules Ferry. Soldier-deputy Ferry had been the undersecretary of state for foreign affairs in the Viviani Cabinet, and for the first six months of the war a second lieutenant at Verdun.[102] Joffre's liaison officer soon perceived that Ferry was certain "to have a serious influence in circles less and less friendly" toward the High Command, for the soldier-deputy "was as brave as his sword, loving danger and inspiring confidence."[103] Abel Ferry was not in the least reluctant to make political use of his personal knowledge of conditions at the front. As early as October 13, 1914, in a letter addressed to President Poincaré, he had called attention to the German superiority in aviation and artillery.[104] When Parliament convened in December, 1914, Lieutenant Ferry returned for a short time to his seat at the Council of Ministers, but soon he "shuttled" back and forth between Paris and his staff assignment with the 2d Army Corps of General Augustin Gérard. On March 22, 1915, Ferry addressed a long memorandum to the Viviani Cabinet, criticizing the High Command for failing to follow up its initial suc-

PARLIAMENTARY INSPECTION

cess after piercing the enemy lines in the Hurlus sector. The High Command, wrote Ferry, changed generals too frequently and located its headquarters too far away from the theater of operations.[105]

Soon after drafting the memorandum, Ferry appealed to President Poincaré to try to cancel the attack ordered for April 12 on the Maizeray-Marcheville front, since it had rained so heavily "that some of the wounded had been drowned."[106] Despite the inundation, the attack was ordered as scheduled, causing "the staff officers to weep," for the anticipated result was realized: "Not a trench taken; three thousand men felled."[107] The criticism of G.Q.G. was renewed on April 27—this time when Ferry, in person, read a note to the Council of Ministers.[108] He charged that G.Q.G. was staffed with officers "who had not foreseen this war, who had not studied it, who had not witnessed it," and as a corrective, he suggested that general staff officers might be required to serve for a time with active commands.[109] Balance could be restored to a general staff overloaded with artillery and engineering officers by adding some infantrymen.

Millerand was inclined to ignore this brashness, but G.Q.G. was concerned over allowing a subaltern officer (albeit a mobilized deputy) to criticize the commander in chief and his staff.[110] G.Q.G. followed the sly course of waiting to catch the lieutenant in an error. A pretext was afforded when Ferry incorrectly listed the serial number of an insolent gendarme whom he reported for disciplinary action.[111] Joffre seized upon this trifling mistake as an excuse to teach a lesson to the young parliamentarian who played at strategy. On May 20, 1915, Joffre ordered Ferry transferred from Verdun to the Nieuport region.[112] Nieuport was not merely a "dead sector" where there would be nothing for Ferry to report upon, but it was too far away from Paris for the sort of "shuttle trips" which the soldier-deputy had made from Verdun. This stratagem alone would have corroborated Captain Basil H. Liddell Hart's judgment of Joffre: "... In a man so devoid of all political interests [Joffre's] interest in politicians was quite as remarkable as his skill in dealing with them, ever alive to incipient intrigues and quick to counteract them through his faithful entourage and press supporters."[113]

Even more summary was the treatment of another prying parliamentarian who tried to enter the preserves of G.Q.G. No less than Senator Charles Humbert, *rapporteur* of the Senate's army commission, attempted to visit his native Verdun on March 28, 1915, but was brusquely ordered to leave the sector by General Sarrail, who reported the incident to Joffre.[114] Joffre airily dismissed the matter with a passing comment in his *Mémoires:* "This was only a trifle to which I attached no more importance than it deserved."[115] Charles Humbert, however, was not so willing to forgive and forget. The rebuff may have been one of the numerous provocations which caused him to make the threat before the army commission that he would "go and proclaim the truth to the people and have himself voluntarily arrested in the Place de la Concorde."[116] This histrionic role of the tribune of the people was never performed—unfortunately for those who enjoy public spectacles.

Such incidents indicated that even yet there was no adequate procedure for civilian visits to the front, for all the fencing between Millerand and the commissions. In yet another passage at arms, Millerand prepared a ministerial circular on June 20, 1915, which he sent to the army commission of the Chamber, setting forth more explicitly the conditions for admission to the various zones. Passes would be issued to designated commissioners upon express request of the war minister. Most difficult to obtain would be a pass to the zone of operations, since the war minister would have to provide special facilities for such a visit. In the event of such a request, the war minister would require the names of the delegates (a new stipulation), their itinerary, and schedule.[117]

Millerand's circular of June 20 was studied for a month by the army commission of the Chamber before the parliamentarians

PARLIAMENTARY INSPECTION

decided to reject it. A letter was addressed to the president of the Chamber on July 22, protesting that compliance with Millerand's formula for admission to the zone of operations would have the effect of nullifying parliamentary inspection, because the requirement of the names of the personnel and the exact itinerary and schedule of the mission would preclude inspections made necessary by sudden emergencies. The army commission, as determined as ever, reaffirmed "its right of inspection at its own time," under the reservation that twenty-four hours advance notice would be given to the minister of war, thus "enabling him to cancel the trip of the delegation in case military operations, which had to remain hidden, [had] begun or [were] in immediate preparation...."[118]

The army commission's intransigence aroused great hostility among those who were partial to G.Q.G. Léopold Marcellin reported that the animus against Pédoya was such that "half of the Chamber was demanding the resignation of that old meddler,"[119] but while it is true that the chief support of the army commission of the Chamber came from the Socialists,[120] the testimony of the atrabilious Rightist must be taken with some reserve.

The "meddlesomeness" of the army commission was by no means unique, since the commissions of navy, hygiene, and finance were quite as vigorous in their efforts—and quite as annoyed in trying to fulfill their tasks. In view of the obstructions encountered by all the commissions, they drew up a joint resolution which they addressed to the president of the council:

The delegates of all the groups of the Chamber affirm unanimously the right and duty of Parliament's exercise of supervision, an essential element in national defense; they invite the government to give definite assurance of its regular and permanent exercise. This supervision functions through commissions which delegate certain of their members for missions which are temporary and with a specific object.

The government has the duty of seconding the efforts of the missions and of assuring them of the full and sincere agreement of the civil and military authorities by giving them the necessary instructions.

Each mission will prepare a written report signed by the *rapporteur*.... Copies of the reports will be transmitted to the president of the council and to the proper ministers who should make known to the commissions, with the briefest possible delay, the decisions taken as a consequence of these reports.[121]

The government could not fail to take cognizance of this joint resolution. René Viviani, the easy-going president of the council, gave the assurance "that the government, which has always recognized the exercise of this legitimate right, accepts this text, it being well understood... that for the accomplishment of the missions, there must be agreement between the government and the commissions."[122] All of the commissions of the Chamber interpreted Viviani's reply as an acceptance of their decision "to make no distinction between the zone of the interior and the zone of the armies."[123]

Viviani and the rest of the Cabinet may have acquiesced in the formula of the commission, but not so Millerand, who seemed to be more mindful of the wishes of G.Q.G. than of Parliament or of his fellow ministers.[124] On August 11, Millerand bluntly informed the army commission that "the solution adopted by the groups relative to inspection was unacceptable," and that there must be compliance with his ministerial circular of June 20. The army commission authorized Pédoya to remind the war minister that President of the Council Viviani had fully approved the joint resolution of the commissions, and that there was no intention of allowing the commissions "to intervene in the domain of the command."[125] The result was stalemate: the war minister must still sanction trips to the front.

Rue St. Dominique's tactics of obstruction probably reached the zenith with the Senate's subcommission of aeronautics. The vice-president of the subcommission, Senator Lucien Cornet representing Yonne, was rendered almost speechless with vexa-

PARLIAMENTARY INSPECTION

tion over the obstacles placed in the path of his mission. Charged on March 31, 1915, with making an inquest into aviation at the front, Senator Cornet applied to Millerand for permission to visit the zone of the armies. Before Cornet was actually allowed to fulfill his mission four months later, he encountered almost every variation on the theme of evasion. First, he was told that he could not go alone to the front.[126] When he asked several colleagues to accompany him, he was then informed that the letter of authorization was in the mail—but, for some reason, the letter never arrived.[127] After hearing his further complaints, the War Ministry sent him "an authorization to visit sanitary formations and warehouses for medical supplies of the health service."[128] A tart reminder to Millerand that he was charged with the investigation of aeroplanes—not medicine—elicited a pass for "air bases in the zone of the interior and the rear"—but not in the zone of the armies. A further protest brought permission to "visit depots and training camps in the zone of the interior."[129] Almost on the verge of apoplexy, the senator, on July 24, received at last the authorization to go to the Armies of the North, but only after he had found it "necessary to write seven letters and two telegrams, to make six requests and to wait four months" to enable one of the most redoubtable commissions to fulfill its duty.[130]

The parliamentarians had learned from repeated experience that Millerand seemed impregnable against frontal assault, so they attempted to circumvent him. The need to overcome the war minister's obstructions was ironically expressed to the Chamber by the Socialist deputy, Raffin-Dugens from Isère: "... the war minister has been swamped, overwhelmed; he has done what he could, but he has no more gift of ubiquity than I have; for him, as well as for others, the day has only twenty-four hours. His time is limited, and how, therefore, can you expect his work to be perfect! How can you expect that complaints will not arise from every part of the country?"[131] Ostensibly to lighten Millerand's load, the parliamentarians decided to split up the war minister's functions into several posts of undersecretary—"a legitimate, constitutional, and effective extension of the control of Parliament over the services."

Albert Thomas, a Socialist deputy from Seine, was appointed to the newly created position of undersecretary of state for munitions,[132] but no sooner had he taken up his duties than he discovered that the Young Turk, Colonel Edmond Buat, and the War Ministry were determined "to paralyze" him.[133] Justin Godart, a Radical Socialist deputy from Lyon, was named undersecretary of state for health, but he immediately informed Poincaré that at the War Ministry he was "visibly" regarded as an "intruder."[134] The post of undersecretary of state for supplies was entrusted to Joseph Thierry, a Republican Union deputy from Marseilles.[135] Lastly, the new portfolio of undersecretary of state for aeronautics was given to René Besnard of Indre-et-Loire, a Radical Socialist deputy.[136] In theory, these undersecretaries of state were supposed to assist the war minister in his manifold duties; in practice, the new appointees served as parliamentary Trojan horses introduced into Millerand's stronghold at rue St. Dominique.

Through persistence, aggressiveness, and a recourse to such stratagems as the creation of the offices of undersecretaries of state, the parliamentarians were able to reduce somewhat the effectiveness of Millerand's barriers separating the military and civilian worlds. After having renounced the intention of going into the zone of the armies on their missions, the army commission of the Chamber bent every effort toward precisely that end. Millerand continued to insist upon an advance notification for each proposed visit, but this retention of discretionary power in the hands of the war minister did not seriously curtail the activities of the commissions. Despite such annoyances, the commissions engaged in a great number of successful undertakings, a partial list of which was supplied by M. Paul Deschanel in his inaugural address of January 13, 1916, the day following his reelection to the presidency of the Chamber.

PARLIAMENTARY INSPECTION

You have expedited ... the manufacture of arms and munitions for land and sea warfare. You have roused from apathy the bureaus which continued to apply in wartime the slower methods of peace. You have sought the best utilization of mobilized and mobilizable man power. You have assured grants to the families of conscripts ... to widows [and] ... orphans.... You have created the Croix de Guerre.... You have obtained furloughs for our soldiers, which, far from harming discipline, have encouraged good spirits.... You have increased the pay of the troops. You have forced an improvement in their barracks, their bedding, uniforms, food, and even in the condition of our prisoners in Germany. You have greatly contributed to perfecting the health service, the treatment and care of the wounded, the postal service, and transportation.

You have extended grants to the civilian victims of the war.... You have modified a great number of the articles of the civil, penal, and criminal codes.... You have undertaken the examination of war contracts....

However, certain criticisms have been directed against you.... Has the Chamber, for example, interfered with the conduct of diplomatic negotiations? No; since the beginning of the war, the military and the diplomats have acted in complete independence; neither their powers nor responsibilities has been hindered. And those who reproach us today for excessive officiousness would reproach us too late for an excess of reserve.[137]

The mere enumeration of the tasks of the commissions inspires not only respect for the parliamentarians' industriousness, but also commiseration for the members of the government who had to answer so many questions. René Viviani, in a conversation with Poincaré, described the ordeal of the average harassed council member. "Physically, I cannot hold out longer," he declared. "Every day I spend three or four hours with the commissions, listening to their interminable discussion, replying to questions which are concerned with infinitesimal details; I return exhausted to my office where I am badgered anew by senators and deputies; I no longer have a single minute of leisure in which to work; I am tired, discouraged, disgusted."[138]

All of the ministers were by no means able to maintain Millerand's impassivity. Had the war minister done no more than answer the deluge of questions showered upon him by the commissions, he would, perhaps, have deserved the reputation given him in Rightist circles. Millerand, they declared, was a "tyrant of toil, an ox of labor."[189] Only an ox could have remained indifferent to the thousand stings of the parliamentarian gadflies, and Alexandre Millerand was well cast in such a role. He had displayed a firm devotion to the High Command which even transcended his sense of obligation to President of the Council Viviani or to his fellow Cabinet members. The war minister yielded ground to the army commissions as begrudgingly and stubbornly as humanly possible. In the absence of adequate regulation of parliamentary inspection, the army commissioners naturally tried many stratagems to advance their missions to the very trenches; that the commissioners were not able to enter the zone of the armies entirely at their own pleasure was due to Millerand's unsurpassed intransigence.

4

L'Affaire Sarrail

THAT GENERAL JOFFRE SHOULD BE JEALOUS OF A popular rival such as General Sarrail was natural; that Joffre should have found convenient reasons for sacking Sarrail was understandable; but what was not fully apparent in July, 1915, when Sarrail was ordered to relinquish his command of the Third Army, was that Joffre had precipitated an issue which introduced a new phase of conflict into the relations between the command, the government, and Parliament. Friction between these agencies had so far been largely confined to the contest which the commissions, in their ambitious efforts to inspect matériel at the front, had carried on with the War Ministry, and to a few isolated encounters between mobilized deputies, such as Abel Ferry, and General Joffre. The abrupt dismissal of the influential Sarrail was to extend the scope of conflict by pitting a substantial part of Parliament itself (the Socialists and some of the Republican Socialists), and even several of the ministers, against the War Ministry and the command. This extension of friction foreshadowed the eventual abandonment of the ministry's resolution to defend the command against parliamentary attack, come what may.

General Sarrail occupied a singular position in the French army. "Sarrail is a flag," a parliamentarian once boasted to Joffre's liaison officer. "They will never be able to touch him. Depriving him of his command would be a slap at Parliament by breaking the only republican general."[1] Apart from his being a freethinker, there was not much in Sarrail's early career to suggest that he was to become a red flag, since he was a graduate

---

[1] For notes to chap. 4, see pages 254–257.

of St. Cyr whose ascent was seemingly orthodox through the rank of captain. Then his anomalous tendency reasserted itself when he married a Huguenot[2] and became an orderly officer for War Minister General André, although he later protested his complete innocence of dubious Freemasonic practices in officer selection.[3] As director of the Infantry School at Ste. Maixent, he acquired a reputation for military Jacobinism by showing a rare friendliness to cadet officers who had risen from the ranks.[4] After a period of political experience as military commander at the Palais Bourbon, Sarrail served as director of infantry at the War Ministry. The outbreak of war in 1914 found him a major general in command of the 8th Army Corps at Bourges.[5]

Sarrail's chief renown was won at Verdun, which he defended in September, 1914, in the most flamboyant tradition of *furia francese*.[6] Joffre had instructed Sarrail to allow his troops to fall back from Verdun under the crown prince's blows if the pressure became too great, but the commander of the Third Army ignored the vague order and "resisted before Verdun and saved the fort."[7] The legend portraying this spectacular officer, with his tall and powerful frame resembling "in a striking fashion a hearty and gallant king,"[8] as a military sport—a regal champion of the people—had effectively endeared him to the working class of France. His éclat in the eyes of the Left was magnified by his bullheaded defense of the Verdun hinge which helped to make the Battle of the Marne possible. Working-class readers of *La Guerre Sociale* were proudly assured by Gustave Hervé: "One can say without offending anyone that... Sarrail is one of the greatest generals the war has produced."[9]

So great was Sarrail's prestige with the proletariat that some of his idolaters drew up two anonymous memoranda which, in the intended interests of the general, they addressed to certain members of Parliament in February and March of 1915. These circulars revealed an intimate knowledge of troop movements, operations, and losses of certain units, which prompted Sarrail's political enemies to charge that only mem-

L'AFFAIRE SARRAIL

bers of his staff could have been the authors—an accusation which the general was later to deny on the grounds that the presence of Madame Joffre's son-in-law on his staff precluded even the possibility of any political secrets or conspiracies.[10] These memoranda were clumsy attempts to proclaim from the housetops the superiority of Sarrail to Joffre, and to urge the entrusting of the French army to the genius of the "red republican." The panegyrics were certain to ruffle the sensibilities of so jealous a commander as Joffre: only a saint could have ignored the invidious distinctions which they drew. The author (or authors) of the memoranda wrote in Joffre's disparagement: "I believe that... if, for a fortnight, General Joffre were not available, and the High Command were given to General Sarrail, the Germans would be expelled from [France], for there would be a vigorous, brutal action which would certainly cost us less dearly than the war of attrition which we have endured for five months and which we shall go on enduring, leaving our richest regions of the north completely ruined."[11]

Joffre undoubtedly knew of these insulting circulars, since in his *Mémoires* he makes a fleeting reference to Sarrail's role as a politician. "As soon as the front had become stabilized," wrote Joffre, "preoccupations of a military nature, which had sufficed until then to engross the attention of General Sarrail, gave way to political and personal preoccupations. He received all the parliamentarians who came into the neighborhood, particularly M. Doumer who... circulated malicious remarks about me."[12]

Despite Joffre's own admission that he was aware of Sarrail's political interests, the general in chief insisted that military reasons called for a change in the command of the Third Army. A two months' lull in fighting along the Argonne front had been broken by violent German attacks beginning on June 30, 1915. Sarrail's army was sent two divisions of reinforcements to enable it to counterattack on July 14. Before any counteroffensive could be mounted, the Germans profited by their momentum to strike again, seizing Hill 285 on the Haute-Chevauchée. Sarrail's counterstroke was begun belatedly, but despite two desperate drives, the Third Army was thrown back to its starting point. Joffre decided that "such a situation could not be prolonged without danger."[13]

General Joffre, knowing that he would have to proceed with caution against this favorite of the Left, displayed an adroitness worthy of a born politician. He selected as an inspector of the Third Army General Yvon Edmond Dubail—a choice of great cunning, for Dubail was widely known as a republican, and if he recommended Sarrail's dismissal it would preclude the Socialists from claiming that such an action was due to a clericalist-monarchist conspiracy. Dubail carried out the "delicate and painful inquiry." In reporting on the case, the inspector wrote that he found bad morale in the Third Army which he attributed to Sarrail's severity toward certain subordinates and partiality toward others.[14] Dubail criticized especially Sarrail's practice of refusing to mix units, so that "bracketed divisions were compartmented into rigid zones" without the commander's keeping adequate reserves on hand.[15] The brusqueness of Sarrail toward generals whom "he did not esteem" damaged the morale of the lower cadres.[16] Dubail thought that a sufficient sanction would be Sarrail's transfer to the command of the less important Army of Lorraine.[17] Joffre was thereby given a justification for changing the command of the Third Army.

A student of *l'affaire Sarrail,* Lieutenant Colonel Emile Mayer, has noted the "paradox" of the "brutal hostility" shown by Joffre and Millerand—themselves republicans—toward such a "notoriously republican" officer as General Sarrail. Mayer attempted to explain the severity of Sarrail's treatment by pointing out that the general in chief and war minister either "had to gag malcontents... or exile them—which was the case with Sarrail."[18] Republican generals who became centers of controversy were far more to be dreaded by Joffre and Millerand than the great number of monarchists on the roster of the High Command for the obvious political reason that the republicans

L'AFFAIRE SARRAIL

were supported by a majority of parliamentarians who would strike back in defense of their cause.[19] The monarchist generals may have been powerful in the army and the *haut monde,* but they commanded only a weak following in Parliament ("three dozen rattlepates," in Clemenceau's words),[20] and hence they were not regarded seriously. But when Chantilly and rue St. Dominique felt that action had to be directed against that rare species, a republican general, the maneuver had to be swift, as silent as possible, decisive, and drastic, or else the political welkin might ring with calamitous results.[21]

General Sarrail received notice of his dismissal at his headquarters at Ste. Menehould on July 22, 1915. He was told that General Humbert would replace him as commander of the Third Army, and that he should report to the War Ministry on July 23. When the outraged general arrived in Paris he did not go directly to rue St. Dominique, but in response to a telephone call went instead to the offices of the minister of interior, M. Louis Jean Malvy, a Radical Socialist deputy from Lot, whose politics aligned him on Sarrail's side of the barricades. Malvy confided to the general some recent scraps of gossip to the effect that he was to be demoted to the command of the Expeditionary Army Corps of the Orient, assigned to the Dardanelles.[22]

Sarrail thus knew what to expect when he made his way to the War Ministry for the appointment with Millerand and President of the Council Viviani. The none too subtle offer of the command of the expeditionary corps was flatly rejected by the general, convinced as he was that Joffre and Millerand had only one objective with regard to him: to have him "thrown out of France."[23] Sarrail bluntly informed Millerand that he intended to withdraw to his home at Montauban to await his retirement from the army. Perceiving that Sarrail was going to be "difficult" about the offer of the Dardanelles command, Millerand ordered the general to go to Montauban within forty-eight hours to await the settlement of his case.[24] Thereupon the brusque war minister departed, and Sarrail was left alone with the more

71

genial President of the Council Viviani, who tried to mollify the general with so many troublesome friends.

Political repercussions were soon forthcoming in *l'affaire Sarrail*. President Poincaré recorded in his journal that there was "a great commotion" in the Council of Ministers when it was learned that Sarrail had been "broken," with some of Joffre's own "personal friends" conceding "that the measure taken was unjustified or, in any case, excessive."[25] Even the conservative financier, Senator Alexandre Ribot from Pas-de-Calais, protested that there was no valid reason for "breaking Sarrail" for the check suffered in the Argonne "when no such sanction followed [similar reverses] at Arras."[26] Despite the regret of the ministers over Joffre's severity, they decided for the time being, at least, not to intervene, lest it provoke the general in chief to resign. Since a precedent had been established for "always leaving to [Joffre] the free choice of his lieutenants," it would not be wise to return just then to a strict legality in accordance with which the war minister would act on his own judgment in making important military appointments. In any case, Millerand would support Joffre. Some of the ministers wanted Sarrail to be given the command of the Lorraine army as a compensation for his rebuff, but Aristide Briand, the minister of justice, thought it would be unwise to leave the general on the western front since he was "discontented, and would become a focus of agitation."[27]

Briand, one of the original "Easterners"[28] (as the advocates of a Balkan front were called), saw in the Sarrail case a heaven-sent opportunity for "reconciling the wishes of the government with [Sarrail's] personal dignity."[29] Joffre was known to be willing to send Sarrail to the Dardanelles: why not assign him to a Macedonian army instead? If Sarrail were given such a command, a convenient means would be found to bring about his removal from France and, by the same stroke, there would have to be created a Macedonian army—"which, in strict truth, did not as yet exist"—and thus there would materialize Briand's

L'AFFAIRE SARRAIL

cherished dream (shared by Gallieni, Franchet d'Esperey, and others) of a Balkan front against the Central Powers.

The ministry had to decide at once what to do with Sarrail, Viviani told Poincaré on July 23. "The Chamber is in an incredible state of agitation. [Republican Socialist Maurice] Viollette on the one hand and the Socialists on the other have been trying to see me all day to protest the action taken against Sarrail. I have hidden out. But the situation is becoming impossible, since Parliament must be reckoned with."[80] Viviani went on to explain to Poincaré that the ministry, for all its reluctance, might have to intervene in military appointments after all. In fact, three ministers, Gaston Doumergue, Albert Sarraut, and Louis Jean Malvy, with the intention of heading off the parliamentary storm of indignation, were planning to visit Joffre at Chantilly to try to persuade him to give Sarrail the command of the Army of Lorraine,[81] which would be less a demotion than a Near Eastern command. Viviani seemed convinced that if Sarrail were not given a good assignment, he would withdraw permanently to his home at Montauban, since the general had said to him: "My career is finished; I am going to be placed in retirement, I know, but I refuse to go to the Dardanelles. They have humiliated me, beginning by relieving me of my command. I will accept nothing in these circumstances."[82]

The ministerial delegation which was to intercede with Joffre had to be selected for its tactfulness—a consideration which ruled out Albert Sarraut and Louis Jean Malvy, for these Radical Socialists were known to be friendly to Sarrail. The Left Democrat Gaston Doumergue was regarded as more neutral, so on July 24 he went to Chantilly, accompanied only by War Minister Millerand. Joffre listened politely to Doumergue's suggestion that Sarrail be given the Army of Lorraine. Joffre's response corroborated Gallieni's verdict that the general in chief was one of "the craftiest of men."[83] Doumergue was blandly informed that the command of the Army of Lorraine had already been assigned to General Gérard[84]—as staunch a republican as could be found. The general in chief added that he had "no objections of a military nature to entrusting to [Sarrail] the expedition of the Dardanelles."[35] Joffre thus cunningly spiked the guns of the Socialists, as no one in his senses could have branded the appointment of republican (but unspectacular) Gérard a "reactionary" measure, and yet Sarrail was thereby excluded from a command on the western front.

Nothing remained for the Council of Ministers except to try to make the Near Eastern command acceptable to Sarrail—his retirement being out of the question, since his Socialist supporters would never peacefully consent to it. The Cabinet decided on July 24 to send the Radical Socialist minister of public instruction, M. Albert Sarraut, on a mission to General Sarrail to ask him to reconsider his refusal to command the Expeditionary Corps of the Orient, in view of the importance of capturing Constantinople as quickly as possible. Sarraut held out to the skeptical general the bait of a vague promise "of an increase in the expeditionary corps."[36] Sarraut's visit was followed by one from Briand who turned upon the general all of his famed powers of eloquent persuasion. Sarrail appeared to relent somewhat and told Briand: "I would accept the command offered if it were augmented, but I would take over only after this increase has been carried out."[37] Quite as encouraging to the government as Sarrail's surprising tractability was the general's parting quip before he left Paris for his furlough at Montauban, to the effect that he "was not the stuff of which Boulangers were made."[38]

Sarrail's justifiable lukewarmness toward the offer of the French Expeditionary Corps of the Orient arose from the fact that it was not really an "army," but a mere "grouping of two divisions" which did not even possess service forces. Sarrail felt, moreover, that the commander of the French Expeditionary Corps, General Henri Joseph Gouraud, had done nothing to deserve his being replaced.[39] The Dardanelles imbroglio had grown out of a series of improvisations, beginning early in 1915

L'AFFAIRE SARRAIL

with Winston Churchill's proposal of an operation against Constantinople which was to have been largely naval until the Chanak Narrows had been forced, when a modest ground army was to be used to consolidate the gains made.[40] The French government had asked the British to convert the naval expedition into a joint Franco-British operation, since the right of command in the Mediterranean theater belonged by agreement to France.[41] On February 9, 1915, the Franco-British squadrons failed miserably in their attack upon the entrance of the Straits, thereby demonstrating the imperative necessity of ground support for the fleet.[42] To meet this need the British created a reserve corps of two divisions of Anzacs, based temporarily at Lemnos. The French government felt that it was only fitting that it should provide troops as well as ships for its share of the attack aimed at Constantinople, but Joffre opposed the sending of even a single French division on the ground that the whole campaign was too offhand. Millerand, in one of his rare gestures of independence of Joffre, went ahead and provided two French divisions from the reserves.[43]

After another unsuccessful naval attack upon the Straits on March 18, the two Anzac divisions under Sir Ian Hamilton and the pair of French reserve divisions under General d'Amade gained a precarious bridgehead on the Gallipoli peninsula, where the whole Anglo-French position came under Turkish enfilading fire. The discomfited Viviani government which had overridden Joffre's opposition to the makeshift campaign thereupon had to ask the advice of the general in chief, who, fully relishing his right of saying "I told you so!"[44] merely suggested replacing d'Amade by General Gouraud as commander of the two French divisions which bore the deceptively impressive title of *Corps expeditionnaire d'Orient*. Gouraud arrived at the Dardanelles only to find the Allied forces "more besieged than besiegers." This dreary state of affairs continued until the end of July, when the anxious Viviani Cabinet tried to palm off the Expeditionary Corps of the Orient upon Sarrail. The general showed an understandable lack of enthusiasm over the doubtful compensation which the new assignment would represent.

Several days after the Jacobin general's arrival at his home at Montauban, Millerand telegraphed Sarrail to appear at the War Ministry on August 3, "in order to make known his wishes."[45] This was an irregular state of affairs, revealing how enmeshed in dubious political considerations was *l'affaire Sarrail*. "Normally, it would have been incumbent upon the government to set the aim of an expedition."[46] Yet in this case, the minister of war was asking a subordinate general officer to draw up his own mission—subject, of course, to the minister's right of rejection of the proposals. Sarrail suppressed his feelings and prepared a list of his "desiderata," which he gave to Millerand: "(1) There would have to be constituted an army which would take the name of the Army of the Orient; (2) I would not wish to be under the orders of English generals, as Generals d'Amade and Gouraud have been; (3) I will not depart except with divisions of reinforcement."[47] Millerand wanted to chaffer over these terms by pointing out that the second demand was within the purview of the Ministry of Foreign Affairs. But Sarrail was adamant, convinced as he was that if he left France without reinforcements, "not a rifle nor a cannon would be sent to him."[48]

This haggling with Sarrail made Millerand impatient, which provoked him into a slip. "The desire to see me removed from the French front and from France," observed Sarrail, "came out in a phrase which escaped the minister: 'If you imagine that I am going to let you remain in Paris until September 15!' "[49] In an attempt to solve the problem once and for all, Millerand notified Sarrail on August 5 that he "was named commander of the Army of the Orient; he did not refer to [his] status of independence or subordination to the English...." As for the requested reinforcements, Millerand promised that Sarrail "would not be sent out to the Dardanelles if the expeditionary corps were not augmented—at least," he added, vaguely, "while Gen-

L'AFFAIRE SARRAIL

eral [Maurice] Bailloud, the commander pro tem, remained."[50] Sarrail interpreted this somewhat obscure reservation as a flagrant violation of "the *modus vivendi* worked out by the minister of justice and the government," but unwisely, perhaps, he did not challenge the ambiguity of the remark then and there. As General Sarrail prepared to leave, Millerand took off the mask of "correctness" and bluntly ordered him: "Do not associate with parliamentarians."[51]

Millerand, it appeared to Sarrail, "was trying to find a means of putting everything in order,"[52] since failure to do so might cause the Viviani Cabinet's downfall.[53] While the war minister grappled with this problem of political expediency, "busy work" had to be assigned to the troublesome republican general who, if left to his own devices, might spend his time in the company of his Socialist cohorts in Parliament, hatching heaven knows what schemes against rue St. Dominique and Chantilly. Accordingly, General Sarrail was "invited to make known to Millerand his opinion of what a French army ought to do in the Orient."[54] Millerand tried without success to induce Sarrail to leave at once for the Dardanelles by reassuring him with the comment, "It commits you to nothing."[55]

While Sarrail was engaged in finding out "what an army could do in the Orient," the three Chamber subcommissions of army, navy, and foreign affairs were anxiously trying to find out what the army corps had actually been doing in the Orient, since "the government had refused to give out any information, even to the commissions. It was from the press that the army commission learned that the Anglo-French fleet had not been able to force the Dardanelles and that the attack by land had miscarried. Such was the situation when [they] learned that there would be constituted an Army of the Orient."[56]

On August 13, a delegation of the three commissions visited President Poincaré to state their unanimous decision that a greatly enlarged expedition to the Dardanelles was urgently needed. Poincaré cautiously replied that he could neither give his opinion, except to ministers, nor engage in debate with parliamentarians,[57] but the three commissions were not to be turned aside. They drew up a long letter on August 25, addressing it to the president of the republic, to the president of the council, and to all the ministers.[58] The letter asserted that the commissions were "astonished" at the delays in negotiations with England and the Balkan states over the Dardanelles policy, and it expressed uneasiness over the indecision with regard to the reinforcements to be sent to the Dardanelles. "At first you spoke to us of more than 100,000 men, then of four divisions, then of two divisions. You have told us at last that military reasons will not allow you to decide before September 15 whether reinforcements will be available for the Orient. However, a general, who formerly was at the head of an army, has been named commander in chief of the Army of the Orient. Despite this, the navy minister has acknowledged that all transport preparations have been suspended. What can this general do then, if he does not know as yet whether he will be furnished a man; what preparations can be made if the transport facilities are not known ... ?"[59]

In conversation with Poincaré, Joffre displayed a "gentle obstinacy" in regard to the Dardanelles imbroglio. The general in chief asked: "What is to be done at the Dardanelles—prepare an expedition for a factious general?"[60] Poincaré tried to show Joffre that it was not Sarrail, but Generals Henri Gouraud and Maurice Bailloud, as well as the commissions of the Chamber and the government, who had "considered necessary the extension of the Dardanelles expedition." Poincaré was uneasy, since Joffre would promise no more aid for the Dardanelles than two army corps, and even they could not possibly be sent before September.[61]

General Sarrail, meanwhile, dutifully prepared his report on what a French army might do in the Orient. He suggested several alternative campaigns including a landing on the coast of Asia Minor at some such point as Adramati[62] or Smyrna, as

L'AFFAIRE SARRAIL

well as a possible debarkation at Salonika which "would permit a truly military action."[63] This prospectus drew no approval from G.Q.G., which protested to President Poincaré that Sarrail's plan "took into account neither the size of the forces which would be needed, nor the chances of success, nor any of the various questions which the organization and the conduct of the expedition might raise...."[64]

Sarrail was willing to concede the validity of much of this criticism, but, as he pointed out, "it is the task of the government to determine the theater where a general should operate and the goal which he must achieve; the minister of war had not been able to state...what was to be done...."[65]

The minister of war had his hands full in combating his political opponents—which might have accounted, in part, for his inability to assign Sarrail to a definite mission. In an address to the Chamber on August 20, Millerand tried in effect to hide from the Socialists behind the ample bulk of Joffre. The Argus-eyed vigilance of "Anastasie," the censor, and respect for the "sacred union" had so far prevented open discussion of *l'affaire Sarrail*, but the vehemence of conversation in the lobbies of the Palais Bourbon induced Millerand to take cognizance of the ill-suppressed fury of the Socialist supporters of the "red general." Millerand began his speech to the Chamber with a recital of the improvements in the health and artillery services, from which point of vantage the war minister launched into praise of Joffre. "...I say that the country is fortunate in having at the head of the armies a general officer of absolute loyalty...." This bouquet infuriated some of the Socialists, who cried out: "No one has attacked him. This is an evasion."[66] Millerand then committed a stupid blunder: he referred directly to *l'affaire Sarrail*. "It was only yesterday," he declared, "that I was asked to account for a change in the command of the armies...." The Socialists interrupted with the question, "Who asked that?" The impervious Millerand continued: "...I would be remiss if I did not oppose [this demand, but] some people have no fear of injecting political interests into debate, apparently without seeing that they create thereby a dangerous precedent in authorizing themselves—and in a time of war!—to judge the chiefs on grounds apart from military considerations...."[67]

This speech annoyed Millerand's fellow ministers who were especially indignant over the war minister's indiscreet allusion to a recent "change in command." At a Cabinet meeting on August 21, the members of the government rebuked Millerand for ignoring the "sacred union" in his ill-considered remarks about *l'affaire Sarrail,* whereby he had broken "the agreement, not only between the Cabinet and the two groups of the extreme left [the Socialists and Republican Socialists], but between the members of the government themselves." Millerand seemed not to care if he gave the deputies a pretext "for discussing everything."[68] Responsible members of the government were deeply concerned at the thought of extending conflict over war policy to the very floor of the Chamber—a presentiment of what was eventually to happen following the mismanaged Verdun and Chemin des Dames campaigns of 1916 and 1917.

Toward the close of September, 1915, there occurred a peripeteia in the Balkans which caused the various Dardanelles campaign plans—serious or frivolous as they might have been—to be discarded in favor of a Macedonian strategy much like that advocated by Briand and the other "Easterners." Bulgaria began mobilizing on September 19, having secretly signed a military alliance with the Central Powers which pledged her to enter the war against Serbia and the Entente Powers by the second week in October, 1915.[69] The French foreign minister, Théophile Delcassé, displayed a fatuous optimism toward Bulgarian mobilization, suspecting merely a "bluff."[70] The Ententophile Greek prime minister, Eleutherios Venizelos, sensing the seriousness of the Bulgarian menace, appealed to France and Britain to send 150,000 troops to Salonika to enable Greece to honor her commitments of aid to Serbia in event of an attack upon the latter. The French and British governments

L'AFFAIRE SARRAIL

consented in a lukewarm fashion,[71] and, as an advance installment, ordered one British and one French division transferred from Gallipoli to Salonika.[72] No sooner had the French division arrived at the Greek port than the Hellenic king, Constantine, abruptly dismissed Venizelos, declaring that his realm would not abandon its neutrality.[73] This reassured Sofia, and the predictable denouement occurred on October 7, when the Bulgarians attacked eastern Serbia with an army of 250,000 while 200,000 Austro-German troops launched an attack from the north. The Serbs were confronted with a well-nigh hopeless situation, attacked thus in front and on the flank by greatly superior forces.[74]

When it had been decided to intervene in Macedonia, the war minister informed Sarrail that he was to leave for the Levant "with a mixed brigade" taken from Belfort, to be followed by a division of cavalry. But Millerand, as mindful of Joffre's wishes as ever, would not agree to send the two divisions of cavalry and one division of infantry which had been sought by the navy minister, Victor Augagneur, as well as by General Sarrail.[75]

Sarrail visited Delcassé, the minister of foreign affairs, on October 5, and Poincaré the following day, in the hope that his "mission might be stated precisely"—but he got no clarification.[76] The government (apart from Millerand) could appreciate Sarrail's vexation and suspicion. Two unofficial emissaries visited Sarrail to learn his attitude toward a possible exchange of command with another general in metropolitan France. Victor Basch, professor at the Sorbonne, proposed—"under governmental inspiration"—that Sarrail become military governor of Paris in place of Gallieni, while Léon Blum, chief of cabinet of the Ministry of Public Works, suggested an exchange with General Franchet d'Esperey as commander of the Fifth Army.[77] Moreover, Deputy Paul Benazet urged Sarrail "not to throw himself into the Oriental wasp nest," while Georges Clemenceau bluntly told the general: "There's still time to change your mind. Tell Millerand you definitely won't go."[78] Sarrail tried to explain to Clemenceau that he "had obtained partial satisfaction and believed in the success of the expedition." This provoked Clemenceau into the brusque remark: "But, my poor fellow, you don't understand, then, that you're being drawn into a trap? There never will be an Allied front in the East.... We haven't enough troops in France. The Germans are at Noyon, and England will never follow us into such a harebrained scheme."[79]

Notwithstanding all these prophetic warnings, Sarrail dutifully embarked at Marseilles on October 7, determined that "it might not be said that [he] had shirked a most unpromising task."[80] Sarrail wryly observed of the circumstances of his departure: "... I did not have the [oft] mentioned reinforcements; I did not have a supply chief, having been denied the one whom I had demanded; graver yet, I still had no directive. But G.Q.G. and the war minister had succeeded in their aim: I was thrown out of France."[81]

Upon Sarrail's arrival at Salonika on October 12, he led the single French division (the only one to reach Greece as yet) ninety miles northward into Macedonia to assist the hard pressed Serbs. Sarrail's puny force was followed by the single British division under General Mahon.[82] The Franco-British troops never progressed beyond Krivoloh, for the enemy was already strongly entrenched in southern Serbia and was pushing the Serbs toward the Adriatic. The question then arose as to whether reinforcements should be rushed to the forces under Generals Sarrail and Mahon. The British government, except for Lloyd George, was doubtful of the wisdom of a Balkan campaign,[83] with General Sir William Robertson urging London not to follow France's example of sending another division to Salonika.[84]

The predictable disaster of the Bulgarian attack upon Serbia, as well as the failure of Joffre's September offensive, jarred the French government, dislodging as the first fragment of the

L'AFFAIRE SARRAIL

Viviani Cabinet Foreign Minister Delcassé. The unexpected gaucherie of Delcassé's handling of France's Balkan policy so gravely embarrassed Viviani that the harassed president of the council, convinced that his Cabinet was at "its last gasp," visited the Elysée on October 25 to request Poincaré to summon a new ministry.

A supple statesman was called to succeed Viviani. Aristide Briand, minister of justice in the outgoing Cabinet, one of those hardy perennials in twentieth-century French politics, was invited to form his third ministry since 1909. Suave, eloquent, flexible, still possessing vestiges of the humanitarianism of his early socialism, the Independent from St. Etienne, at Poincaré's request, agreed on October 29, 1915, to form a government, retaining for himself the foreign affairs portfolio.[85]

Briand decided to replace the intractable Alexandre Millerand with General Gallieni in the post of war minister. The military governor of Paris was reluctant to take over at rue St. Dominique. "I do not know politics," he had told Viviani, just before the latter's fall. "...I do not know how to speak....I am an authoritarian....I am not able to abide discussions, commissions, palavers...."[86] Victor Augagneur, former naval minister, and Millerand (once more a mere deputy and no longer the chief paladin of the military) "created a storm" when they learned of Briand's decision to name General Gallieni as war minister. They protested to Briand that Gallieni "would foment a *coup d'état*"; that he "would have the ministers shot"; finally, that he "was a Corsican."[87] For Millerand—of all persons—to be expressing concern over the danger of undue military ascendancy was piquant, but it did not disguise his obvious wish to spare his friend Joffre any possibility of umbrage, whether from Sarrail or Gallieni. Joffre, however, was urgently in need of restoring his popularity, so with an astuteness alien to Millerand, he put aside his private feelings toward his rival for fame as the "victor of the Marne" and blandly told Poincaré that Gallieni "was the best choice which he could make. He is an organizer...."[88] He hoped thereby to mollify his political enemies whose hand had been strengthened by the Serbian fiasco.

The problem of aiding Serbia beset Joffre like the Erinyes—poetic justice for one who had all along opposed any sort of eastern diversion. Since the swift catastrophe which overtook Serbia jeopardized not only the French Cabinet but Joffre's prestige as well, the general in chief developed a belated interest in sending the 150,000 Anglo-French troops to Salonika in fulfillment of the promise given to Venizelos. But Joffre wanted to send only two French divisions, hoping that the British would "supply the balance needed to complete the contingent up to the 150,000 men mentioned."[89] The British Cabinet and General Staff turned down the French request, Lord Kitchener of the War Office expressing reluctance to furnish even a single British soldier.[90]

Without immediate reinforcements, the Anglo-French troops in Serbia had no choice but to make a dreary and dispiriting retreat down the Vardar Valley to Salonika,[91] while the harassed Serbian army made its way to the Adriatic as best it could. Once Generals Sarrail and Mahon reached Salonika, they set to work fortifying the environs of the port,[92] determined to make it an entrenched camp which could be a future base for offensive operations. Sarrail's political enemies in France immediately tried to capitalize upon the defensive nature of the Salonika fortifications by insinuating that the Sarrail faction—determined to keep the general's prestige intact so that he might yet become France's commander in chief—would not allow their hero to take a chance on an offensive until victory was guaranteed.[93] This malicious interpretation of Sarrail's actions is not borne out by enemy testimony, General Erich von Falkenhayn emphasizing in his memoirs the ease with which the Central Powers held the mountainous terrain of the Balkans, which was so disadvantageous to an offensive drive from the direction of Salonika.[94]

The parliamentary commissions in Paris fully understood the

L'AFFAIRE SARRAIL

precarious position of Sarrail's Army of the Orient. On December 1, 1915, the Chamber's foreign affairs commission sent to the army commission a copy of a note which it had addressed to President of the Council Briand: "The commission of foreign affairs calls the government's attention to the fact that the safeguarding of Salonika is ... essential. ... It does not appear that this result can be obtained without a great increase in the forces which constitute the Army of the Orient. These troops urgently need to be reinforced, with our allies reminded at once of their responsibilities."[95]

President of the Council Briand, in one of his characteristic flashes of political intuition, saw in Sarrail's predicament an opportunity to cut through a tangle of problems. In the first place, General Joffre had been chagrined over the fact that Sarrail, as commander in chief of the Army of the Orient, had been taking his orders directly from the War Ministry rather than from G.Q.G.[96] By extending Joffre's authority to include the Army of the Orient, Briand could be sure that the Joffre faction would be pleased that their hero had become a generalissimo. Furthermore, by making Joffre responsible for the Army of the Orient, the general would be given a personal commitment in that army's success, and, consequently, he could be expected to take an interest in it which was notably lacking so long as this army's prestige was tied primarily to the reputation of Sarrail."[97] It could be surmised further that the Sarrail faction—for all the irritation which they would undoubtedly feel at first over their favorite's direct subjection to Joffre—could be won over eventually when they learned that Joffre would be sending to Salonika great quantities of matériel and numerous reinforcements for the puny Army of the Orient. Thus Briand could please Joffre by aggrandizing his command; he could probably dispel the opposition of the Sarrail faction by facilitating a victory for French and British arms in the Balkans; lastly, the president of the council could realize his own "Easterner's" dream of attacking the Central Powers through their back door. Ingenious solution! On December 2, 1915, President of the Republic Poincaré and War Minister Gallieni issued a decree stating that General Joffre had been elevated from "general in chief of the Armies of the North and Northeast" to the rank of "commander in chief of the French Armies"—except for the colonial corps in Algeria, Tunis, and Morocco.[98] France now had no less than a generalissimo.

Briand's act of including the Near Eastern Command under Joffre's direct authority may have been clever, but it sorely displeased the members of the Chamber's army commission, who drew up a note of protest which General Pédoya gave to War Minister Gallieni. The army commission called attention to the difficulties which inhered in the new system, according to which Generalissimo Joffre would be expected to direct from Chantilly, in the heart of France, complex military operations in remote Greece, with its peculiarities of terrain and its uncertain political contingencies. "Granted that the government can give directives—that is its right, its duty; but is it not a military heresy to expect a chief [inside] France to be responsible for military operations in the Orient?"[99] President of the Council Briand rather skillfully parried this objection by reminding the commission on December 15 that "in the theater of operations in the Orient diplomatic considerations [were] as important a matter as military considerations," and that in foreign countries General Joffre still had a "prestige and authority"[100] which had been won through the "Miracle of the Marne."

Now that the Army of the Orient was directly subordinate to G.Q.G., the generalissimo lost no time in putting Sarrail in his place: he sent as inspector general to Salonika his newly appointed chief of staff, the archclericalist General Edouard de Castelnau,[101] whose very name was anathema to the Left.[102] To the surprise of everyone, the "red republican" and the "booted Capuchin" behaved with commendable correctness toward one another as long as the inspector general remained at Salonika.[103] But upon leaving for Paris, General de Castelnau sent Sarrail

L'AFFAIRE SARRAIL

a carping note which summarily ordered him to modify his plans of fortifying the entrenched camp, to create a reserve, and to change the location of his headquarters.[104] Sarrail reacted to this provocation by writing the president of the council a furious letter in which he reminded Briand of his numerous requests for reinforcements: "... You know that you wanted to form the Army of the Orient; you know what you wanted in issuing the decree of December 2. I ask you consequently to regularize a situation which ... affects me deeply in my initiative ... authority and ... in my military honor...."[105] The only "regularizing" of Sarrail's situation was the brusque order from G.Q.G. that he cease corresponding directly with the government instead of with Chantilly.[106] Furthermore, he was to give up his usurped "right" of bestowing Croix de Guerre and making promotions in the Legion of Honor. The partisans of Sarrail protested against these petty acts of malice by insisting that the remoteness of Salonika had caused Sarrail to become *de facto* commander in chief in that theater; that the British had deferred to Sarrail in Salonika, although in the field their generals had been autonomous; that Sarrail's umbrage would damage his prestige with all the Allied forces in Macedonia.[107] All of these complaints fell on deaf ears, however.

L'affaire Sarrail was an unpleasant reminder of the precariousness of the "sacred union." Confronted with the German invasion, the political groupings in France had closed ranks—at least, in outward appearance—but with the reaching of a military stalemate the peacetime struggle between the classes was resumed. The French Left wanted a commander in chief of its own stripe, and Sarrail seemed made-to-order for such a purpose. The furtive campaign in the general's behalf did him no good, however, since such clumsy tactics as the circulation of anonymous memoranda praising Sarrail played into the hands of Joffre and the war minister, Millerand. A commander could hardly be expected to condone a politico-military campaign designed to bring about his own replacement, and Joffre had already demonstrated his awareness of such possible stratagems. But Joffre and Millerand, despite their adroit use of republican officers in removing Sarrail, bungled their handling of the affair, especially in the case of Millerand's tactless speech to Parliament, and in the long delay in deciding what to do with the red republican after his removal from the Third Army. This gaucherie redounded to the political advantage of the Socialist supporters of Sarrail, and an open rupture of the "sacred union" was narrowly averted. The Sarrail faction was bought off with vague promises of future reinforcements for the Army of the Orient, and the general was sent packing to Salonika. Despite his new and impressive title of generalissimo, Joffre's victory over his rival was a Pyrrhic one, since a precedent had been set in *l'affaire Sarrail* for a parliamentary free-for-all in discussing military affairs—an ominous portent.

5

The Verdun Crisis

THE MASSIVE GERMAN DRIVE AGAINST VERDUN ON February 21, 1916, threatened not only to capture the French stronghold on the Meuse, a symbol of national pride, but to destroy a legend—the invincibility of Joffre, "France's savior." Had Joffre tried deliberately to provoke parliamentary criticism of his cocksureness with regard to Verdun, he could not have done better than to say to his liaison officer, Colonel Herbillon, shortly before the bombardment: "I ask only one thing, and that is that the Germans will attack me, and if they do attack me, that it will be at Verdun. Quote me."[1] This comment reflected as much irony as overconfidence, since Joffre, considering narrowly the map rather than the possibilities of psychological warfare, was firmly convinced that Verdun had no strategic advantage for the Germans because it was remote from Paris—far more so than such reasonably tempting points of attack as the Valley of the Oise, Reims, or the Champagne region.[2] The generalissimo failed to guess the German purpose in attacking Verdun: to damage French morale through the attrition of man power rather than a mass break-through, or even the capture of scraps of territory.[3]

Joffre had lost confidence in the defensibility of forts since the rapid fall of Liége and Namur, and during 1915 he had, in effect, declassed "Verdun as a fortress...[and] thenceforth drained it of its men and armament."[4] A degree of security was still afforded Verdun by the French control of both banks of the Meuse for a distance of eight to ten kilometers north of the city's girdle of forts.[5] But unfortunately, the French forces "were not

---

[1] For notes to chap. 5, see pages 257–259.

rooted in fortified works" in this important buffer zone. "Letters from officers and soldiers, information gathered by the representatives of the department of the Meuse, drew the attention of the army commissions of Parliament to this none too reassuring situation."[6]

Whatever rationalizations Joffre might have advanced in explanation of his dawdling at Verdun, he could never have said that he had not been forewarned of the sector's unpreparedness for a threatened German attack. No less than five different warnings were given the government and command before the deadly onslaught began. The first cautioning was given to army commissioners in July, 1915, by General Coutanceau, military governor of Verdun, who braved the wrath of his superior, General Dubail, by calling attention to the need for maintaining the defensibility of Verdun's existing forts.[7] General Dubail, commander of the Army Group of the East, had given the army commissioners the official view of the High Command—namely, that the existing forts in and around the city were little more than shooting gallery targets, and that a citadel like Verdun could be defended only by advancing its artillery parks to a wide perimeter far enough removed from the city's center to nullify the enemy's firepower.[8] For contradicting his superior by asserting that the forts in Verdun's immediate environs could and should be adequately armed and protected by outer works, General Coutanceau was removed from the post of military governor, being replaced by General Herr, an Alsatian artilleryman of repute.[9]

The reconnaissance aviators of General Herr brought him "terrifying information" about German preparations around Verdun in the days preceding the attack of February 21, 1916. The enemy, declared General Herr,

had so many batteries that it was impossible to count them. To resist the German thrust, I had altogether only 65 battalions.... Most terrible for me were the Young Turks of G.Q.G. Upon each demand for artillery reinforcements which I would address to them, they would reply by withdrawing two batteries or two batteries and a half: "You will not be attacked. Verdun is not a point of attack. The Germans do not know that Verdun has been disarmed." They had no excuse for so deceiving themselves: all of my information agreed on the imminence of a formidable attack, and the questioning of Polish, Russian, and Belgian prisoners, escaping through the German lines, each day supported my conviction. Verdun was, in fact, declassed; only G.Q.G., while completely stripping the place, did not have the courage to pronounce it declassed.[10]

Further anxiety over the unpreparedness of the Verdun sector was expressed on November 30, 1915, by the well-known soldier-deputy, Abel Ferry, recently released from his rustication at Nieuport. Ferry cautioned the army commission of the Chamber about the disturbing amount of German railroad construction near Verdun in contrast to French inactivity.[11] General Pédoya likewise called attention to the danger of no less than fourteen German rail lines which converged upon the Verdun salient. Pédoya had been told by some of the field officers that "because of the lack of double tracks the transport of [French] troops would be extremely slow; reserves would arrive late at the point of attack; all the railroads out of Paris ran perpendicularly to the frontier; in their construction they were designed only for a defensive war. This information was turned over to the commission and the minister of war."[12]

Of all the warnings about the dangerous position of Verdun, the most authoritative came from an observer who enjoyed vast respect, Colonel Emile Driant, a Liberal Action deputy from Meurthe-et-Moselle and the son-in-law of General Boulanger. Colonel Driant was a career soldier who had seen much fighting near Verdun.[13] Although a member of the army commission of the Chamber, he was quite safe from any suspicion of being a mere caviling politician who was at heart a "Socialist-pacifist sniper." On November 30, 1915, when soldier-Deputy Abel Ferry appeared before the army commission of the Chamber to indict the High Command for inactivity, Colonel Driant listened attentively to the account of Verdun's neglect.[14] The next day Driant unexpectedly corrobated the testimony which Ferry had given to the commission.

> At the beginning of hostilities [he said] I was hardly disposed to see Parliament concern itself with military matters, but since Parliament and the inspection of the army commission have ... made great progress, I now recognize my error—I do not hide it—I, who once wanted only a single director during a time of war—the general in chief. The organization of our front is not secure at certain points. I demand that a delegation of the army commission be sent to inspect these regions since—who has not said it—the terrain is at the mercy of a German attack. It is necessary to go and see it; what I did not understand three months ago, I comprehend today.[15]

Historic words! "The end of Joffre was still distant, but [it] ... had its inception in the session of the army commission of the Chamber at which Driant made his 'pronouncement.' "[16]

Driant's surprising support, coming as it did from a professional soldier, entranced the other commissioners who listened with rapt attention to the famed colonel. "With documents and statistics in hand, [Driant] revealed that the sector which he had defended was entirely unorganized, lacking in fortifications and means of supply, and awaiting an enemy attack against which no effective resistance could be offered except at the cost of the most heroic sacrifices."[17] The army commission of the Chamber immediately assigned Colonel Driant and General Pédoya to an inspection tour of the Lorraine sectors. The renowned new convert to parliamentary inspection as well as the commission president reckoned without Chantilly, however. Driant and Pédoya dutifully submitted to the War Ministry an itinerary for an inspection tour of the Nancy-Lunéville region.[18] But, "upon their arrival in the sector, the delegates were notified that G.Q.G. had given orders forbidding their visit."[19] Nevertheless, they heard reports which confirmed their impression "that there was only a single line of defense, that even this line was incomplete at certain points, and that no line for falling back had been prepared."[20]

Word soon reached President Poincaré that Colonel Driant had "alarmed" the army commission by his charge "that in the [Verdun] fortified region, we nowhere had a second line." Poincaré asked his officer of liaison with Chantilly, Colonel Jean Pénelon, "to notify Joffre," but the president of the republic considerately "refrained from exposing Driant."[21] Poincaré likewise asked War Minister General Gallieni "to draw Joffre's attention to what had been said... about the insufficiency of certain lines of defense."[22]

Gallieni had already spoken privately with Driant, even before the colonel made his sensational "pronouncement" to the army commission.[23] Without doubt Driant's indictment was the principal inspiration of a historic letter from Gallieni to Joffre.[24] President of the Council Briand, perceiving the political as well as the military import of the warnings about Verdun, asked the war minister at a Cabinet meeting on December 16, 1915, to write a note of caution to the generalissimo. Gallieni thereupon ventured the opinion that any such governmental intervention would probably provoke Joffre into another threat to resign. Someone at the council table cried out: "Very well, so much the worse. We shall have to exercise our duty of supervision." "Yes," replied Gallieni, "but let it be well understood that if General Joffre goes, I shall go also."[25] This pledge of "loyalty" to a personal enemy would be most implausible in a civilian, but as one disciplined in correct military form, Gallieni knew that it would be unseemly for him to appear to be trying to unseat the commander in chief, whom so many persons wished to replace with Gallieni himself[26] despite the fact that as war minister he was already theoretically above a generalissimo. With some misgivings, therefore, Gallieni consented to address the following letter to Joffre.

GENERALS & POLITICIANS

Paris, December 16, 1915

The Minister of War to M. the Commander in Chief, G.Q.G.:

From different sources have come reports on the organization of the front, calling attention to certain defects in the defenses.

Particularly, in the region of Meurthe, Toul, and Verdun, the network of trenches is not as complete as on the greater part of the front.

This situation, if it be correct, incurs the gravest risk. Any breakthrough by the enemy, occurring in these circumstances, would challenge not only your own responsibility, but that of the entire government.

The most recent information from the front itself proves conclusively that first lines can be forced, but that the resistance of the rear lines can stop an attack, even after its initial success.

I know that you will want to enable me to give assurances that all along our front the organization of at least two lines has been anticipated and provided with all the defensive devices necessary (barbed wire, moats, abatis, etc.)

GALLIENI[27]

The generalissimo's reply, sent December 18, registered offended grandeur and ponderous rage—as might have been expected. Joffre loftily reminded the war minister that as early as October 22, 1915, he had instructed the commanders to improve the front and second lines of trenches, preparing fortified zones well to the rear of these.[28] Necessary measures had already been taken to speed up the transport of reserves by rail.[29]

Joffre concluded his letter with a crushing rebuke which, according to Basil H. Liddell Hart, "might well be framed and hung in all the bureaus of officialdom the world over—to serve as 'the mummy at the feast.'"[30]

... Since those fears [which you express] are based on reports calling your attention to deficiencies in the readiness of defense, I demand that you send me these accounts and that you name their authors.... The soldiers who write know that the government makes use of their correspondence concerning their chiefs. Authority is impaired; the morale of everyone suffers from this discrediting.

I shall not be a party to the continuation of this state of affairs.

THE VERDUN CRISIS

I need the full confidence of the government. If it grants me this, then it will neither encourage nor condone practices which diminish the moral authority indispensable to the exercise of my command and, in the absence of which, I shall not be able to continue to assume responsibility.
J. JOFFRE[81]

This perverse letter of Joffre's addressed to a legal superior thoroughly exasperated the war minister who prepared a blistering rejoinder, but Briand, ever the peacemaker, persuaded Gallieni to put aside his first draft and write a soothing note.[82] Evidently Briand felt that the official warning given Joffre was a reasonable enough precaution on the part of the government. If the ministry could not accept Joffre's assurances as to Verdun's readiness, then it should dismiss him. But as yet, Briand believed that Joffre's technical judgment and competence should be trusted, pending events which might prove the contrary. Meanwhile, Briand saw no point in allowing a feud to break out between Gallieni and Joffre. The war minister's thankless task of writing a conciliatory reply to Joffre was made no easier when Minister of State Léon Bourgeois openly criticized Gallieni "for losing time in personal caviling."[83] The gravely ill and sorely tried old general swallowed his anger and wrote Joffre a letter which mollified the Lion of Chantilly:

I have submitted your letter to the Council of Ministers. It has accepted your statements and has taken note of your careful foresight in those matters concerning the defense of positions occupied by our Armies of the Northeast.

It assumes that the work which still remains to be done will be pushed with all possible diligence and care, and it asks you if you will proceed with whatever supervision and inspection you might consider useful, with this in view.

The government has full confidence in you; it recently gave you a brilliant proof of that by conferring upon your person the unified command of the French Armies of all fronts. Its desires to be informed on the condition of our armies, from every point of view, should not be considered as a sign of distrust....
GALLIENI[84]

As events were soon to prove, it was unfortunate for France that Joffre's complacency was not in itself enough to prevent the Germans from mounting one of the war's greatest offensives by their attack upon Verdun. In the middle of January, 1916, French agents in Denmark and Switzerland reported that the crown prince had massed fully 400,000 Germans in the Verdun salient, while French military intelligence estimated that at least seventeen divisions had been withdrawn from other fronts for this purpose.[35] German deserters reported to the Third French Army on January 17 that an attack would be launched against Verdun at the end of January or the beginning of February. The chief of staff, General Edouard de Castelnau, having recently returned from his inspection of Salonika, decided to investigate for himself the defenses of Verdun. When his tour of January 23–26 took him to the outlying woods of Caures and Cumières, he was disturbed to see how "insufficient" and "sketchy" were the defensive works.[36] De Castelnau's "conclusions fully confirmed the alarms of Gallieni...."[37] It seemed as if Joffre and the Young Turks were almost the only ones who did not expect the impending storm, despite all the warnings that had been received.

The elaborately prepared German assault, delayed by rain until February 21, 1916,[38] was launched with the firing of a fourteen-inch shell into Verdun's spacious Bishop's Palace. Soon the whole sector was engulfed in artillery fire.

Nowhere before, on any front, in any battle, had anything like it been seen [wrote General Henri Philippe Pétain]. The Germans aimed to create a "Zone of Death" within which no troops could survive. An avalanche of steel and iron, of shrapnel and poisonous gas shells, fell on our woods, ravines, trenches and shelters, destroying everything, transforming the sector into a charnel field.... It would be impossible to describe an action of the kind. I believe that it has never been equalled in violence, and it concentrated the devastating fire of more than two million shells in the narrow triangle of land between Brabant-on-Meuse, Ornes, and Verdun.[39]

THE VERDUN CRISIS

On the first day of the attack, the enemy quickly breached the Bois des Caures and the Herbebois sectors, north of Verdun, killing, ironically, as one of their first victims the prescient soldier-deputy, Colonel Emile Driant.[40] By February 23, Wavrille was in German possession and Samogneux, Haumont, and Ornes were gravely threatened. Joffre immediately sent two army corps as reserves to Verdun, but he was reluctant to alter the position of his twenty-six reserve divisions which were "echeloned behind the entirety of the front" because he still could not be convinced that Verdun was to be the chief point of attack.[41] Joffre was utterly blind to the German strategic plan which, according to Winston Churchill,

> was founded upon Falkenhayn's appreciation of French psychology and German artillery. [Falkenhayn] believed that the French regarded Verdun with sentiments which had no relation to material facts. Verdun was the historical scene of the triumph of Gaul over the Teuton. It was regarded throughout France as the corner-stone in the French rampart against Germany. To preserve Verdun the French ... would be bled white.... Honour would compel them to defend positions which a cool view of war would have yielded at a certain price. The brave would be slain, and Paris, accepting defeat, would sue for peace.[42]

On the night of February 23, the news from Verdun continued to be so grave that Joffre sent his personal aide, Colonel Claudel, to study the situation on the spot.[43] February 24 brought even worse reports to the effect that the Germans had captured the wood of Fosses, that Ornes had to be evacuated, and that the German advance along both banks of the Meuse might necessitate a French withdrawal from the Woevre region. Joffre instructed General Langle de Cary, the commander of the Army Group of the Center (to whose authority Verdun had recently been assigned), to use his own judgment about evacuating the Woevre, but, in any case, to retain the French hold on the east bank of the Meuse.[44]

In Paris, meanwhile, Briand had been following the dismaying reports of the German advance. With a nightmarish vividness, he realized that all the grim warnings about an impending German attack upon Verdun were proving well founded. It was obvious that not only was the reputation of Joffre at stake, but the prestige of Briand's government was called into question, since it was the president of the council's responsibility for having accepted Joffre's ill-tempered assurance to War Minister Gallieni that all was in a state of perfect readiness at Verdun. If the city should fall, the scandal would undoubtedly provoke a parliamentary investigation, and no president of the council would enjoy contemplating the political capital which ill-disposed deputies could make of all the unheeded warnings about Verdun's defenses.

Thoroughly agitated, the usually unruffled Briand summoned his chauffeur on the night of February 24 and set out for Chantilly, unannounced and unbidden. Despite one of the most formidable attacks of the war, Joffre, as usual, was "sleeping like a child"[45] when the president of the council arrived at G.Q.G. Briand demanded that Joffre's most inviolable order—"that he should not be awakened under any pretext"—be disregarded, and the comatose generalissimo and his staff of Young Turks had to assemble in Joffre's study at the Villa Poiret to give Briand "a complete and detailed account of the situation."[46] The Young Turks spoke for their chief, using as their text the report of Colonel Claudel[47] which had evidently convinced Joffre of the infeasibility of trying to hold the east bank of the Meuse as he had so recently ordered Langle de Cary to do. The staff officers advanced the beguiling argument that "Verdun was only a geographical point, not all of France. There was no need for superstition in regard to terrain."[48] This "essentially military thesis" was elaborated in detail: "We have our back to the Meuse; there are four bridges which the Germans can destroy whenever they want; Verdun, a heap of ruins, would then lie beyond reach of our supply columns; so we might just as well abandon this salient and rectify the line."[49]

THE VERDUN CRISIS

Joffre may have been sleepy, but he had not lost his peasant cunning, since he was letting his protégés bear the responsibility of trying to persuade Briand to risk political suicide by abandoning Verdun. But neither had Briand lost his political bearings, for his assistant director of political affairs, M. Philippe Berthelot, had repeatedly called his attention to "the role of morale in the war and to the capital importance to France of not giving up Verdun...."[50] As the exasperated president of the council listened to the detached analyses of the technical experts, he tried to remonstrate with them: "For you it is understood that the abandonment of Verdun would not be a defeat, but for the whole wide world it would be one. And rest assured our soldiers would receive a rude shock on that day."[51] The technicians obstinately brushed aside such "political" objections until at last Briand was so thoroughly irritated that—possibly for the first time in his life—he "shouted" at his antagonists:[52] "If you surrender Verdun, you will be cowards, cowards! And you needn't wait till then to hand in your resignation. If you abandon Verdun, I sack you all on the spot!"[53]

Never before in the war was there so dramatically illustrated the difficulty of finding a formula which would automatically differentiate between the spheres of policy and strategy. The president of the council possessed the legal right to order the defense of Verdun, because the question directly impinged upon state policy, both foreign and domestic (for the city's capture unquestionably would have been a blow to French prestige abroad as well as morale at home). Yet from the strictly military point of view, Joffre and the Young Turks had a plausible case: by giving up the Verdun salient (which was far from Paris and strategically expendable) the French line could be shortened and held with relative ease and with a reduced loss in man power. The command, however, had inexcusably wavered between abandoning the Verdun salient voluntarily at a suitable time, and continuing to go through the motions of maintaining its defenses. Either Verdun should have been abandoned earlier at a time of France's own choosing, or, if it was to be held at all, the command should have heeded the repeated warnings about its neglected defenses. To abandon it in the face of a carefully prepared and long-forewarned German assault would shatter French morale; to maintain the city by belated efforts at defense which could be carried out only with staggering losses would impair the French will-to-victory only slightly less. Since the High Command had not made up its mind in time as to what it should do, Briand was fully justified in trying to salvage a bad situation by demanding that Verdun be held, for its loss in the existing circumstances would have prejudiced the hope of ultimate victory. Joffre must have appreciated the extent of Briand's unwonted fury and the extreme shakiness of his own position; he realized that the strictly military argument for abandoning Verdun would have to be discarded for the political considerations which called for the city's retention. From bottomless depths of sleepiness and craftiness, the generalissimo amiably spoke up at last: "The president [of the council] is right. I share his point of view. No falling back on the left bank. We fight to the end."[54] France's course was set.

Having been shockingly negligent about Verdun's defenses before the attack, Joffre made partial amends through his belated efforts to hold the citadel. He readily agreed to the proposal of his Chief of Staff de Castelnau that a new Army of Verdun be constituted from the existing Second and Third armies, and that it be entrusted to the commander of the former, General Henri Philippe Pétain.[55] The career of Pétain had been singular. The outbreak of the war had found him an aging colonel stationed at St. Omer. He had not endeared himself to the command by his lectures at the Ecole de Guerre in which he had advanced the defensive thesis of the decisiveness of fire power,[56] a doctrine abhorred by the school of the *offensive à outrance*. However, in the Battle of the Marne, his defense of Montceau-les-Provins had won him an advance within six weeks from colonel to major general.[57] From June, 1915, this cold, aloof, and conservative general officer commanded the Second Army until he was given the new Army of Verdun.

Pétain set to work at once solving Verdun's supply problem by hastily improving the departmental road which connected the partially surrounded city with Bar-le-Duc.[58] The "fire-power fetishist" then had a long-awaited opportunity of putting his favorite theories into practice. Whenever the liaison officers of the various army corps under Pétain's command met him at his headquarters at Souilly to give their reports on the fighting, he invariably interrupted them with the question: "What have your batteries been doing? We will discuss other points later."[59] Pétain insisted on rotating the units thrown in at Verdun, thus using in succession no less than seventy-eight divisions to prevent the annihilation of any one of them.[60] In this he ran counter to Joffre's wish to keep sufficient reserve divisions free to try to relieve Verdun by mounting a joint Anglo-French offensive on the Somme which had been scheduled for the end of June, 1916.[61] An agreement for such a combined offensive had been reached earlier at an inter-Allied war council held at Chantilly on December 6, 1915.

Joffre and Pétain engaged in a tug-of-war for all available guns and divisions—Pétain fully determined to hold Verdun in the face of the immediate danger, Joffre equally resolved to save it through the diversionary offensive on the Somme which had been previously arranged with the British. The generalissimo finally became so irritated over Pétain's "insatiable demands" for troops that he brusquely ordered him to make out as best he could with "the forces already at his disposal."[62] The result of this order was that a reduced number of troops had to endure more frequent intervals of punishment under the German guns. "Men began to be worn out on certain parts of the Verdun front" and French morale flagged.[63]

It is possible that one reason Joffre had been caught unprepared at Verdun was that a generalissimo had too much to do. This problem of a commander in chief's burdensome responsibilities had been laid before Parliament on December 15, 1915, by Léon Accambray, a Radical Socialist deputy from Laon, an admirer of Gallieni and Sarrail, and a merciless critic of Joffre.[64] Accambray was bold enough to refuse to vote for war credits even in 1915 "because the government did not have his confidence."[65] This audacious deputy had no hesitancy in publicly demanding of President of the Council Briand a full accounting of what precisely were the legal powers of the commander in chief of the armies, "especially in matters of organization and military administration.... What texts define the character and consequent relations with the higher military authority, charged with the conduct of operations, in the cases of: A) the minister of war, charged with anticipating and providing all the needs of the armies; B) the government in general, vested with a high mission of administration and negotiation, of organization and coördination, of direction and long-range motivation?"[66]

Briand blandly ignored this probing, confident in his knowledge that a conservative bloc in the Chamber did not want to open a general discussion of the High Command.[67] Furthermore, Briand probably felt that he had sufficiently patched up the difficult relationship between command and government (as well as it could be improvised) through his recent creation of the *Conseil supérieur de la défense nationale*. It is true that this body was merely "the Council of Ministers reduced by some of its members and reinforced by the addition of the general in chief,"[68] but, in any case, it presented an impressive façade to potential critics.

The question of the broad and amorphous powers of the commander in chief was again brought up at the Chamber's session of February 18, 1916, by Deputy Abel Ferry, who tried vainly to draw Briand out on the problem of parliamentary inspection. Briand skillfully and persistently parried debate on this topic, claiming the necessity of avoiding "grave inconveniences" and "mischievous words" which might echo throughout the country.[69] Undaunted by Briand's refusal to discuss military

THE VERDUN CRISIS

questions, Ferry directed an attack against the anachronistic nature of Article 2 of the Field Service Regulations of December 2, 1913, which vested Joffre's vast powers in him. In this attack Ferry stated:

What is bad in the strict application of this out-of-date text is that it burdens with a thousand petty details of daily administration the gigantic task of the general in chief, who has to lead an army three or four times the size of that of Napoleon I; to assure unity with the Allied armies; to wage the daily battle; to interrogate personally, not only generals of armies, but the executors, generals of divisions, of brigades, colonels, to see even majors and captains; to combine in himself the experiences of the entire French army; to be at the same time a permanent inspector of the trenches, of defensive and offensive organizations; finally, to be in person at the decisive points on the battle field.

So be it! This state of affairs will continue. So be it! It is to be understood that they will go on waging the war as before; they will go on with their paper work, their documents, their orders, and an officer will not be judged by his exercise of command—the only good criterion in a time of war—he will be judged by the orders he issues, and by his bookkeeping.... All of this, gentlemen, is the result of an initial error, because the government has assigned functions to the High Command which do not properly belong to it. General headquarters ought to be only a command post, but you have made it a ministry. Do you want that to continue? Very well! Yours will be the responsibility.[70]

The most penetrating analysis of the role of the High Command and of its nebulous relationship with the government was supplied on March 7, 1916, by one who should have been well informed on the topic, War Minister General Gallieni. Greatly displeased with the General Staff's recent negligence at Verdun despite his own formal warning, Gallieni read to a startled and increasingly apprehensive Council of Ministers a fifteen-page "Note on the High Command" in which he explained the commander in chief's functions in theory and in practice.

The rights and duties of the commander in chief are limited to directing operations, of which the political aim has been previously determined by the government. The commander in chief has entirely at his disposal the resources given him by virtue of his prescribed function; he is in charge of these means and is responsible for their use; but all the texts agree in leaving to the minister [of war] the responsibility for creating and providing these resources, thereby relieving the commander in chief of the burden of the so-called administration of the army. There is no doubt about the executive power's having the sole right of determining the political, economic, and diplomatic conditions within which the armed conflict takes place, nor of the minister of war's assisting... in the deliberations of the government, thereby relieving the commander in chief from all concern with interdepartmental communications which must be in accordance with the conduct of operations. From the point of view of administration of the army, the law of 1882 declares formally that the minister of war is solely responsible, constitutionally speaking.[71]

General Gallieni briefly reviewed the legislation affecting the command and the government which had been passed between 1882 and 1913. He called particular attention to the minister's power of dividing the country into the commander in chief's zone of the armies and the minister's zone of the interior, as given in the decree of December 2, 1913.[72] He reiterated that while the government determines the policy of the war, "the execution of this plan, insofar as it concerns military operations, is entrusted to the general or commander in chief who becomes responsible henceforth for its execution, as the resources are put at his disposal. The minister of war remains, all the while, responsible for the administration of the army."[73] Such was the relationship between the High Command and the government in theory.

As to actual practice, Gallieni cited numerous instances of encroachments of the High Command upon the domain of the government. Military control of production was understandable in the early weeks of the war when the government was at Bordeaux, since there "was left in the zone of the armies a major part of the natural resources,"[74] but a policy justifiable in a temporary emergency threatened to become permanent, long after the crisis had passed. The undersecretary of state for munitions had testified as to the inefficiency of the duplication of efforts, with the High Command as well as the government letting out contracts for aviation, artillery, and engineering supplies.[75]

The High Command, according to Gallieni, had shown a "repugnance" toward accepting the parliamentary inspection established by the law of 1882, for it sought to "impose upon every inspection mission authorized by the minister the obligation of going first to *Grand Quartier Général* before any investigation could be made in the zone of the armies." This practice circumvented "immediate and direct" inspection, which was the only effective supervision by Parliament.[76]

The war minister declared further that the decree of December 2, 1915, creating the post of commander in chief of the French Armies, was supposed to have assigned to the chief of the general staff [de Castelnau] all of the auxiliary services under the jurisdiction of G.Q.G. But such was not the case in actual practice, the chief of the general staff being left with an empty title while the commander in chief himself continued to have direct contacts with the medical officers and with the chief of the personnel bureau, for example.[77]

Gallieni reminded his restive colleagues that the government had notified Joffre on December 16 that reports from the armies had called attention to defects in the defenses of Verdun. "Recent events tend to prove that the government was well informed." Thus warned of German movements at least two months before the attack upon Verdun, the High Command should have studied the terrain through map investigations and reconnaissance to determine Verdun's needs in troops, cannon, food stocks, transport, barbed wire, aviation, and the adequate organization of its general staff. A standard gauge railway between Bar-le-Duc and Verdun should have been built by the High Command a year before. "In short, for at least two months—if not five months—they should have anticipated the defense of the region of Verdun against a tremendous German offensive, either on the east or west bank of the Meuse."[78] But all of that was already past. General Gallieni concluded his long indictment with three recommendations:

1) Put the High Command back in the place where it belongs and withdraw from it all of its concerns except the direction of military operations.
2) Restore to the minister his administrative control....
3) Eliminate those chiefs who adhere to anachronistic ideas and outmoded procedures, who cannot adapt themselves to the circumstances of the actual struggle.[79]

General Gallieni's trenchant criticism of the High Command greatly irritated his fellow Cabinet members. Despite the fact that Briand had been ready to sack the entire General Staff a fortnight before, he paradoxically rallied to Joffre's defense Apparently the supple and opportunistic politician felt that the government should maintain closed ranks with the command now that the worst crisis seemed past and France's course had been set for Verdun's retention. Any continuation of criticism of the command issuing from within the government would eventually leak out and become political capital for carping deputies. Briand went so far in rebuking Gallieni as to declare that the war minister had "bored" his colleagues with his long memorandum—an "insult" which brought the Cabinet's second warrior, Navy Minister Admiral Lucien Lacaze, into the discussion in General Gallieni's behalf. In his own account of the incident, Gallieni dismissed the matter with the dry comment: "Decidedly, if the military do not understand the parliamentarians, the parliamentarians do not understand the military."[80]

Notwithstanding his seeming detachment, Gallieni was suffering from an ailment soon to prove fatal. In great physical pain, and disgusted with the command's presumption and the government's vacillation, he insisted upon resigning to undergo an operation. He ignored the protests of Briand and Poincaré, who were aghast at the thought of the government's losing so distinguished a member before the Verdun fighting had subsided completely.[81] Gallieni could not be dissuaded from his resolution, but he stoically agreed to wait until he could be replaced.

Finding a successor was an urgent matter, because some prying parliamentarians might reasonably suspect that Gallieni's resignation signified something more than illness, however bona fide. After briefly considering as possible choices the politicians Charles de Freycinet and Louis Barthou, and Generals Lyautey, Dubail, and Famin, Briand acceded to Joffre's suggestion that a suitable war minister could be found in General Pierre Auguste Roques.[82] That Briand should still be taking seriously Joffre's wishes after all that had happened was not surprising in view of the president of the council's easygoing and conciliatory nature. Then too, apart from the somewhat shopworn General Sarrail, the name of no great military captain came to mind as a serious alternative to Joffre, who with all his limitations now so patent continued to profit from his earlier reputation as France's savior. Accordingly, Joffre had his way once again in the choice of a war minister. Joffre related that he had only one misgiving about General Roques: "... I feared, somewhat, his lack of character vis-à-vis the parliamentarians...."[83]

Offsetting such doubts was the friendliness existing between Joffre and Roques, who had been classmates at the Ecole Polytechnique and campaigners together in Indo-China.[84] At the beginning of hostilities in 1914, Roques was inspector general of military aviation. Assigned at once to a field command, Roques' army corps had cut a sorry figure in Belgium and again at the Marne.[85] This did not prevent Joffre from giving him the command of the First Army in January, 1915. "In political circles [Roques] passed for a military man able to play the game according to the accepted rules. Conciliatory, gentle, affable, with no more obstinacy than authority, he could frighten no one. As a private individual he was an excellent man, but nothing marked him as a man of state unless it was the 'suppleness' which was expected of him."[86]

But "supple" Roques proved a source of astonishment and dismay to Joffre. In fact, it was Joffre's "old friend" Roques even more than his known rival Gallieni who served notice upon the generalissimo that the epoch of the war minister's eager deference to the command (which characterized the Messimy-Millerand period) had ended. The first inkling that Roques could be capable of an attitude of independence toward Joffre appeared in a conversation which the new war minister had with Colonel Herbillon. In referring to the commander in chief, Roques declared: "If our old and solid friendship will not permit us to go arm in arm, then it is doubtful whether such a thing as agreement is ever possible. I will defend him with all my power if he is attacked, but, for his part, he ought to aid me. I do not want to be a sub-Joffre, but rather a ministerial friend of Joffre's...."[87]

Roques was to be strengthened in his determination not to be a "sub-Joffre" by the effect of the mounting casualties at Verdun. When Gallieni had criticized the command only a short time after the decision had been made to hold the city, Briand's government had treated the war minister as if he were querulous and disloyal. But every day, every hour, of March, April, and May of 1916 brought reports of such huge losses at Verdun—casualties which could have been minimized had the command only made up its mind earlier—that no government could have continued much longer to act as if the generalissimo were infallible. War Minister Roques, consequently, was to be allowed a much freer hand than Gallieni in reproving the general in chief for his mistakes or presumption.

Scarcely a fortnight passed after Roques' appointment (with Joffre's blessing) before there appeared the first hint of the new

THE VERDUN CRISIS

war minister's intentions. On March 31 General Roques asked Colonel Herbillon to notify the generalissimo that "certain points in the vicinity of Verdun did not seem . . . to be fortified strongly enough."[88] When Joffre heard of Roques' action, he flared up and indignantly asked Herbillon what the war minister was "meddling in." Herbillon replied tactfully that ". . . in Paris they are beginning to say that secondary defenses are not sufficiently laid out everywhere; it would be well to find out if everything has been done according to orders." Joffre decided to let the matter rest. *"C'est bon,"* he replied guardedly.[89]

Joffre soon received another rude jolt from the short, affable, and seemingly ineffectual war minister when Roques introduced a new procedure for promoting generals—or rather returned to a legal prescription which had fallen into disuse. The government, according to legist Joseph Barthélemy, possessed beyond question the right "to select the chief of the army and other generals." Nevertheless, indulgent War Minister Millerand had given the commander in chief carte blanche in promoting general officers. Gallieni had been willing to grant Joffre the initiative in nominating officers, subject to the war minister's veto, but even in such a case Joffre was allowed to fill out new lists of candidates until his proposals were finally acceptable.[90]

Unlike his predecessors, War Minister Roques boldly assumed the initiative and on March 23, 1916, proposed the "rejuvenation of the officer cadre" by withdrawing commands from Generals Langle de Cary, Dubail, de Villaret, and d'Urbal, and by giving an army command to General Gérard.[91] There was no fundamental disagreement between Roques and Joffre over the proposed changes in command, but Joffre was accustomed to making the appointments himself—with no "officious" interference from any quarter, not even from rue St. Dominique, and least of all did he expect it from Roques.

Meanwhile, the devastating fighting at Verdun went on unrelentingly. In the words of Winston Churchill, the German "attacks on Verdun had subsided into a prolonged concentrated struggle in the crater-fields around the fortress. Each side crammed new divisions into the limited arena of the death-grapple, and fed their guns with unstinted shells. The Germans had performed prodigies. [Forts] Douaumont and Thiaumont and Vaux were in their hands. The possession of '304-metre hill' was disputed with blood and assertions. But the world sustained only one impression, namely that the French held Verdun...."[92] Such may have been the world's impression, but the French government had deeper insight: it knew the incredible cost in lives of the defense of the stronghold, and it was aware of the questionable behavior of the High Command before the attack, as well as during its opening days.

The Briand government must undoubtedly have feared the effect upon public opinion of the forthcoming reports of the slaughter at Verdun. Since so many divisions had been rotated in this sector, it was only a question of time until numberless eyewitness accounts of the carnage on the Meuse would be broadcast throughout the nation. To enable the Briand government to survive the storm of criticism which was bound to arise, a scapegoat was needed, and who better than Joffre, for was not his complacency in large part responsible for the high casualties?

Instead of acting forthrightly in sacking Joffre, the Briand government appears to have connived at the undermining of his prestige through press criticism of the High Command—something without precedent in the war. The French political world was incredulous when there unaccountably appeared two anonymous newspaper articles which dared take Joffre to task for his role at Verdun. By some means, *Le Petit Parisien* managed on May 8, 1916, to publish an account of how Verdun had hung in the balance for a few critical days after February 21. "Some persons thought [the German attack was] a feint, and delayed in sending reinforcements." This was an obvious slur upon misguided Joffre. The writer went on to explain that when French covering troops were forced to fall back, there was even contemplated the abandonment of the east bank of the

Meuse. "However, there was a chief who, from the first hour, had an intuition of danger and who sounded the alarm...." Thus was Chief of Staff de Castelnau singled out for having made a fateful decision which, we can say thirty-five years after the event, could more properly have been ascribed to Briand. The article declared that the chief of staff on February 24 telephoned "the imperative order to change the plans adopted and to assure, at any cost, the defense of Verdun on the right bank of the Meuse."[93]

Hardly had the shock of this first disclosure worn off when there appeared another in *Le Matin* on May 10. As in the first instance, the anonymous writer traced the crucial events at Verdun immediately following February 21. He contended that when the three French covering divisions had to fall back before five German army corps, those who had all along been complacent about Verdun's defenses were suddenly seized with pessimism and demanded the evacuation of the entire right bank of the Meuse. At this juncture Chief of Staff de Castelnau arrived at Verdun, "looked about him, exercised his judgment, and decided upon a counterplan of holding the enemy on the plateau of Douaumont, at all costs. Thus Verdun was saved." The article praised General Pétain for his organization of the supply route from Bar-le-Duc, and concluded with a thinly veiled warning that one day "responsibilities would be assessed" for what had happened at Verdun.[94]

As anyone could have predicted, the High Command was "furious" over the publication of these unflattering articles.[95] One would have to read for himself the French wartime press to appreciate completely the brazen tone of the exposures which was in such marked contrast to the awed respectfulness of all previous references to the High Command. Joffre's indignation reached unparalleled heights when he heard the rumor that the person responsible for letting these lampoons slip by the censor was none other than War Minister Roques! Joffre must have felt as if he had been stabbed in the back. Gone were the days of Messimy and Millerand, when the war minister served primarily as a buffer between the command, the government, and Parliament. Now it appeared that rue St. Dominique had become an outpost in the hands of the parliamentary critics of Joffre rather than the commander's principal bulwark. But the loss at Verdun of 250,000 Frenchmen in killed, wounded, and captured within the two months between February 21 and April 25[96] was a shattering reality which the government could not keep hidden for long. A "vigorous" ministry, such as the future Jacobin rule of Clemenceau, would probably have acted openly against Joffre, but such devious politicians as Briand and Roques could hardly be expected to pursue such a course. War Minister Roques had access to the files of his predecessors at rue St. Dominique, and he could hardly avoid learning the unheeded warnings about Verdun's vulnerability. In view of these facts, the rumor was credible that Joffre's "old friend" had offered no opposition to the publication of the critical newspaper articles,[97] and, according to one version, had even "appended a note of favorable comment to them."[98] The surprise over the publications was so great that all sorts of speculation ensued, with one report even asserting that Briand had inspired the articles "to claim credit for the battle of Verdun."[99] This particular rumor, noted by Poincaré, misrepresented the purport of the articles which ascribed the credit to Chief of Staff de Castelnau, but it did take into account the fact that such an evasion of the censorship twice within three days could hardly have occurred without the connivance of someone high in the ministry.

The army commission of the Chamber was so disturbed over the excitement aroused by the disclosures that it asked Briand and Roques to appear at its session of May 13. All that the commissioners could extract from the wily pair was Briand's assertion that the person responsible for the exposures was André Tardieu, a Union Republican deputy from Seine-et-Oise, who had been assigned to the staff of Foch.[100] Briand contended that M. Tardieu "had suggested the articles to M. Henri de Jouvenel

THE VERDUN CRISIS

and to an editor of *Le Petit Parisien*."[101] Evidence is not at hand to authenticate this statement, but even if its accuracy be granted, it still does not explain how the articles, appearing three days apart, managed to evade the censorship. But it was the only explanation which the army commission received.

The question of the "defamatory" articles came up again at a meeting of the Council of Ministers at which President Poincaré insisted "that the censorship ought not to allow the High Command to be attacked during hostilities...."[102] The whole affair, in the opinion of the president, was enough "to make one weep." Joffre had demanded that a communiqué of correction be issued at once. Briand, whose behavior during the entire affair had been very devious and none too creditable, proved himself again to be a temporizer by docilely agreeing to Joffre's request.

Briand's compliance with Joffre's demand for what amounted to an "apology" did not mean that the president of the council was going to protect Joffre from all parliamentary attack. In fact, Briand forthwith joined a chorus of demands that Joffre dismiss certain of the Young Turks who were held especially responsible for the bloody strategy at Verdun. Particularly hated by parliamentary critics were General Pellé, chief of general headquarters theater of exterior operations; Colonel Buat, the former chief of the Cabinet of Millerand; Lieutenant Colonel Bel, who was the chief of the personnel bureau.[103] Not only Briand, but Roques and even Poincaré insisted that Joffre drop the members of his staff who were the especial objects of parliamentary attack. Colonel Herbillon tried to remonstrate with the government by pointing out that dismissing the principal Young Turks "would not disarm the adversaries" of Joffre, who "would return to the attack with all the more violence."[104] Herbillon was partially correct in the prediction, since the dropping of Colonel Buat by Joffre on May 13 did not silence the clamor.

The sacrifice of one Young Turk was not enough to prevent the Socialist deputies as well as Left Democrat André Maginot and the Left Radicals Paul Benazet and Abel Ferry from demanding a session of the Chamber in secret committee[105] for a full discussion of the High Command which was held responsible for the sickening casualties at Verdun. Briand undoubtedly heard the rumor circulated in the corridors of the Palais Bourbon that if he tried to prevent a discussion of the command, he would be overthrown for a Barthou or a Clemenceau cabinet. The opportunistic politician saw no reason for sacrificing his ministerial life for a general who had proved a disappointment. Thus Briand consented to hold a secret committee, which meant that no longer could the generalissimo assume that the war minister and president of the council would defend him, as in the past, by a studied policy of ignoring or shutting off all criticism. Joffre's parliamentary enemies, who had been closing in on him for months, were soon to be baying at his very heels.

6

Parliament's Ascendancy over the Ministry and Command

FOR THE FIRST TIME SINCE THE OUTBREAK OF THE WAR, France held a session of a parliamentary secret committee on June 16, 1916. On three previous occasions (August 12, August 13, and December 15, 1915) demands for a secret committee had been voted down by the Chamber, primarily because the conservatives wanted to avoid any criticism of the command; in addition, it was feared that a possible overthrow of the government during a closed session might affect morale, since the public could learn the reasons for such action only by rumor and hearsay. The critics of Parliament would be sure to ascribe a ministerial upset in these circumstances to irresponsible political intrigue rather than to a sincere concern with national interests.[1]

The customary supervision which Parliament exercised over the government in peacetime had been greatly curtailed, since budgetary review, temporarily suspended by the legislative branch during the five months of "military dictatorship" from August to December, 1914, had never been fully reasserted since then. Interpellation in public session was out of the question during a national emergency, the government naturally refusing to debate openly the "delicate" questions of the prosecution of the war—questions which would have delighted the enemy intelligence. Yet the procedure followed between December, 1915, and June, 1916, had proved unsatisfactory, for while members of the great parliamentary commissions could obtain information on the government's war policy by directly questioning the ministers in camera, those deputies and senators who were not

---

[1] For notes to chap. 6, see pages 259–262.

members of the army commission, or the finance commission, for example, were left officially unenlightened.[2]

By the middle of 1916, a majority of the parliamentarians felt that it was high time for the Briand government to submit to questioning on such serious issues as the rumored loss of 250,000 casualties at Verdun, as well as "the immobility of the front, the futility of partial offensives, the warnings of Colonel Driant, the reports of the army commissioners."[3] The demand for the extraordinary procedure of a secret committee was advanced by such well-known enemies of Joffre—and friends of the late Gallieni—as Senators Paul Doumer and Charles Humbert, and Deputies André Maginot, Abel Ferry, Léon Accambray, Maurice Viollette, and André Tardieu.[4] Opposed heart and soul to the secret committee were Ministers Jules Méline and Charles de Freycinet, as well as President Poincaré who had glumly predicted at a council meeting "that if the Chamber wished to discuss the Verdun affair, as it appeared, they would fall into complete anarchy."[5] Sanguine and opportunistic Briand refused to take "such a gloomy view," and he yielded to the demand for a governmental airing of war policy, preferring characteristically to take his chances by tacking before the wind.

The first secret committee was called to order on June 16, 1916, by the president of the Chamber, M. Paul Deschanel, who reminded the deputies of the "inviolable nature" of the sessions. "Everyone," he said, "is pledged to reveal absolutely nothing of what will be said in the course of the secret committee. The text of our deliberations will remain in our archives, after being sealed immediately...."[6]

The first speaker was a Democratic Left deputy from Bar-le-Duc, André Maginot, a war veteran who had been wounded at Verdun in November, 1914. "The war," Maginot declared, "can last a year longer; if our forces melt away at the same rate as in the preceding months, France may emerge victorious from this struggle, but she will be exhausted and condemned to become a nation of second rank."[7] Maginot assailed the "deceitfulness" of the government's announcements concerning attrition. The fighting at Verdun had raised German total losses by June, 1916, to 2,940,195, of whom 800,000 were killed, while "in the number killed the French were not at all below this figure."[8] Germany, said Maginot, had experienced hardly more deaths on two fronts than France had suffered on one, yet France was far below Germany in total population and birth rate. Maginot attributed the magnitude of French casualties to an inferiority in matériel and to the mad plan of "uninterrupted partial offensives which result in no appreciable change of strategic importance, but only in murderous losses...."[9] We must change [our] methods.... The Verdun affair definitely condemns the... High Command in its conduct of operations. It has revealed the degree of unpreparedness and inertia which our High Command has reached!"[10]

André Maginot was followed on the rostrum by Deputies Espivent de la Villeboisnet, Paul Benazet, and Pierre Renaudel. It was a foregone conclusion that inveterate foes of the High Command would avail themselves of every opportunity of blasting Chantilly,[11] but the role of Espivent de la Villeboisnet caused surprise. This deputy of the Right defended the procedure of sending parliamentary delegations to the armies with all the warmth which the Socialists and Radical Socialists were accustomed to display.[12] When Deputy Paul Benazet inveighed against the usurpation of general headquarters which had made it "a government in miniature," and when he demanded that Chantilly be restricted to its normal functions—military operations—Briand ironically congratulated him "on his excellent memory, since he was merely repeating facts cited by Briand himself before the army commission."[13] After this sally, Briand briefly reassured the deputies that the government had already begun to recover control of "essentially governmental" services (such as letting out contracts for matériel), and general headquarters would be reduced "little by little to a mere organ of command."[14] Briand was resorting to his favorite stratagem of trying to ridicule a critic by acting as if his complaint had been considered and disposed of long in the past, when in reality the concession was in the very process of being made.

The following day Briand informed Poincaré that he was "very satisfied" with the way things were going in the dreaded secret committee. Poincaré wrote happily in his memoirs that "none of the orators had the slightest success."[15]

Deputy Abel Ferry delivered the principal indictment against the command and government on the second day of the secret committee, June 17.

We cannot escape the impact of facts. At Verdun no second line was organized and this has all but cost us the capture of the city. This has cost us, in the past three months, tens of thousands of sublime soldiers whom foresight could have saved. Even in victory—if there is to be victory!—the heroism of the soldier does not absolve so grave a neglect....

For twenty months the High Command has sacrificed the best of our army in piecemeal and useless attacks. Consider ... Verdun ... bloody and tragic.... What more flagrant proof could there be that for twenty months there has been no command![16]

Ferry concluded his attack with what had become a sort of refrain: "There are two Frances, two Frances which struggle separately, each in its own zone. There are two ministries: a Ministry of War in Paris and another ministry in the zone of the armies at Chantilly...."[17]

How was Joffre to be defended from his critics? In view of the vacillating attitude which War Minister Roques and President of the Council Briand had recently shown toward the command in the rather shabby affair of the exposures published in *Le Petit Parisien* and *Le Matin,* it would have been difficult to predict the course which they would follow in the secret committee. So far, they had shown a strong tendency to run with the hare and to hunt with the hounds. Had the government openly thrown Joffre to the parliamentary critics, the Socialists and Radical Socialists might have been appeased, but such a cynical

PARLIAMENT'S ASCENDANCY

course would have outraged the conservatives who, notwithstanding their doubts about Joffre's infallibility, were nevertheless opposed to a direct parliamentary intervention in the removal and appointment of commanders. Briand had to tack to avoid the complete alienation of either extreme in Parliament. Moreover, it was taken for granted that a government would try to defend the technicians subject to its control, unless it could be clearly demonstrated that these functionaries, military or civilian, were guilty of serious faults or misdeeds. A government could easily be tarred with the same brush as that applied to its technicians, since it was responsible for policy, and this responsibility could not be lightly evaded by summary dismissal of its executants who happened to be under attack. Briand was more of a political tactician than strategist, preferring to work out his plan of action on the spur of the moment. Encouraged by the seeming ineffectiveness of the fire of Joffre's critics, Briand and Roques came to the defense of the commander in chief.

The war minister spoke first in Joffre's behalf. Roques extracted from his portfolio great stacks of circulars and decrees concerning Verdun which he proceeded to read to the Chamber until the deputies were "prostrated."[18] He quoted statements from German newspapers to the effect that the French defenses before Verdun were "a veritable labyrinth of trenches."[19] War Minister Roques droned on and on for two days, recapitulating in tedious detail the whole history of the Verdun campaign, and taking to task those critics who engaged in "condemnations en bloc."[20]

Friends of Joffre were encouraged as the secret committee entered its third day, because the attacks upon the command seemed to them to be mere "sword thrusts in water."[21] The Rightist journalist, Léopold Marcellin, wrote that the secret committee was not really concerned with serious questions "of the nation, of the war, but only with parliamentary jousting.... In the last analysis, the Chamber is too feckless to run the risk of disapproving of the High Command. It is going to end where it began, by leaving responsibility to the government."[22] Discounting Marcellin's antiparliamentary bias, it must be granted that there was much truth in his charge. Parliament was justifiably dissatisfied with the way the war was being conducted. It had good reason for being critical of the Verdun campaign and of Joffre's strategy of "nibbling" or attrition, which was more wasteful of French man power than German. But by no stroke of magic could Parliament have produced in 1916 a great military captain to take the place of Joffre. Even had General Foch been appreciated at this period, he would have lacked the necessary resources for his strategy of the *offensive à outrance*. Nor could a strong Jacobin government like the Clemenceau ministry of the following year have so ordered policy that isolated America could have been drawn automatically into the war on France's side, thus tipping the scales of man power and resources to a Western Allied preponderance—which ultimately was to be the decisive factor in victory. There was little which the parliamentarians could do in the summer of 1916 but complain against Joffre's strategy and Briand's policy. Surely they could offer no effective alternative, apart from a passive defense which might have saved man power or made possible a negotiated peace, but which, in itself, could not have brought a decisive victory. A year later when the United States had been drawn into the war, the defense plan of Painlevé and Pétain was the only sensible course pending full American participation, but no such remote contingency as the involvement of the New World could have been taken for granted in 1916.

The session of June 19 was entirely given over to the interpellation of Briand by Maurice Viollette, a Republican Socialist deputy from Eure-et-Loir, who was regarded as the chief "instigator of the secret committee." Challenged by Viollette's truculent questioning, Briand made a long speech, describing his attempts to promote a "unity of the front, a unity of efforts, under a single direction."[23]

PARLIAMENT'S ASCENDANCY

Our concern has been to establish the relations of the government and the command on ... the principle that ... the government has the political direction ... the general supervision of military operations.... The command has the execution ... in full independence, under the direction of the government which, in its turn, is responsible to you [of Parliament]; [the government] must give you an accounting of its superintendence....[24] It is the general in chief who has control of military operations, who has charge of drawing up the plans.... The commander in chief has as executants—and we must give them as much autonomy as possible—the commanders of the army groups, who are themselves under the orders of the High Command. The supervision of the government ought to extend over the whole [hierarchy], from summit to base....[25]

Briand continued the defense of his policy by arguing that he had tried to facilitate parliamentary inspection by allowing army commissioners "to go everywhere on the front." He had willingly discussed their findings with them, appearing fifteen times before the Senate's army commission and five or six times before the Chamber's.[26]

In peacetime [said Briand] there was a *Conseil supérieur de la guerre* which was made up in a manner already known to you. In a time of war, the principal generals who constitute it must lead their armies. It is thus impossible to convene the *conseil* itself, but we have tried to do something similar. Each time a great military problem has arisen, it has been settled only after a kind of *Conseil supérieur de guerre* has met, at which the president of the republic, the president of the council, the minister of war, the general in chief, his chief of staff and the commanders of the army groups have taken part. They examine and discuss the problem. How else would you conceive of the command?[27]

Confident that the parliamentarians had no ready answer for this rhetorical question, Briand launched into a eulogy of the command, praising especially its plan of rotating the sixty divisions already used in the Verdun sector.[28] This bouquet naturally pleased the conservatives, but with complete impartiality Briand next made an appeal for Socialist support by naming the generals who had been dismissed as a result of the reverses at Verdun: first, the small fry, the divisional commanders, Bapst and Bonneval, and then the important figures, Generals Langle de Cary, Dubail, d'Urbal, and Dubois.[29] At the seventh session of the secret committee Briand concluded his defense with a review of events in the Near East, commenting upon the difficulties encountered there: the fall of the Ententophile Cabinet of Venizelos, the Serbian defeat, and the reluctance of the British to support the Salonika expedition.[30]

According to prior agreement, a vote of confidence on the government's war policy was delayed until Parliament reconvened in public session on June 22. After considering six "orders of the day," the Briand government staked its life on the one proposed by the Democratic Left deputy, Maurice Sibille:

The Chamber... declares its intention of continuing... close collaboration with the government in the most vigorous defense of the country. While strictly abstaining from... intervening in the conception, direction, or execution of military operations, it intends to see that... the military needs of these operations are supplied with thoroughness, vigor, and foresight corresponding to the heroism of the armies of the republic.

In view of the fact that the secret committee has enabled [the Chamber] to become informed on the general conduct of the war, the right to return to this same procedure is reserved if the need should arise. [The Chamber] is resolved to institute... a direct delegation which, with the aid of the government, will exercise effective supervision on the spot over all the services charged with providing the needs of the army. It takes note of the efforts already made and the commitments already undertaken by the government, in which it has confidence; aided by this past experience, it will continue to exercise its authority over all the organs of national defense, and will make every effort to have an effective supervision of the war....[31]

The order of the day was adopted by a vote of 440 to 97.

PARLIAMENT'S ASCENDANCY

Briand was so encouraged by the vote of confidence that he decided at once to force the hands of his senatorial critics by asking a friend of Joffre's, M. Jean Bepmale, a Left Democrat from Haute-Garonne, to call for a senatorial secret committee. The friends of the command responded with alacrity, and the Senate sat behind locked doors from July 4 to July 9, 1916, hearing many of the same complaints against Joffre which had been expressed in the Chamber. The Senate's secret committee differed from the Chamber's chiefly in the lavishness of the praise which some of the senators heaped upon General Sarrail.[32] But after the fifth day of debate, the Briand government won an even larger vote of confidence than the Chamber had given it, 251 to 6.[33]

Despite the safe votes of confidence, Poincaré was deeply displeased, especially with the Chamber's order of the day of June 22 calling for a more adequate parliamentary inspection. According to the president of the republic, "the Chamber [was] going to appoint commissioners directly charged with missions which [were] very vague and very dangerous to the armies."[34] Poincaré had probed into a most delicate issue. On this topic Professor Pierre Renouvin of the Sorbonne advanced the view that "the Chamber, according to constitutional theory, could not, of its own authority, exercise a *direct* supervision, which was the prerogative of the government alone; it could not name 'delegates to the armies'; but the government could *invest* certain deputies with inspection missions, on the proposal of the competent commissions, which could draw up the program of inquiries."[35]

Unmindful of such legalistic quiddities, the army commission of the Chamber drafted several plans for improving parliamentary inspection. The one which at first appeared most plausible to the parliamentarians was that drawn up by M. André Tardieu, the rapporteur of the Chamber's army commission. Tardieu proposed a "permanent and general" delegation of thirty inspectors, chosen by the Chamber for ninety-day periods, who would exercise a direct supervision of the armies, while abstaining from the drawing up and execution of military operations.[36] Tardieu's plan was debated from July 18 to July 24, 1916, during which the fear was expressed that a "permanent and general" inspection delegation would probably conflict in jurisdiction with the long-established commissions such as army, navy, and finances,[37] not to mention an inspection delegation which the Senate might likewise create.[38] The deputies were also warned that the thirty inspectors might in fact turn into political commissars comparable to the "representatives of the people on mission with the armies" of the period of the convention.[39]

The deputies weighed all the arguments and counterarguments concerning M. Tardieu's proposal, finally voting in favor of it on the first reading. The next day, "frightened by its own audacity,"[40] the Chamber reversed itself and voted for a counterproposal drawn up under the direction of the Democratic Left deputy from Gironde, Charles Chaumet,[41] which was framed as follows:

The Chamber delegates to its great commissions the necessary powers to exercise an effective inspection on the spot, in accordance with their vested authority, and within the conditions envisaged by the order of day of June 22.

The government is invited to assure the inspection delegates the free and complete exercise of their mandate, as well as to provide all the facilities necessary for its execution.

The delegates will submit a written record of each of their missions to the proper commissions, which will transmit the accounts to the government and bring them to the Chamber's attention by a full report, at least once a quarter.[42]

This moderate resolution merely strengthened the commissions already in existence—army, foreign affairs, finances, as well as such relatively obscure commissions as agriculture and public works—by "spurring on their activity, increasing their authority, and by making the delegates the true proxies of the

PARLIAMENT'S ASCENDANCY

entire Chamber."[43] "The only innovation was that the commissions had to address a quarterly report to the Chamber."[44] The appointment of a panel of thirty permanent inspectors, as recommended by Tardieu, would have been a *direct parliamentary* supervision of the armies, since it would have by-passed the War Ministry. Such a plan undoubtedly would have subtracted from the government many of its administrative duties. Parliament may have been ready to criticize the government, but it had no desire to take over the government's responsibilities.

Parliamentary inspection had been an object of heated contention ever since January, 1915, but now it was regularized to a greater extent, encountering only minor obstacles henceforth. The president of the army commission of the Chamber, General Pédoya, conceded that from the moment of the adoption of the Chaumet procedure, "the work of the delegates was facilitated; the reports filed by the delegates upon the return from [their] missions stated enthusiastically that most of the military chiefs had shown a willingness to satisfy legitimate curiosity, and a strong desire to assist in their efforts."[45] Especially was this true of Generals Ferdinand Foch, Emile Fayolle, and Adolphe Guillaumat.[46] "Rest assured," General Foch told a group of army commissioners, "I am not one who will obstruct your view."[47] Nevertheless, general headquarters still ordered generals not to turn over to the commissions documents concerning "the conception and execution of military operations," or bearing upon military works or lines of defense.[48]

A sovereign remedy for any further friction between the politicians and the military would obviously have been a decisive success of French arms (or even Allied arms), since the bickering arose primarily from the prolonged stalemate. Such a *deus ex machina* solution was allowed to slip away in the battle of the Somme. This long-awaited Anglo-French offensive had been agreed upon as far back as February 14, 1916. The attack was to begin on July 1, 1916. But the prospects of the Somme campaign were none too bright, since the British desired more time for preparation, and the French had found it necessary to throw in at Verdun many of the reserve divisions which General Ferdinand Foch was supposed to employ on the Somme as reinforcements for his Army Group of the North. Nevertheless, the ill-starred campaign began on schedule, following a weeklong artillery barrage.

The Anglo-French objective on the Somme, according to Chief of Staff General de Castelnau, "was first to pierce the enemy's line and then to enlarge the gap by continually bringing up fresh troops on the flanks. The movement aimed at Bapaume, Maubeuge, Liége and Luxemburg."[49] Despite the fact that the twelve German divisions on the Somme sector were outnumbered at the beginning by two to one, the Allied advance was only four miles deep along a thirteen-mile front,[50] nor were the Anglo-French able to follow it up because of their lack of reserves.

It was quickly realized by the French that the battle of the Somme, like so many others, was not to lead to a decision. Colonel Jean Pénelon, Joffre's liaison officer with the Elysée, gave Poincaré "the impression that the command [was] hesitant and [did] not have a sure and definite plan."[51] Even Joffre conceded that while the attack of July 20 "had partially succeeded, that of July 30 had completely miscarried"—a sad state of affairs which he attributed to the fact that General Fayolle's Sixth Army was expected to continue attacks both north and south of the Somme—a campaign beyond its resources.[52]

There was not to be a quick victory, then, which above everything else could have relaxed the tension between the command and the politicians. Joffre, rather than being humbled or chastened by the dwindling chances of military success, "became more and more jealous of his authority and autonomy."[53] Scarcely a fortnight had gone by since the first secret committee when there occurred what Colonel Herbillon—a man not prone to exaggeration—styled a "violent incident" in the increasingly difficult relations between G.Q.G. and the War Ministry. In

PARLIAMENT'S ASCENDANCY

early July, War Minister General Roques visited the headquarters of General Pétain, now commander of the Army Group of the Center. Roques, proceeding upon the assumption that as war minister he was directly responsible for military supplies, had made "certain observations to General Pétain and promise[d] different things.... It was a question of artillery batteries which the commander in chief had ordered sent to the Somme, but which the minister had suggested to General Pétain ought to be sent to Verdun. General Joffre had repeated his order but, naturally, G.Q.G. had taken umbrage at this ministerial intervention."[54] This was a complicated issue in which Roques was probably in error, for if the war minister's responsibility extended over the provisioning of the army, it did not customarily include the allocation of military equipment among the various battlefields, since that was a technical question ordinarily left to the judgment of the commander in chief.

Joffre wrote in his *Mémoires* that on several previous occasions Roques had encroached upon the command by allowing local commanders to submit demands or questions directly to rue St. Dominique, in violation of hierarchical procedure. "A typical example ... [was] the report which General Pétain submitted directly to the war minister, [which] caused the government to write me a letter bringing great pressure to bear upon me to force me to change my decisions. This resort to governmental authority, over my head, appeared to me to be hurtful to my authority over my subordinates."[55]

Determined to guard his prerogatives as commander in chief, Joffre found a pretext for putting Roques "in his place" when the war minister wrote him on July 11 that he and President Poincaré would visit the Verdun and Somme sectors "to congratulate the troops."[56] Joffre gave Colonel Herbillon a letter for Roques in which he stated that at a suitable time he would accompany the war minister and the president of the republic personally over the sector in order to inform them "on the spot of the decisions taken in each particular case, and of [their] reasons...." Elsewhere, concluded Joffre, "military action already under way does not allow projects or trips.... I demand instantly that, for the time being, you postpone your trip to the armies."[57] Colonel Herbillon was laconic in his description of the way in which Roques received this highhanded letter: "Change of physiognomy. Veritable explosion." But Roques recovered his composure sufficiently to say to Herbillon: "How can he write me in this fashion... after the way I defended him in the secret committee!... It is the negation of my authority; it is his determination to assert his independence vis-à-vis the government, to be the government himself. He does not even seem to realize that, without Briand and me, he would have fallen long ago."[58]

Roques was known to be "sweet and affable," which he proved on this occasion, for on July 14 he wrote Joffre a letter in which he was willing to *tutoyer* the general. He tried to remonstrate with the commander in chief: "I must tell you that if I accept what you propose, namely, that I cannot go to the armies unless you accompany me, and if I forego my visits when you cannot accompany me, neither the government nor Parliament would consent, since they would regard it as an abdication.... We can do much together, provided each fulfills his own duties. Please understand that this condition governs the order of the day of the Chamber and Senate. If this is not realized, there will be shipwreck within two months.... It would be better for you to ask me to return your letter of yesterday...."[59] Roques told Herbillon that if "Joffre does not withdraw his letter, I will be forced to submit it tomorrow to the Council of Ministers, and then I do not know what will happen, but it is certain that the government will not accept his attitude."[60]

Colonel Herbillon received a bristling response from Poincaré when the liaison officer visited the Elysée to ask the president, as well, to postpone his visit to Verdun and the Somme. "I will not put it off," Poincaré asserted. "[General Joffre's letter] is

PARLIAMENT'S ASCENDANCY

flagrant proof of the state of mind which prevails in G.Q.G.; it is the encroachment of the military power upon the civil, of a power which wishes to avoid all supervision and which creates a government apart from the real government, the authority of which it does not wish to accept."[61]

As Herbillon returned to Chantilly, he felt "the necessity of... avoiding a catastrophe." Joffre's attitude was not reassuring, for when he read Roques' conciliatory reply, the generalissimo remarked to his liaison officer: "So much the worse; I shall not withdraw my letter. He is wrong; he is meddling in what is not his business. I am the one who commands; since I do not want him to criticize me before my subordinates, I shall accompany him when he goes to the armies, or he shall not go at all. In any case, I shall not withdraw my letter."[62] Herbillon had a fund of resourcefulness and tact which equaled Briand's, and he cajoled Joffre into a willingness at least to discuss the matter with Roques, if the war minister would come to see him at Chantilly.[63] Roques reluctantly agreed to make the trip.[64] The interview led to a simulated reconciliation, and Joffre's letter was returned to him. Poincaré and Roques made their visit to Verdun, where de Castelnau served as cicerone for them.[65] Joffre himself guided them about the Somme sector,[66] and thus ended an imbroglio which revealed that as the generalissimo lost face through the prolongation of the stalemate, he was more determined than ever to recover his former omnipotence.

The Briand ministry, more mindful than Joffre of the command's waning prestige, saw the necessity of informed answers to parliamentary questioning, especially since the battle of the Somme was proving just another costly offensive with no strategic gains. To keep abreast of a more vigorous activity on the part of the parliamentary inspection delegates since the adoption of the Chaumet proposal, War Minister Roques felt the need of being briefed regularly on what was happening in the armies. With this in mind, he wrote Joffre a letter, dated August 1, 1916. In this letter War Minister Roques stated that by the orders of the day ... voted by the Chamber and Senate, Parliament has given notice that it intends to ... make certain that all material needs are provided for ... the defense as well as for ... offensives. ... Parliamentary inspection cannot be exercised over the High Command ... [but] parliamentary delegations will have the right of conducting their investigations in all the army services. Even if the object of their mission does not allow them to concern themselves with operations, they will obtain data of a military nature—whether one wishes it or not—which they will not fail to use in conversation with the members of the government, either in the commissions, or on the tribune during secret sessions. Consequently, it is necessary ... that the government be kept constantly informed as to what happens in the armies. ... [67]

Colonel Herbillon considered this letter as tantamount to a declaration by Roques that, so far as the war minister was concerned, the parliamentarians could have carte blanche in visiting the front.[68] Joffre regarded Roques' letter as a provocation; it served him as the stimulus for what had become by now a kind of conditioned reflex: the generalissimo stormed into Paris to see Briand, greeting him with the angry refrain: "If it is my resignation which you want, I give it to you."[69] Briand was dramatic, even when caught off guard; he "raised his arms toward heaven" and declared that he did not know what was the cause of Joffre's displeasure. The generalissimo gave Briand Roques' letter to read. The president of the council looked at it, and agreed that the war minister's declaration was "inadmissible." Briand promised to speak to Roques about it.[70] When Briand did so, the war minister showed "stupefaction" over the request that he withdraw the communication, since Roques "had believed that in sending this letter he had only carried out the suggestions of his colleagues."[71] Colonel Herbillon, in summing up the incident, expressed the opinion that if the government and the command "talked over matters before writing one another," much friction would be obviated. "Otherwise, it is always the same comedy. Discussion, threat of resignation, re-

PARLIAMENT'S ASCENDANCY

conciliation lasting until the next time. The scenario is becoming well known."[72]

President of the Council Briand was increasingly tired of his double task of placating Joffre and holding off the parliamentarians. He was greatly relieved when the Chamber and Senate decided to adjourn their sessions until the middle of September, 1916. Briand hoped that by the time Parliament reconvened, he would have some first-rate news for his critics: the entry of Rumania into the war against Austria.

After months of negotiations, Rumania concluded on August 17 a political alliance and a military convention with France, England, Russia, and Serbia.[73] The Rumanian government of Ioan Bratianu had been assured that on August 20 General Sarrail's Army of the Orient would effectively pin down the Bulgarian forces by moving northward against Macedonia, thereby leaving the Rumanians free to penetrate Transylvania without unnecessarily exposing their southern flank to a Bulgarian attack. The Russians, moreover, would take the offensive into the Dobruja. To carry out his share of the strategy, Joffre telegraphed Sarrail to begin an offensive against the Bulgarians in the Albanian sector on August 20.[74] But the Bulgarians snatched the initiative from Sarrail by suddenly attacking his forces on August 17 along the Struma as well as in the Florina sector, actually capturing the latter stronghold.

Sarrail explained in his apologia that one of the chief reasons for the swift Bulgarian success was the perfidy of Germanophile King Constantine of Greece and his Minister Zaimis. When the Bulgarians began their attack on August 17, "the Greeks, upon orders from Athens, gave way everywhere, both at Xanthi and at the forts covering Sérès."[75] Simultaneously, the Bulgarians assaulted Cavallo, Florina, and the Ostrovo sectors. "Confronted by this general attack," wrote Sarrail, "it was necessary to renounce the offensive expected for August 20, and I decided to pursue a new plan. Abandoning all effort in the Vardar region, I reoriented everything toward invaded western Macedonia and Monastir."[76] This improvised strategy did not get under way until September 10 when there was an Allied attack in the Ostrovo sector. The campaign was not a success because of the malarial condition of the troops of General Cordonnier, Sarrail's field commander, the difficulties of supply and transport, and the insufficiency of reserves.[77]

The failure of Sarrail to take the offensive against the Bulgarians punctually on August 20 greatly irritated the Rumanians, but it did not prevent them from declaring war upon Austria on August 27. Instead of following a reasonably cautious strategy of holding off the Austro-Hungarian forces by posting guards in the Carpathian passes until the bulk of the Rumanian army could strike Bulgaria simultaneously with blows aimed at it by Russia and Sarrail's forces, the Rumanians foolishly invaded Transylvania at the outset to liberate their "oppressed brothers."[78] Southern Transylvania fell to the Rumanians in the first two weeks of September, but the following fortnight brought the predictable contretemps of an irruption of General Mackensen's Bulgarian and German troops into the Dobruja region. Before the Rumanian command could come to its senses, the forces of General Falkenhayn wiped out the illusory gains by overrunning all of Transylvania, pushing through the Carpathians, and engulfing Wallachia—all by the first of December.[79]

The Rumanian government and command—and the French—reeled under the impact of these disastrous events. Briand and Joffre were both caught in the catastrophe, since Briand had optimistically urged the Rumanians to come into the war, and Joffre was widely regarded as the *de facto* commander of an Allied coalition. General Joffre had sent to Rumania much matériel and a military mission under the direction of General Henri Berthelot. Moreover, he had apparently condoned the questionable Rumanian strategy of attacking Transylvania first, despite the exposure of Rumania's southern flank to Bulgarian attack.[80] Joffre appears to have been misled in this

PARLIAMENT'S ASCENDANCY

matter by the false Russian promise to send 60,000 troops to aid Rumania, a figure double the actual number of Slav troops belatedly sent to the Dobruja sector.[81]

L'affaire Sarrail was reopened when the commander of the Army of the Orient failed to obey Joffre's order to attack the Bulgarians on August 20. Enemies of Sarrail at once attributed his "inactivity" to his "dabbling in politics" in support of the republican Greek Colonel Zimbrakakis who had led a revolt at Salonika, setting up a *de facto* government which sought to enter into relations with the French.[82]

At a meeting of the Council of Ministers in Paris on August 26, there came up for discussion Joffre's proposal to send Chief of Staff de Castelnau to Salonika once more to find out what—if anything—General Sarrail was doing.[83] When the wealthy shipowner, Navy Minister Admiral Lacaze, demanded an investigation into the reasons for Sarrail's "inactivity," the Leftist minister of public instruction, Paul Painlevé, replied that Sarrail was being attacked because he was a republican. "As for me," declared Painlevé, "I can take no part in action against General Sarrail before the charges against him are clearly set forth and before the general is given a chance to explain."[84] To this challenge of "radical" solidarity, Minister of Colonies Gaston Doumergue retorted: "One can't speak of political persecution of General Sarrail. It is because he *is* a republican that he has a command. Politics is at his service. Anyone else in his position would have been removed long ago...."[85] A measure of harmony was restored when it was finally agreed that Sarrail, who had frequently asked for reinforcements, should be given a new brigade of French troops. Action was postponed on Joffre's demand that de Castelnau be sent on an inspection trip to Salonika.[86]

Several days later, at a meeting of the *Conseil supérieur de la défense nationale* held at the Elysée to "advise" the government, Sarrail was again the object of attack. General Joffre read a list of Sarrail's alleged deficiencies: an inadequate garrison at

Florina, recently captured by the Bulgarians; disobedience to the command to take the offensive on August 20; haggling over orders; misunderstandings with France's allies; constant complaints about the insufficiency of troops and supplies.[87] Once again Joffre requested that de Castelnau be sent to Salonika on an inspection trip.[88] Briand was sufficiently astute as a politician to perceive that sending clericalist de Castelnau on a second tour of Sarrail's sector would all but destroy the "sacred union," because the Socialists would be thrown into paroxysms of rage over such a provocation.[89] Anxious above everything else to avoid strife, Briand postponed a decision for weeks, instructing Sarrail meanwhile "to maintain order in Salonika and to tolerate neither revolution nor trouble."[90]

After careful deliberation, the Briand government decided on October 25 to send War Minister Roques to Greece as inspector general. Sarrail cordially welcomed Roques, as he related in his memoirs: "I had known him when both of us were directors at the War Ministry.... I knew his qualities of industry, frankness, and integrity, and I felt sure that he would see and appreciate that everything possible had been done."[91] Sarrail had momentarily disconcerted his critics by capturing Florina on September 18,[92] and even more discomfiting to the Joffre faction was the news of November 20—the Army of the Orient had captured Monastir, the most important French (or Allied) victory in months![93] Briand, having in mind Joffre's recent fiascoes in the Verdun, Somme, and Rumanian campaigns in contrast to Sarrail's surprising success, gave an ironical greeting to the generalissimo's liaison officer: "It is the general in whom there was no confidence who is the victor, whereas on your side, what do we find?"[94]

Still more to Sarrail's favor and to Joffre's discredit was the tenor of War Minister Roques' report on the Army of the Orient. "Sarrail has been vigorous, active, and intelligent," wrote General Roques, "but very personal.... With insufficient forces ... he has obtained all the results which one could hope

PARLIAMENT'S ASCENDANCY

for...."[95] Roques estimated that Sarrail needed at least thirty more divisions as reinforcements[96]—which in itself sufficiently explained Sarrail's so-called "immobility." The final recommendation of Roques was that the decree of December 2, 1915, ought to be rescinded, thereby transferring Sarrail from Joffre's command back to rue St. Dominique's.

The war minister's unforeseen defense of Sarrail[97] as well as the disappointments over the Somme campaign and the Rumanian reverses so seriously discredited Joffre and Briand that they had to endure a second secret committee which was announced by the Chamber for November 28, 1916. The harassed commander in chief and president of the council tried to anticipate some of the forthcoming Socialist criticism by hastily transferring to field commands two of the most execrated Young Turks, General Pellé and Lieutenant Colonel Bel, and by sending clericalist de Castelnau on a mission to Russia.[98]

The parliamentary critics of the command and government were not to be lightly turned aside by the sacrificing of small scapegoats: they were now hunting big game—no less than the generalissimo himself. They began their attack in the second secret committee by criticizing the decree of December 2, 1915,[99] which had made Joffre generalissimo by placing him over Sarrail's army as well as the forces in metropolitan France. It was argued that the direct subordination of Sarrail to Joffre instead of to the War Ministry had hamstrung the commander of the Army of the Orient and had exposed him unfairly to all sorts of vilification on the part of Joffre's reactionary supporters.[100]

Briand, in his reply to the criticism, exhibited an opportunism which surpassed anything which he had previously displayed. He began the defense of his war policy by asserting that Joffre's title of generalissimo had in the past proved of inestimable value in various conferences with Allied generals.[101] Yet Joffre could continue to have as much prestige, insinuated Briand, if the decree of December 2, 1915, were rescinded.[102] With this brazen self-contradiction, Briand revealed that he was yielding to the critics by removing Sarrail from Joffre's control. He explained further that he was giving Joffre a new rank, that of general in chief, technical adviser of the government.

The critics of the command and government were deeply suspicious of Briand's sudden capitulation with regard to Joffre. They tried to pin the slippery president of the council down to a specific statement as to Joffre's new status. "What will be the duties of the general in chief, the technical adviser of the government; will he have a purely consultative role, or the power to make decisions?" "How will authority be divided between the technical adviser of the government and the minister of war?"[103] Briand began to show some signs of fretfulness in his reply, indicating that he had not fully clarified Joffre's status in his own mind: "I cannot allow you to try to force me to go into details, under the pressure of incessant questions, after the explanations which I have given you here in secret committee. I have said what is essential. The autonomy of the commands will be assured to the greatest extent. And the authority of the government will be exercised constantly over the whole front...."[104] This statement provoked further protest: "That is not precise! You are not answering the question!"[105]

Briand made a final effort to silence his critics. Joffre, as technical adviser of the government, would consult with the ministers of war and navy to prepare the decisions of the government, and to supervise their execution. The field commanders, such as Sarrail and the general who would lead the Armies of the North and Northeast, would be given the government's general "directions," but they would be left entirely free to carry them out on the battlefield.[106] Some of the deputies were still dissatisfied with these ambiguous remarks. "Will General Joffre continue to sign the battle orders?" asked Abel Ferry.[107] "Will they be signed by the government?" inquired Socialist Pierre Renaudel.[108] But Briand refused steadfastly to offer any additional clarification.[109] Wisdom suggested that before committing himself further, Briand should consult Joffre, who, after all, might resign with a

PARLIAMENT'S ASCENDANCY

flourish rather than accept his new status. In view of what followed, Briand appears to have had the intention of gradually pushing Joffre into a pretentious-sounding but nugatory appointment which would surely disappoint him, and, after a politically safe interval, provoke him into resignation. Such a devious stratagem came naturally to Briand.

In a disingenuous conversation Briand appealed to Joffre's patriotism "to save the government" by accepting the changes in the command which the ministry had just promised Parliament. Joffre wrote in his *Mémoires* that Briand misled him by assuring him that he "would have the general direction of the war and [his] purview would extend at the same time over the commander in chief of the Armies of the Northeast and over the *commander in chief of the Army of the Orient.*"[110] Briand did not tell Joffre outright that he was to be merely the presiding officer of a species of military advisory body which was to replace the *Conseil supérieur de la défense nationale.*[111] Joffre, failing to perceive the ruse, began organizing his new general staff which was to aid him at his headquarters at Neuilly, near Paris. With Joffre still nominally in active service, although a mere technical adviser of the government, Briand succeeded in winning a vote of confidence upon the close of the secret committee on December 7.

Having survived the trying experience of interpellation in camera, Briand prepared further changes to consolidate his somewhat strengthened position. First, he went through the motions of offering his resignation to Poincaré who refused to accept it.[112] Then Briand imitated Lloyd George in forming a "War Cabinet," appointing three more undersecretaries, but reducing his regular Cabinet by eight portfolios, although he allowed Lacaze, Doumergue, Viviani, and Ribot to retain their former posts. The important change was in the War Ministry. Briand was angry with Roques for having embarrassed him with his unexpected defense of Sarrail,[113] which had been one of the causes of the harassing second secret committee. He abruptly dismissed Roques and replaced him with a war minister who would undoubtedly please the conservatives—General Hubert Lyautey, the royalist proconsul of Morocco, who had won great fame through his administrative talents.[114]

Balancing the appointment to rue St. Dominque of a royalist of the purplest hue was Briand's selection of General Robert Nivelle as commander in chief of the Armies of the North and Northeast, the field command of the French armies on the western front. General Nivelle had previously succeeded Pétain as commander of the Second Army in the Verdun sector, and was often spoken of as the true victor of the reconquest of forts Douaumont and Vaux.[115] Nivelle, a Protestant with an English mother, was very popular with anticlerical politicians of the Left Center, who were cordially received at his headquarters.

Briand felt secure in crowding out Joffre altogether after these adroit appointments and his second successive vote of confidence at the close of a senatorial secret committee on December 23.[116] "France's savior" was shocked to learn that "the 1917 plan of operations of the French armies in the western theater was profoundly changed by General Nivelle, *without [Joffre] being consulted in the least.*"[117] Finally, on December 23, the last illusion left to Joffre was shattered by a letter from the acting war minister, Admiral Lacaze, which bluntly stated that Generals Nivelle and Sarrail would receive their orders directly from the War Ministry rather than from the technical adviser of the government.[118] The new war minister, upon arriving from Morocco, was very impatient with Briand's mummery in creating the post of technical adviser of the government, which, in Lyautey's opinion, encroached not merely upon the authority of Generals Nivelle and Sarrail, but upon the duties of the War Ministry as well.[119] Lyautey, consequently, was ready to demand Joffre's retirement after giving him the solace of a marshal's rank.[120] Fortunately, this open dismissal was made unnecessary by Joffre's dignified resignation, which was accepted with weary gratitude. President Poincaré lost no time in naming him

PARLIAMENT'S ASCENDANCY

"marshal of France," and thus, at last, in the words of Finance Minister Ribot, Joffre was "embalmed under flowers" and laid to rest.[121]

The removal of Joffre represented the appeasement of Parliament by the ministry, an indication of how much authority the chambers had recovered since the initial period of parliamentary abdication. A succession of military reverses and frustrations had made cunning Briand so fearful of his ministerial life that he had not hesitated to sacrifice (with appropriate ritual) a general whose fame had been dimmed by two years of bloody but inconclusive combat. France thus entered a new phase in the relations between the politicians and the military, a period in which Parliament and the ministry were to vie with one another for dominance over a command no longer sure of itself.

7
The Tragedy of Chemin des Dames

A MORE ATTRACTIVE FIGURE THAN ROBERT NIVELLE, the new commander in chief of the French Armies of the North and Northeast, was hardly to be found on the roster of French generals. "Tall, youthful looking, of elegant bearing...proud and clean-cut, this *divisionnaire* made a good impression...."[1] There was no career comparable to his spectacular rise in the third year of the war and his equally abrupt descent into official and popular disfavor. For five months Nivelle exercised command with exemplary delicacy and restraint, which did not spare him grave complicity in the bloodletting of Chemin des Dames—a campaign which posed for both strategists and policy makers an almost insoluble dilemma.

Born of Protestant parents at Tulle in 1856, Nivelle was trained at the Ecole Polytechnique and the Ecole Supérieure de Guerre, following which he had a tour of duty in China and Algeria. He distinguished himself with his swiftly unlimbered artillery batteries in the battle of the Ourcq in August, 1914. Several years later it was Nivelle's army corps, fighting before Verdun, which recovered the Bois de la Caillete and the great fort of Douaumont. These bold feats won him the command of the Second Army in May, 1916, when Pétain was transferred to the Army Group of the Center. The very embodiment of the offensive, Nivelle led the Second Army in ceaseless counterattacks against the Germans at Verdun. As a fiery tactician, he enjoyed a well-merited fame; as a strategist he was woefully lacking in experience, never having commanded a unit larger than an army. There was considerable surprise when he was

---
[1] For notes to chap. 7, see pages 262–266.

CHEMIN DES DAMES

appointed successor to Joffre in December, 1916, as this represented the advance of a mere major general over the heads of experienced commanders of army groups—Foch, de Castelnau, and Pétain.[2] Nivelle, however, was a friend of politicians, especially the anticlericalists who were attracted by his Protestantism. A gracious host, he had warmly welcomed to his Second Army headquarters visiting ministers, senators, and deputies.[3] "... In the halls of Parliament Nivelle's visitors... celebrated his merits, sang his praises...."[4] Briand was thoroughly aware of the general's popularity. Only Nivelle's skeptical (and jealous) comrades-at-arms failed to share the prevalent enthusiasm, for the general was "commander in chief by choice of the government, not by the acclamation nor even the tacit assent of all his subordinates."[5]

Nivelle was not to be allowed to forget his indebtedness to the politicians. Scarcely had he installed himself in Joffre's old headquarters at Chantilly when he was visited by M. Auguste Gervais, the Democratic Left senator from Seine. "Well, General," was Gervais's abrupt greeting, "you are going to move from Chantilly?" Nivelle explained that there "was no military reason" for such action, which would require several weeks and would prove expensive. "Perhaps," replied Senator Gervais, "but all the same, there is the consideration of moral dignity."[6] This civilian's insinuation that G.Q.G. was a place of iniquity infuriated Nivelle—professional soldier that he was—but upon reflection, the successor to Joffre decided it might be a wise plan to move away from all the emotional connotations attached to the very name of Chantilly. "Parliament scored a victory."[7]

Nivelle's susceptibility to the opinions of politicians did not make him amenable to all of the wishes of the army commissions and the minister of war, who, for example, wanted general headquarters to move at least part of its staff to Paris.[8] Instead, Nivelle selected Beauvais as the new site of G.Q.G. He did this in the rather naïve hope that the remoteness of Beauvais from Paris would spare him further parliamentary visits, but Nivelle still had the politicians in mind when he quartered his staff in two separate buildings—in an agricultural institute which had been founded by an abbé, and in a new, secular lycée.[9] By this Solomonic division, he sought to avoid alienating either the clericalists or the anticlericalists in Parliament.

All of Nivelle's famed tactfulness and patience were needed for him to get along well with the new war minister. General Lyautey's long colonial experience in Algeria, Indo-China, Madagascar, and his sweeping authority as a proconsul in Morocco made it virtually impossible for him to be content with former War Minister Millerand's role of the general in chief's devoted acolyte, holding no discernible opinions of his own. No sooner had Lyautey assumed control at rue St. Dominique than he began touring the various fronts, "visiting the army commanders, and calling for the plans of attack."[10] According to the letter of the law, no serious complaint could be raised against this practice, for Lyautey had been away from metropolitan France for the first two and a half years of the war and it was obviously necessary for him to familiarize himself with the new tactics and problems. But the army commanders correctly judged the new war minister to be a man of decision and independence. Such a state of affairs practically invited the subordinate commanders to go over Nivelle's head and appeal to the dominating figure of the war minister. This likelihood was quickly perceived by Senator Charles de Freycinet, who on January 7, 1917, begged Poincaré "to be on his guard that Lyautey, having become minister of war, did not try to direct operations himself."[11] De Freycinet said Lyautey had such an ambition, "even more than Gallieni had. The Cabinet must thwart him and you must help us."[12]

In the realm of politics War Minister Lyautey was as inept as he had been capable as a colonial administrator. He had no awareness whatever of parliamentary views and preconceptions. For example, he proposed appointing a chief of staff who would be a "technical adviser," subordinate to the war minister, and charged with the responsibility of providing the government with the military data that it needed.[13] The scheme appeared to some to resemble the office which Briand had created in December, 1916, but which Lyautey had opposed when the incumbent was to be Joffre, whom the war minister despised. These objections Lyautey seemed to have forgotten when it dawned on him that he might assign to this new post his coreligionist, de Castelnau, the bête noire of the Left. The proposal held a different meaning for Colonel Herbillon. "What the devil," he wrote, "all this looks like an effort to return in a devious fashion to the decree of December 2, 1915."[14] Was Lyautey trying to create a generalissimo in disguise, assigning to the office a congenial soul whom he might control? Such an interpretation occurred to some of the members of the government, who were displeased by it. After Lyautey had already drawn up a decree naming de Castelnau as chief of staff, the whole scheme collapsed because of the strong opposition of anticlericalist Interior Minister Louis Malvy and his Radical Socialists.[15]

The greatest dilemma posed for any war minister in the four years of struggle was the question of authorizing the hazardous "Nivelle plan," the ambitious strategy which the general in chief had worked out for the spring of 1917. The broad outlines of this campaign had first been sketched by Joffre after a conference on November 16, 1916, with the Allied military missions at Chantilly.[16] It was tentatively agreed that a Franco-British offensive would be undertaken in February, 1917, with the British striking eastward between Bapaume and Vimy, while the French attempted a massive break-through by pushing northward from the river Aisne toward the Oise. The commitment to this joint campaign devolved upon Nivelle as part of the responsibilities of his new assignment. He encountered at once the reluctance of the British command to extend their line from Bouchavesnes to the Route de Roye in order to free sufficient French divisions to make possible the break-through.[17] The French, obviously, would win the lion's share of the glory with the spectacular rupture which was expected. When Field Marshal Haig showed lukewarmness toward the supernumerary role expected of him, Nivelle "was obliged to negotiate directly with the English War Committee. A great innovation—which marked in both countries the restoration of governmental authority over the military...."[18]

Assured of British ministerial support, Nivelle sent to the chagrined Haig on January 25 a completed draft of the offensive. There were to be three phases of the battle. First, on March 15 the British were to drive eastward toward Cambrai, to be followed four or five days later by General Franchet d'Esperey's Army Group of the North striking in a parallel direction toward St. Quentin.[19] These initial attacks were to divert German attention. Second, "two French Army Groups, under Generals Micheler and Pétain respectively, were, a few days later, to carry out the main offensive on Franchet d'Esperey's right, attacking in a northerly direction"[20] from the river Aisne toward the Oise. This northward thrust of Micheler and Pétain would strike from the rear the German divisions already engaged by the preliminary offensive of the British and Franchet d'Esperey. Finally, there would ensue "the resumption or the continuation of the offensive ... by all the attacking armies, supported by all the reserves which could be mustered (both fresh and reconstituted units) for the purpose of completing the disorganization and the defeat of the enemy."[21] Such, in rough outline, was the titanic "Nivelle offensive" which would break the prolonged stalemate on the western front.

General Nivelle entrusted to Colonel Georges Renouard, the head of the 3d Bureau of Operations, the mission of explaining his audacious campaign plan to the minister of war,[22] which the colonel did "in the manner of a disciplined and impersonal officer...."[23] With mounting anxiety, the war minister questioned Colonel Renouard especially about the "new army," *une masse de manoeuvre,* which was to exploit the breach made possible by the initial Anglo-French attack which would throw the Germans off balance. Lyautey was stupefied to learn from Renouard that the much-puffed "army of maneuver" of Nivelle's was to be composed largely of units "drawn, during the actual fighting, from the attacking troops themselves."[24] "But surely, Renouard," protested the war minister, "this is a plan for the Grand Duchess of Gerolstein!" Colonel Renouard ignored the comment as he explained that Laon would be reached on the first bound. Lyautey refused to allow Renouard to seek refuge behind hierarchical correctness.[25] "Come, come, my dear Georges.... Just fancy that you're once again my confidential officer at Ain-Sefra, and tell me the truth.... What do you think of [the plan]?" Renouard, for the first time during the conversation, revealed his private feelings. "General," he replied, "I think as you do.... It is mad."[26]

Lyautey was in a quandary, wondering whether he should replace Nivelle or hand in his own resignation. He decided to await a suitable opportunity for resigning—at a time which would not be likely to compromise "the conduct of the war in the eyes of the enemy informers."[27] This decision would have been unimpeachable had Lyautey controlled his tongue. But the war minister was not skilled in the art of dissimulation, and Colonel Herbillon quickly noted Lyautey's obvious distrust of the soundness of Nivelle's views. On February 8, 1917, Herbillon recorded in his journal: "A rumor is current concerning the advisability of our offensive.... In General Lyautey's entourage they seem skeptical about the results which can be obtained. Moreover, after his visits to the front and his conversation with several of the great chiefs, the minister himself feels shaken in his confidence...."[28] Herbillon feared that "the situation of General Nivelle was becoming untenable." Already certain field commanders were following Lyautey's example by speaking of Nivelle's plans, "criticiz[ing] them and mak[ing] comments upon them to visitors who often prompted them."[29]

In a conversation with President Poincaré, General Nivelle registered a complaint against Lyautey's tactlessness. Nivelle drew an unflattering portrait of the war minister who traveled about with a cavalcade of staff officers, "stepping on everyone's toes, despite the best of intentions." He described Lyautey as "a man who quickly converts his colleagues either into his servants or else into irreconcilable enemies. He need not let his officers invade the front, question the chiefs, and offer support to malcontents." Poincaré was distressed to see that "the misunderstandings which have troubled G.Q.G. since the time of Joffre and Gallieni have changed casts, but remain the same."[80]

As if the friction between the War Ministry and the command were not difficulty enough, a feeling of resentment developed in the British General Staff over their being subordinated to Nivelle for the duration of the joint offensive. Before Field Marshal Haig and General Robertson could be mollified, it was necessary to hold two Anglo-French conferences, the first at Calais on February 26 and 27, 1917, and the second at London on March 12 and 13. At Calais, General Nivelle told General Robertson in private that "the idea of placing the British armies under my command did not originate with me. It was the subject of a communication between the two Governments... and I was instructed to work out the details of the scheme and lay them before the conference for consideration...."[81]

The London Conference was called to assuage the resentment of Field Marshal Haig whose sensibilities had been ruffled by the peremptory tone of a battle order from G.Q.G., which, to everyone's relief, turned out to have been written by a subordinate rather than by General Nivelle.[82] Before the conference adjourned, Alexandre Ribot, the head of the French delegation, made the unexpected proposal that General Nivelle explain the plans of the coming offensive. This would have publicly demonstrated the ascendancy of the French politicians over the military. The French statesmen were in the position of *arrivistes,* unable to resist the temptation of flaunting their newly won dominance over the military. The British were more subtle, feeling no need of an ostentatious display. Consolation for the generals came, therefore, from Bonar Law, the British chancellor of the exchequer, who broke in with the question, "... Are the generals in agreement? *M. le Commandant en chef,* are you in agreement with the field marshal?" Nivelle and Haig expressed assent. Thus reassured, Bonar Law brusquely dismissed Ribot's proposal: "Well then, we shall not consider it!" Ribot made no effort to hide his surprise at Bonar Law's "supine" attitude toward the military by protesting, "But the government has the right to know...."[33]

The Briand Cabinet, which had miraculously recovered its equilibrium so many times in the past, was overturned soon after the London Conference by the congenital inability of War Minister Lyautey to understand the thought processes of the politicians, especially those of the Left. He declined to speak at a session of the Chamber's secret committee which, on March 14, was investigating military aviation. But upon the resumption of the public session, Lyautey surprised the deputies by asking at once for recognition by the chair. "Gentlemen," he began, "I confess that I first thought that this debate had better not take place." Lyautey wanted to explain, in general terms, that he had already taken necessary steps to improve aviation by such means as unifying the radio and air services.[34] "I have accepted this debate because it appears repugnant to me to avoid it, and because I felt no less strongly that it was possible to say something of importance by which we should be the first to profit.... But you will allow me not to follow you on technical ground as my officers had to do, because even in secret committee, I consider, in full responsibility, that this would expose national defense to risks.... (Lively exclamations on the benches of the Socialists, Radical Republicans, and Radical Socialists.)"[35] The war minister was not allowed to finish his speech, since he had been tactless enough to "insult" Parliament by broadly insinuating that there might be traitors in its midst.[36] The Left interpreted Lyautey's comment as meaning that the military alone could be entrusted with the sacred arcana of national defense.[37]

Royalist Lyautey had unleashed all the dogs of class war by his ill-considered remark. Deputies of the Left cried out in chorus: "What do you mean by that?"[38] The deputy from Isère, Socialist Raffin-Dugens, shouted at Lyautey: "All you have to do is to suppress Parliament!" President Deschanel tried in vain to restore order by pleading: "The words of the war minister, I imagine, were merely the justification of the secret committee." The Left refused to accept this palliation. The Radical Socialist deputy from Basses-Alpes, M. Jugy, exclaimed: "The minister's words are nothing less than a provocation." When Deschanel invited Lyautey to explain his statement, the Socialist deputy from Puy de Dôme, Joseph Claussat, retorted: "There is no explanation to give; rather he should be called to order. We have not yet arrived at a regime of the saber!"[39] M. Albert Grodet, a Republican Socialist from Guyane, wanted to know whether the government had seen and approved in advance the war minister's speech. "The Germans are at Noyon," the conservative Deputy Jules Delahaye tried to remind the assembly. "Parliament cannot be insulted!" roared Raffin-Dugens. The din in the Chamber was at last harmonized into a cry of "Vive la république!" and the deputies voted for an immediate resumption of the secret committee.[40] In an antechamber, meanwhile, Lyautey observed in bewilderment to a friend: "I can't understand a thing about it.... I have never understood anything of this race.... I'd hardly begun when they started shouting—I don't even know why...."[41]

What might have been incomprehensible to a colonial general like Lyautey, in half-conscious search for a pretext for resigning, was transparent enough to Briand, who knew that the bell had tolled for his entire Cabinet. After accepting Briand's resignation on March 18, Poincaré decided to entrust the formation of a new government to the outgoing finance minister, Alexandre Ribot, a Union Republican senator from Pas-de-Calais, once described by Field Marshal Haig as "a tall old man of eighty years...a dear old thing...."[42]

CHEMIN DES DAMES

Although Ribot was regarded as an "aged, conservative financier," his choice as president of the council was applauded by the Left for the very reason that he was supposed to be weak. He was expected to yield passively to the Chamber's wishes.[43] Ribot set to work assigning the various portfolios, retaining a number of the former incumbents, and keeping for himself the Ministry of Foreign Affairs. He was at first undecided whether he should appoint as war minister the mild Socialist Albert Thomas or Paul Painlevé. Thomas did not want the office, so the way was left open for Painlevé, concerning whom Ribot felt some misgivings. In the first place, Painlevé was known far and wide as a devoted disciple of General Pétain and of his doctrine of the defensive.[44] Once before Painlevé had been considered for the War Ministry, but when Briand had made him the offer in December, 1916, he had posed as his terms of acceptance the appointment of Pétain as the French commander in chief.[45] Consequently, old Ribot, "an excellent patriot, a resolute partisan of the war *à outrance*,"[46] was doubtful of Painlevé's attitude toward General Nivelle, an exponent of the school of attack.[47] Ribot anxiously questioned Painlevé about his views. "He promised not to work against Nivelle," wrote Ribot, "and to consult me on all important questions, so I invited him to serve."[48]

The new war minister was a Republican Socialist deputy from Seine, who, at twenty-five years of age, had taught on the Faculté des Sciences at Lille, following which he had rapidly progressed to professorships at the Sorbonne and the Ecole Polytechnique.[49] Elected to the Chamber in 1910, the prodigy carried into the asymmetric realm of politics an attitude of mathematical precision, producing results which were not always happy.[50] As a scientist-politician, Painlevé held the post of minister of public instruction and military inventions in the Briand Cabinet from October 30, 1915, until December, 1916. He had been a critic of Joffre and a supporter of Gallieni and Sarrail. While minister of inventions, he had fully utilized the opportunity of visiting the fronts and conversing with the various commanders of the army groups, armies, and corps. "This civilian...put at the head of the army, would be no novice.... With him, the 'civilian power' would be no fiction."[51]

Even before installing himself at rue St. Dominique, Painlevé had learned *par la voix publique* that D-day for the Nivelle offensive would be April 8.[52] That the date of a campaign supposedly planned in secret should have reached a French politician through the channels of rumor should cause no great surprise, if one considers that the Germans themselves were quite well informed about Nivelle's plans, having captured a battle order of the 2d French Infantry Division "clearly pointing to a great French offensive on the Aisne for April."[53]

Painlevé was worried by the fact that he had so little time to consider the Nivelle offensive, since the British were to begin their bombardment on April 4 in accordance with the plan which had been worked out only with the greatest of difficulty by Nivelle, Briand, and Lyautey. Still more disturbing was the realization that, contrary to previous expectations, the Chemin des Dames offensive would be undertaken as an isolated effort on the western front, since the Russian Revolution was paralyzing the eastern ally of France.[54] Germany before long would be able to shift the overwhelming bulk of her forces to the French sector. Furthermore, it seemed to Painlevé that the whole strategic situation envisaged by the Nivelle plan was already radically changed by a clever German gambit—the drastic shortening of their line on the western front through the voluntary withdrawal known as the "Alberich movement." The Alberich operation had begun on February 9 with "demolition" and "clearance" in the Arras-Soissons salient, after which the German troops had fallen back across the devastated countryside to the shelter of the Siegfried Line, anchored a short distance west of Cambrai and St. Quentin.[55]

Painlevé was very uneasy over the effects of the Alberich strategy. "...The retreat of Hindenburg," he wrote, "created a situation in which three-quarters of our projected attack would

CHEMIN DES DAMES

fall upon a void. The two sides of the famous square (Vimy-Soissons and Soissons-Reims) which were to enclose and capture the contents of the vast pocket previously outlined by the German lines, now enclosed only empty space. In these circumstances was it necessary to carry out the anticipated offensive, come what may? Was it better to renounce it, or, without giving it up entirely, to modify the objectives and the method?"[56]

Although War Minister Painlevé had inherited Lyautey's skepticism about the offensive, the government did not clearly understand its exact responsibility in the vexing question of the military effects of the Alberich movement, the Russian Revolution, and the probable entry of America into the war.[57] Of these three new factors, the first (the Alberich movement) was unquestionably a technical matter of strategy. The effect of the Russian Revolution and the prospect of immediate American intervention, beyond a doubt questions primarily of foreign policy, possessed nonetheless an immense strategic significance for France. Before undertaking another bloody offensive, should the overtaxed nation wait until a full-scale participation of the Americans would be able to offset her own weakness and thus correct the imbalance made worse by Russia's imminent collapse? These vast imponderables were quite as much questions of policy as strategy: no French government could reasonably decide on their political significance without taking into account their strategic calculus. Likewise, no command could work out an intelligent plan of strategy without considering the total political context.

A declaration which President of the Council Ribot delivered to the Chamber on March 21 only confounded a problem already complex:

The question of the High Command, which has caused so much debate, is definitely regulated in the simplest manner. The government, which has the political direction of the war under the supervision of the Chamber, controls everything pertaining to the organization and maintenance of our armies. It is the necessary means of contact with the Allied governments.... It maintains a watch over its prerogatives, which are the measure of its responsibilities, seeing to it that they are not diminished. But once the government has chosen the chief who ought to lead our troops to victory, it leaves to him full liberty in the strategic conception, preparation, and direction of operations."[58]

The spring offensive had gone far beyond the stage of conception and preparation and awaited merely the execution. Was the war minister to order the commander to call off the offensive, or to modify his plans, at the very time that the president of the council was offering public assurances that "full liberty" would be left the general in chief in "the strategic conception, preparation, and direction of operations?" According to his own contention, General Nivelle was given no hint that such doubts had ever arisen when he had his first conference with Painlevé. "The first time I saw the new minister of war," he said, "on March 22, he spoke to me only of choosing a chief of the General Staff; he said absolutely nothing to indicate that he did not share my point of view on the subject of the offensive."[59] This assertion was flatly contradicted by Painlevé in *Comment j'ai nommé Foch et Pétain*. Painlevé admitted that he and Nivelle had discussed General Pétain as a possible chief of the General Staff, but he declared that he also had reviewed the "great events [which] had overturned the military situation," including the probable entry of America into the war—a prospect of incalculable importance."[60] He insisted that he had informed Nivelle that such factors as the expected American intervention, the Russian Revolution, and the Alberich movement "raised the question as to whether the plan adopted should not be greatly changed. The government demanded that the general in chief examine this question, in full independence, without considering himself bound by the hopes ... which he had previously expressed. A new situation ought to be considered anew."[61]

Which account is to be believed, Nivelle's or Painlevé's? The weight of the evidence is against Nivelle. The general in chief surely must have learned (at least indirectly) of Painlevé's doubts about the offensive, for Nivelle's subordinates were well aware that the new war minister shared the misgivings of his predecessor, Lyautey. General Charles Mangin, commander of the Sixth Army, and one of the generals to be "broken" for the Chemin des Dames tragedy, testified in his apologia that "M. Painlevé questioned those army chiefs whom he thought he could influence by his arguments against the projected offensive, and no others. He increased their hesitancy, without even giving an explanation [of his actions]. These conferences took place in the absence of the general in chief, who was informed by his subordinates and not by the minister. General Nivelle knew, moreover, that a superior officer in the minister's Cabinet had been instructed to keep a dossier [of arguments] against the projected offensive...."[62] In view of this testimony, Nivelle could hardly have been unaware of Painlevé's skeptical attitude.

Painlevé readily acknowledged in his book that he privately examined the three commanders of the army groups as to their views of the offensive. Franchet d'Esperey told him of the difficulty of quickly rebuilding the roads devastated by the adroitly retreating Germans, who had fallen back behind the Siegfried Line.[63] General Pétain, commander of the Army Group of the Center, emphasized the need of good weather and an "intensive artillery preparation." He described as "chimerical" the hope of seizing more than the first six lines of trenches, since they would be "boxed in" by German reserves. General Micheler, of the Army Group of Reserves, surmised that Laon might possibly be reached—at a very high cost—but *la grande exploitation stratégique de la rupture* was only a "dream."[64] Painlevé also asked the opinions of Generals Mangin (Sixth Army) and Mazel (Fifth Army). In contrast with the skeptical attitude of the army group commanders, both Mangin and Mazel were as optimistic as Nivelle himself, Mangin expressing supreme confidence that his Sixth Army "could reach Laon at a bound."[65]

The conflicting views of the generals placed Painlevé in a

quandary. The war minister believed that dismissing Nivelle in *advance* of his campaign would disgrace the hero of Vaux-Douaumont before he was given a fair chance,[66] besides angering the British whose agreement to the joint campaign had been so laboriously won.[67] Painlevé felt it wise in the circumstances to hold a conference at rue St. Dominique to try to induce Nivelle to scale down his grandiose scheme sufficiently to restore unity to the High Command. With this intent, Painlevé invited to the War Ministry on April 3 the general in chief, President of the Council Ribot, Navy Minister Admiral Lacaze, Minister of Armament Albert Thomas, and Nivelle's personal friend, Minister of Colonies André Maginot. Painlevé told the group of his deep anxiety in regard to the offensive, referring in passing to the similar views of the commanders of the army groups.[68] Nivelle, on the contrary, "affirmed his unshakable faith" in a quick break-through, to be followed by a mop-up which, within three days' time, would surely advance Micheler's army group to the Serre, thirty kilometers from the starting point.[69] Nivelle conceded that the weather would have to be good, and that the battle "ought to be decided within twenty-four hours, forty-eight hours at the most."[70] Given the binding assurance by the general in chief that "under no pretext would he repeat a battle of the Somme," the gathering adjourned, with Painlevé and Ribot "estimating...that there had been reached as complete an agreement as the circumstances permitted."[71]

Nivelle was being subjected to searching interrogation which civilians had not often risked with French generals. But seldom has a government been burdened with such responsibility in sanctioning so hazardous an offensive. Nivelle's patience was to be tried by further interventions. On April 5, Colonel Adolphe Messimy, the war minister during the first month of the war, and of late the commander of a division under General Micheler's army group, carried a letter of warning to President of the Council Ribot.[72] Messimy asserted that the letter "was practically written at the dictation of General Micheler" (which

CHEMIN DES DAMES

Micheler later denied), and he vowed that it expressed "the opinion of the most reputable chiefs of the French army."[73] The letter recapitulated all of the arguments against the offensive: it conceded that the campaign might result in the capture of some prisoners, cannon, and possibly a strip of territory from ten to twelve kilometers wide, "but at the cost of the heaviest sacrifices and without any possible strategic result." The offensive was especially risky in being planned for a spring which had already turned out to be cold and rainy, and even after the return of fair weather the French army would be paralyzed from lack of reserves. "The most urgent conclusion: without an hour's delay, give the order to await fair weather before beginning offensive operations in France."[74]

Ribot showed Messimy's letter to President Poincaré, who was informed that it had shaken all the more the resolution of the minister of war.[75] Poincaré noticed that Ribot likewise had "become very hesitant."[76] The president of the republic sternly reminded Ribot that "these continual interventions of the government in the command could lead to the gravest difficulties."[77] Although Ribot expressed agreement, he nevertheless asked Poincaré to join him in a meeting with Painlevé, Thomas, and Lacaze for further discussion of the matter. At this meeting Painlevé told his colleagues that he had heard from various sources such as Senator Charles de Freycinet,[78] General Pétain, and Colonel Messimy that there might be a reasonable hope of localized tactical success in the campaign, but that fair weather was essential and that there must be no blind efforts at a strategic exploitation, which could waste all the French reserves. Poincaré thereupon warned the ministers that postponing the offensive too long would give the Germans the initiative by allowing them to move their troops from the Russian front to the French. Ribot and Painlevé nonetheless favored delay, especially at a time when America with her tremendous untapped resources seemed ready to enter the war. In view of the harassing uncertainty, it was deemed sensible to go directly to Nivelle and his subordinates at Compiègne, there to thresh out once and for all the whole question of the offensive.[79]

The French government has been excoriated for holding the Compiègne Conference and placing a commander in the position of Nivelle—having to answer questions about his laboriously wrought-out plan in the presence of jealous and captious subordinates.[80] This interrogation, moreover, was to take place only ten days before the beginning of the offensive (rain causing another postponement from April 8 to April 16). The critics of the conference tended to overlook the external but compelling reasons for the meeting. "It was not the French government which determined the date of the Russian Revolution, nor the probable entry of the United States into the war, nor the Hindenburg withdrawal."[81] These were new factors of incalculable importance which the government could not ignore without criminal negligence, for they were inextricably interwoven with France's general war policy. Had they been disregarded, General Nivelle would have been given a free hand to work out his strategy in a vacuum, which would have meant the bankruptcy of policy.

The conference was held in Poincaré's railroad car at Compiègne on April 6. The historic gathering was attended by the president of the republic, the president of the council, the three ministers of national defense, Painlevé, Lacaze, and Thomas, the general in chief, and the commanders of army groups, Micheler, Pétain, Franchet d'Esperey, and de Castelnau.[82] "There is perhaps some question," began Painlevé, "as to a governmental intrusion into the actual execution of operations, of which the general in chief is solely in charge; but the government is responsible for the general conduct of the war and that is why it is essential, before deciding upon an operation in which the very fate of the nation is at stake, that everything should be carefully weighed and considered by the government and the commander in chief."[83] Painlevé reviewed the recent changes in the over-all context of policy and inquired whether they did not

CHEMIN DES DAMES

call for a modification of the plans for the offensive.[84] General Nivelle was then asked to speak. He enumerated the occasions on which laborious negotiations had been undertaken with the British to prepare for the offensive.[85] He declared that whenever he had met with the *Comité de guerre* he had been repeatedly asked to advance the date of the offensive, lest the Germans steal a march. "Bound by these directives, the commander in chief had no right to call off the offensive."[86] The government possessed full authority to express its views as to the probable effects of the Russian Revolution or American intervention. The *Comité de guerre* could order him to maintain the defensive, or to call off the offensive altogether, and he could either obey, or if the new directives seemed militarily unacceptable to him, he could simply resign. He did not have responsibility for the "general conduct of the war," which rested with the government and the *Comité de guerre*. But he could not set aside formal instructions to speed up the campaign until they were at least superseded by other directives.[87]

General Nivelle explained why he was opposed to delaying the offensive. Russia, it was true, was in revolt, but its troops still pinned down three fourths of the Austrian army and a third of the German. By waging his offensive, the French and British could relieve the pressure on tottering Russia and thereby keep her armies in the field. Similarly, Italy could risk an attack on the Carso only if she had the assurance that the French offensive would divert from her the greater part of the enemy forces. To wait for active American participation would, in effect, be a renunciation of all hope of ending the war in 1917, and would thus leave the initiative to Germany who could use her forty-three divisions for an attack at a time of her own choosing (which is what later came to pass). As for a "limited" offensive, it was unthinkable for him to begin a battle without having at hand all available forces, ready for use, if the necessity should arise.[88]

The commanders of the army groups were then asked to state

their views. Micheler, "in formal contradiction" to Messimy's letter of warning which he was alleged to have inspired, expressed the opinion that: "It is necessary to attack as quickly as possible, as soon as we are ready and the weather is favorable."[89] Either Messimy had exaggerated Micheler's misgivings about the offensive, or else the general was more hopeful than formerly. But in any event, Micheler doubted the likelihood of a complete rupture, seeing little prospect of dislodging the Germans from their third and fourth positions.[90] De Castelnau, who had been in command of his Army Group of the East for only three days, declined to speak.[91] Pétain was dry and laconic, expressing hope for a piercing, but none for the "strategic exploitation."[92] Franchet d'Esperey, already well aware of the formidable strength of German resistance from his "pursuit" of them across the devastated countryside, stressed the difficulties of maintaining supply lines over the ruined roads. However, since the English had agreed to the offensive, and, in fact, had already begun their part of the preparatory bombardment, he did not think it wise to cancel the plans.[93]

General Nivelle felt at this point that he had shown patience enough. "Since I am in agreement neither with the government nor with my subordinates, the only thing left for me to do is to offer my resignation to the president of the republic."[94] A tragicomedy followed. President Poincaré was aghast, since (in his words to Herbillon) he "had been the promoter of this meeting" with the intention of ending underhanded intrigues by allowing General Nivelle to explain himself, and by assuring him of the government's confidence.[95] And the upshot of it threatened to be Nivelle's abrupt resignation! "Poincaré, Ribot, and Painlevé at once surrounded the General in one corner of the car and succeeded in calming him."[96] Poincaré brought the inauspicious meeting to a close by summarizing the points agreed upon: an offensive battle would be waged with a prudent use of reserves if the rupture of the enemy front could be effected—otherwise, the drive would be halted if the front were

CHEMIN DES DAMES

not substantially broken by the first efforts.[97] Ribot, in his *Lettres,* wrote that Nivelle clearly promised that "... if contrary to my expectations, the enemy front is not broken in depth within forty-eight hours, I shall most decidedly not persist in the operation."[98]

Bad weather caused one final postponement of the offensive until April 16, but further delays were unthinkable, the British having loyally begun their preliminary bombardment of Arras on April 6, the very day of the Compiègne Conference.[99] The tragic campaign of Chemin des Dames seemed destined to begin in the worst possible circumstances—April 16 being a day when it "rained in torrents, a veritable tempest deluging Compiègne," the new site of G.Q.G., where the staff officers awaited the reports in a "deadly" silence.[100] As if to mock fortune, Nivelle's offensive defied the weather on the first day by scoring a considerable success[101]—a victory judged sufficient to encourage continued effort. Ludendorff conceded that the French "broke through at various points on the Chemin des Dames and forced us to withdraw with heavy losses from the Vailly salient to the heights of the Chemin des Dames. ... Due east of the Aisne our troops held their ground. Towards Brimont another breakthrough was made, but was neutralized by a push on the part of our counter-attack forces."[102]

Such was the somewhat favorable strategic picture of the French gains on the first day of the attack. But Ludendorff's account did not bring out the tactical cost which the French units suffered. President of the Council Ribot acknowledged the consequences of having to begin the assault in rainy weather, which made it impossible for aerial reconnaissance to regulate the French artillery fire with the proper degree of accuracy. Consequently, "when the troops, full of *élan* and enthusiasm, reached the first enemy positions, they threw themselves on defenses which had not been destroyed."[103] Worse still, the French artillerymen, deprived of adequate range finding, mistakenly shelled trenches seized by their own troops, particularly the

Senegalese.[104] The result was a massacre, especially in the 18th Army Corps of the Sixth Army.

By the next day, April 17, even confident General Nivelle recognized that Mangin's Sixth Army was all but foundering, so he commanded it to limit its operations to "consolidating the conquest of the heights south of the Ailette."[105] However, Mazel's Fifth Army was ordered to continue attacking between Reims and Craonne,[106] and General Anthoine's Fourth Army was told to go on with its assault upon the *massif* of Moronvilliers.[107]

Meanwhile, Poincaré, a strong defender of General Nivelle,[108] was experiencing alarm and disgust over rumors of parliamentary "meddling" in the affairs of the command. He was told by Ribot that Deputy Pierre Renaudel, the Socialist editor of *L'Humanité,* "had spent the entire first day [of the attack] at G.Q.G. with Nivelle. Other deputies have followed the course of the battle from his observation post, while still others have gone to the various headquarters."[109] Poincaré pointed out to Ribot the necessity of preventing the deputies from doing this during operations. Ribot described for the president "the incredible turmoil in the Chamber," where reports were bruited about to the effect that the battle had miscarried, that Nivelle was threatened by Painlevé and defended by his friend M. Maginot, and that the Cabinet was ready to resign.[110] Thoroughly irritated by this sort of gossip, Poincaré gave short shrift to Deputy Albert Favre who rushed from the front to ask him to call off the offensive. Poincaré was even more brusque in turning Favre away than General Micheler[111] and War Minister Painlevé[112] had been when that deputy pleaded with them not to bleed the army to death by prolonging the drive.

The fighting continued with great violence on April 18, with the Fifth Army of Mazel encountering "a murderous and insurmountable resistance"[113] in its attack between Reims and Craonne, but farther to the west, the Sixth Army of Mangin, which had been ordered to consolidate its hold on the south bank of the Aillette, made unexpected headway, capturing 17,000 prisoners and 83 cannon.[114] Even so, Mangin's army was still far from its objective of Laon, and at the end of a week's struggle "it had not completely taken the territory, which, on April 16, it was supposed to seize in three hours."[115] Nevertheless, on April 21 the undaunted General Nivelle sent to Field Marshal Haig a confident report in which he stated that "while the progress of our attacking armies is slower than we had counted upon ... there is to be no halting of the operations."[116] This letter was to reassure Haig who was quite opposed to calling off the offensive, since such action would, in the field marshal's opinion, let the enemy "transfer troops to other theaters which call for counter-measures on our part. This will mean increased demand for our shipping and help the German in his submarine campaign. He would also have troops available for threat against England."[117]

On the same day that Nivelle wrote so confidently to Haig, April 21, he received a gloomy message from General Micheler who complained that the attempts "to seize the heights north of Craonne and the line along the crest of the hills from Sapigneul to Mont Spin have come to naught; our advance toward the northeast risks exposing our flanks. Apart from the considerable losses suffered, the fatigue of our troops, made worse by the weather, forces us to relieve a large part of the units in action. Consequently, fresh reserves of the Army Group of Reserves are reduced to four infantry divisions. ... On this sector [we] might rest satisfied with operations which would round out our present situation ... while holding down the enemy."[118]

Painlevé contended that Micheler's pessimistic letter caused Nivelle to reconsider his plans.[119] It prompted the commander in chief to confer immediately with Generals Micheler, Pétain, and Mazel,[120] following which he issued revised orders abandoning the attempt at a strategic exploitation, and substituting instead four limited operations to be undertaken toward the end of April on the sector of Moronvilliers by the Fourth Army of

Anthoine, at Mont-Spin-Brimont by the Fifth Army of Mazel, at Craonne by the Sixth Army of Mangin, and at Chemin des Dames by Duchêne's Tenth Army.[121] Painlevé emphasized that these revised plans were suggested by the military themselves and not by the government.

One can find in this [wrote Painlevé] no trace of intervention by the government or Parliament. And, in fact, during the entire week of the offensive, no intervention of this kind, under any form, took place in the [affairs] of the High Command. Allow me, then, to treat with disdain all the legends inspired by the day of April 16, especially the stupid story—which was bruited about the world—that parliamentarians, terrified by the sight of battle, extorted from a weak minister the telephonic order to halt the victorious drive.[122]

Despite its previous indecision about Nivelle's campaign plans, the government had acted with commendable correctness in giving the general a free hand in carrying out his strategy, once the offensive had been finally reaffirmed at the Compiègne Conference. Even Nivelle's most spirited apologist, Commandant de Civrieux, had to concede that "from April 16 to 23 no *official* opposition was shown to the waging of the offensive."[123] It should be recalled that Poincaré and Painlevé had turned deaf ears to the complaints of a deputy like Albert Favre who wanted to call off the campaign. But the very Poincaré who had been so indignant over Favre's ineffectual attempt to "meddle in strategy" was guilty of just such officiousness at the close of the first week of the drive. Acting upon the instance of General Edouard Hirschauer who served under General Duchêne in the Tenth Army, President Poincaré had a warning telephoned to Nivelle's liaison officer. Colonel Herbillon was told that the officers of the Tenth Army thought "the date for resuming attacks upon Craonne and the plateau of Vauclerc to be altogether premature and impossible. The artillery preparation will be quite insufficient...." Poincaré urged headquarters to consult at once with General Duchêne and with General Hirschauer.[124]

CHEMIN DES DAMES

When Colonel Herbillon gave the message to General Nivelle, the commander in chief angrily protested that neither the exact date of this new attack nor the allotment of ammunition had as yet been determined,[125] as the war minister himself could verify since he had been present when the revised plans were being discussed with Generals Micheler and Pétain.[126] In his dictated reply to Poincaré, Nivelle said that "the general in chief can only express regret and surprise that these rumors—unauthorized and groundless—have been credited by the president of the republic. It is not possible to exercise a command in such conditions." Nivelle demanded that the officers responsible for this sort of rumor (which was destructive of "all discipline in an army") be subjected to a "sanction" as an object lesson.[127] President Poincaré rather lamely tried to explain to Colonel Herbillon that he "had merely wished to inform himself" through his intervention.[128] When Duchêne, Hirschauer, and Mangin were asked by the commander in chief to explain their parts in the breach of discipline, the generals "were harrowed to the point of tears," according to Nivelle.[129] "All three swore on their honor that they had never received any order concerning the date of operations; that they had never complained about the scarcity of munitions—all their demands on this score having been satisfied."[130] The whole imbroglio, in the opinion of Colonel Herbillon, left Nivelle in a state of "complete exasperation" at a time when calmness was essential.[131] But the incident had no consequence, so diminished had become General Nivelle's authority.[132]

War Minister Painlevé had never been enthusiastic about Nivelle, although during the first week of the Chemin des Dames offensive he had at least kept his promise to Ribot that he would not work against the general. However, by April 24, Painlevé was convinced that Nivelle had amply demonstrated his inability to win the victory so confidently and so repeatedly promised. The war minister was aware of the difficulty of removing the commander in chief, for his fellow Cabinet members, André Maginot, Léon Bourgeois, and Louis Malvy, were strongly "Nivellist,"[133] and the British were deeply suspicious of Painlevé's known devotion to General Pétain, a defensive strategist who, as Nivelle's successor, might leave the British in the lurch.[134] The war minister, therefore, moved obliquely to dismiss Nivelle, requesting a conference with Field Marshal Haig on April 25. The British commander saw at once that "Painlevé was evidently anxious that [he] urge dismissal of Nivelle."[135] Haig gave him no encouragement, since, as he explained afterward to Ribot, "any change in command during a battle was to be deprecated."[136]

A demand from the army commissions for sanctions against the generals responsible for the failure of the offensive strengthened Painlevé's hand by allowing him to demonstrate his "judiciousness." He told the army commission of the Chamber on April 27 that he was opposed to "breaking indiscriminately the incapable general and the victim of misfortune who had done his duty," since such arbitrary punishment would "destroy initiative." He promised sanctions only after faults had been definitely verified.[137]

Had Painlevé been a quixotic figure, he might have dismissed Nivelle (who, with the best of intentions, was apparently driving the French army to destruction) and then offered his own resignation, since he, Ribot, and Poincaré were all responsible for finally authorizing the risky campaign at the Compiègne Conference. But Painlevé took a narrowly legalistic view of the tragedy. Nivelle had promised substantial victory within the first forty-eight hours; he had won some initial gains, it was true, but hardly enough to justify continuation of a drive which had already filled the hospitals with 95,000 wounded,[138] not counting the killed on the battlefield. Painlevé's defense of his action in removing the general is interesting: "It was often said that the turmoil in the two chambers forced me to change the High Command. Nothing was less true; violent as have been the attacks upon my behavior, it does not please me to seek refuge behind an assembly. Since I alone possessed all the authentic information necessary for appraising the situation, it was I who had to make decisions. And if my decision was to replace the general in chief, it was because I had become convinced that this measure was necessary for the good of the army."[139]

Painlevé followed the strategy of yoking Nivelle with a chief of staff who was soon to succeed him—the cold and ironical exponent of the defense, General Pétain. When the war minister brought up the question of the High Command at a Cabinet meeting on April 26, not a single minister supported Painlevé in his half-revealed wish to withdraw Nivelle's command, but, with the exception of Ribot, they all favored making Pétain Nivelle's chief of the general staff.[140] General Nivelle, who was as good-natured as Joffre had been magisterial, showed his magnanimity once more by "demanding" Pétain's appointment.[141] Thus, on April 29 there was re-created for Pétain "the functions of military technical counselor of the *Comité de guerre* which Joffre had exercised during a week in December, 1916."[142] Pétain, as chief of the General Staff, "would have no authority of his own outside the Ministry of War; as technical counselor, he would go as seldom as possible to the front unless accompanied either by the minister of war or by the general in chief." The plans of Nivelle were supposed to remain subject to a governmental veto, but once the plans were adopted, "the general in chief was to be absolute master of the direction of operations."[143]

It required only one day's time for Nivelle to sense Painlevé's determination to ease him out of the command altogether. "Yesterday evening," the general told Herbillon on April 30, "M. Painlevé telephoned me that, by the order of the government, I must halt the projected attack upon Brimont."[144] Nivelle said that he had obeyed, despite the protests of General Micheler who had already begun the bombardment. "My first thought when I received these instructions," Nivelle continued, "was to hand in my resignation.... I did not do so because I considered it my duty to remain at my post. My leaving would put us in a bad light with the English; [and furthermore] I ought not to appear to my country to be defeated when I was the victor...." The general in chief addressed letters to Painlevé, Ribot, and Poincaré, asking them for *written* confirmation of the order to call off the Fifth Army's attack between Berry-au-Bac and Reims, and of the command given to the Eighth and Tenth armies to follow their prescribed course.[145]

Painlevé appeared surprised upon reading his copy of Nivelle's letter. "But I never told him not to make the attack upon Brimont," he declared to Colonel Herbillon. "I telephoned him that it had been decided at the Council of Ministers that, before making this attack, he should reach an agreement with General Pétain as a consequence of the new functions [which Pétain had assumed] as technical counselor of the government. I will not permit [Nivelle] to unload upon me a responsibility which I have not assumed, thus allowing him—if things go wrong—to say that it was my fault...."[146] When the liaison officer delivered a copy of Nivelle's letter to Poincaré, the president came to Painlevé's defense in the dispute, pointing out that the war minister's situation was difficult. "The halting of our offensive has caused great disillusionment, since General Nivelle himself dangled before our eyes undreamt-of results; in full *Comité de guerre*, he promised 200,000 prisoners. In parliamentary circles opinion is turning more and more against the general, and under this influence the military engage in intrigues and the nation is nervous and deceived...."[147]

In his efforts to discover what was at the bottom of the government's anxiety over the expected attack upon Brimont, Nivelle learned of an interview in which General Mazel, commander of the Fifth Army, gave Painlevé the mistaken impression that the Brimont operation would cost 60,000 casualties.[148] Mazel, under questioning, assured Nivelle that he had intended the war minister to understand that 60,000 troops would be needed for the operation, "but [he] never wished to say that the losses would be 60,000 men—obviously that [was] impossible." Nivelle was furious over the interview, regarding it as a violation of the hierarchical order as well as a suspicious misrepresentation on the part of a subordinate. He insisted upon Mazel's dismissal, but the government shrugged off his demand.[149]

As if determined to rub salt in Nivelle's wounds, the Council of Ministers refused at first to comply with the general in chief's request that General Charles Mangin also be dismissed because of the bloody outcome of the Heurtebise attack of the 2d Colonial Corps of the Sixth Army. The war minister extenuated Mangin's share in this reverse, since General Micheler had repeatedly warned Nivelle against recklessly throwing Mangin's Senegalese into this dangerous sector.[150] Painlevé suspected that Nivelle was searching for a "scapegoat" to sacrifice because of a mistaken strategy which was primarily the fault of the general in chief himself, rather than of his subordinates.[151] However, when the army commission of the Chamber added its criticism of Mangin to Nivelle's, the Council of Ministers reconsidered, and on April 29 Mangin was removed.[152] The next day General Nivelle made himself ridiculous by telephoning Painlevé "that Micheler had declared... Mangin indispensable," and Nivelle asked that he be restored to his command.[153] This was done several months later, but Nivelle's apparent vacillation weakened his position still further.

The next "scapegoat" to be immolated was General Micheler, whose Army Group of Reserves was dissolved in May, thus leaving him without a command. Colonel Herbillon admitted in his *Souvenirs* "that everyone knows that General Micheler gave a bad reception to the general in chief, who reproached him for keeping open house for parliamentarians and critics."[154] Micheler wrote a furious recrimination, which he sent to his friend, Senator Antonin Dubost, explaining why he lost his command: "I know why this disgrace was forced upon me. I am accused of taking part in politics. Not so! I have received deputies and senators, sent by G.Q.G., and that is all. For two months,

I have observed the hatred of Nivelle and the maneuvers of Mangin. As for the famous plan, I wrote to call attention to its dangers, but they replied that I must carry out the orders."[155]

The relations between the government and the command had by now reached a point of unbearable tension. At a conference with the British held in Paris on May 4, it is true Painlevé had declared: "The battle will go on with all the resources in our power."[156] But the war minister expected defensive Pétain to be the one to dole out those resources—and with a far greater degree of frugality and caution than Nivelle had shown. Painlevé was even prepared to hand in his own resignation if Nivelle should be kept on any longer.[157] The confirmed anticlericalist minister of interior, Louis Malvy, held out to the bitter end as a defender of Protestant Nivelle,[158] but on May 10 the Cabinet empowered Painlevé to ask Nivelle to resign. This was to be followed immediately by the appointment of Pétain as general in chief, with General Foch as his chief of the General Staff. One can imagine the dismay of those Cabinet members who sought to avoid a scandal when Nivelle—normally so tractable—refused to resign! Nivelle described his plight to Colonel Herbillon, telling him that Painlevé had first "dragged [him] in the mud" before the army commissions of the Senate and the Chamber, and then had the effrontery to ask him to resign. "I shall never resign," Nivelle declared. "They can replace me if they wish. But for me, of my own will, to admit that I am defeated—that's too much—and the results are there to prove it. If I no longer possess the confidence of the government, let them say so outright and give me a successor, but I shall not go voluntarily!"[159]

It was hard to realize that this proud general, less than half a year before, had assumed command in such a glow of confidence—an expectancy which was quenched in a blood bath for which no single person could justly be held responsible. With almost frantic effort Nivelle tried to cling to a few shreds of authority, but he had promised too much and had paid too high a price for the moderate gains of the Chemin des Dames offen-

CHEMIN DES DAMES

sive. At last, on May 15, a face-saving formula was found: General Nivelle was assigned to the command of an army group—which, as yet, did not even exist for him (nor was it actually to be created).[160] He had "placed himself at the disposal of the government," and could no longer refuse. So closed one of the most troubled chapters in the war's record of friction between the civilians and the military. Nivelle was a victim of tragic circumstances. Professional pride may have made him unduly persistent in trying to carry through his "strategic exploitation," yet his idea of a coördinated series of attacks was basically sound, as Foch was later to demonstrate. This strategy, however, presupposed an overwhelming preponderance of man power and matériel, and these factors could be supplied only by America, the new belligerent who was still to enter the lists. A fatal complex of circumstances had foredoomed the attack of April 16, 1917: the Russian Revolution, the capture of the campaign plans by the Germans, the Alberich movement, and bad weather. Yet further Allied passivity pending American intervention seemed to Nivelle and the harassed government to be as dangerous an alternative as a partially successful offensive.

The Nivelle offensive, according to British General E. L. Spears, "stands as a monument to the inefficiency of democracy at war, to the helplessness of Ministers facing technicians, and their total inability to decide between professional opinions.... The Prime Minister and Painlevé... had power to over-ride the Commander-in-Chief in whose plan they had no faith; yet they were incapable of pointing out the failings of that plan or suggesting alternatives, impotent even to call a halt. The Cabinet... supreme in name only... was hobbled by its lack of technical knowledge and fettered by public opinion which, aware of its ignorance in military matters, would have been intolerant of civilian intrusion in the military sphere. April 16, 1917, epitomizes the terrible disability from which democracies, even when fighting for their existence, are unable to free themselves."[161]

8

The Fabian Policy of Pétain and Painlevé

THE DISASTROUS CAMPAIGN OF CHEMIN DES DAMES HAD the compensatory effect of harmonizing relations between the command and the government to a greater degree than at any time since the opening months of the war. Joffre, Messimy, and Millerand were united in no more single-minded point of view with regard to strategy and policy than Pétain and Painlevé. After the failure of Nivelle's ambitious drive, only one course of action seemed sensible to General Pétain and War Minister Painlevé: to maintain a vigilant defense until the active intervention of America. A British observer contemptuously remarked that the strategy of Pétain was to "squat, do little and have small losses,"[1] but this verdict failed to take into account France's desperate need of rest and recuperation after the loss at Chemin des Dames of 61,000 killed, 95,000 wounded, and 9,000 prisoners,[2] bringing the total casualties in killed to 1,100,000 since the war's outbreak.

The general strategic situation in which France found herself in May, 1917, was a precarious one. The High Command and the Ribot government were convinced that the exhausted French armies would have to postpone any major offensive against the Germans until the remote date of July 1, 1918, when a million American troops would be available on the western front. But what if tottering Russia—deprived of French aid by a policy of containment on the western front—should succumb before the Americans arrived? That was the calculated risk which Pétain and Chief of Staff Foch decided to take with the full approval of the war minister.[3] Pétain, Foch, and Painlevé

---

[1] For notes to chap. 8, see pages 266–268.

counted upon a Fabian policy of a year's delay and rehabilitation, during which time the French army could be equipped with vast supplies of pursuit and bombing planes, rapid-fire heavy artillery, 2,500 small tanks, and "an enormous number of poisonous gas shells."⁴ By the time the Americans arrived in the promised numbers, the French army would be thoroughly rested, its morale restored, and enough matériel accumulated to launch a final, joint effort with the Americans and British.

Painlevé described as follows the identity of opinion held by himself and the top-ranking generals, Pétain and Foch:

Never, from May 15 to November 13, 1917 (the day when I left office), was there so much as a shadow of dissent between General Foch, General Pétain, and myself on the subject of the general conduct of the war. General Foch, as technical counselor of the government, was a member of the *Comité de guerre* and assisted at all of its sessions. In the case of an important decision to be taken, General Pétain was summoned and participated in the discussion. All the military projects and general plans of operations were studied by the two chiefs, defended by them in broad outline at the *comité*, and once adopted, were followed by them. Never during this period did the government paralyze or shackle any initiative whatsoever of the High Command. It is a fact, then, that the war policy followed between May 15 and November 13, 1917, has been the policy advocated in agreement with Foch and Pétain.... It is I who chose... these two supreme chiefs of the French army... and precisely because of the qualities and conceptions which I knew to be theirs.⁵

There was no more effective means of insuring coöperation between the military and the government (whatever Parliament might think of the matter) than for the war minister, acting for the Cabinet, to select as commander in chief a general whose views of strategy and policy coincided with his own. In such a case, the war minister could allow the commander a free hand, protecting him in the event of parliamentary criticism. Such had been the attitude of Messimy and Millerand toward Joffre, and such was to be the case with Painlevé and Pétain.

GENERALS & POLITICIANS

The urgent need to heal the wounds of the French army, so recently aggravated at Chemin des Dames, was underscored by the threat of mutiny at the very time Pétain was appointed to his command. Insubordination first flared up on May 3 in the 2d Colonial Division which had been severely battered at Heurtebise on the opening day of the Chemin des Dames drive. The survivors of the attack posted placards on the walls of their cantonments proclaiming, "Down with the War! Death to those who are responsible!"[6] Troops gathered around the leaders of the *émeute*, listening to their harangues on the plight of the combat soldiers as contrasted with the good fortune of the munitions workers, who were lining their pockets with 15 to 20 francs a day.[7] The division's officers intervened at once, easily quelling the disorders.

Several weeks later, on May 20, mutiny broke out in earnest, this time in the reserve troops of the 32d Corps who sang the "Internationale" and forced an entrance into the home of the camp commander, committing acts of vandalism.[8] This demonstration set off a succession of disturbances which soon affected no less than sixteen divisions.[9] The disorders were marked by widespread drunkenness, the singing of the "Internationale," the random shooting of rifles into the air, vociferous demands for furloughs, and refusals of troops in rear echelons to go up to the firing line.[10] The disturbances were especially grave in the regions of Soissons, Fismes, Châlons, and the suburbs of Paris. Almost without exception, the mutinous troops were members of the Fourth, Fifth, Sixth, and Tenth armies—those units most brutally mauled in Nivelle's offensive[11]—or else they were in the corps stationed in the rear nearest Paris.[12] Of the 115 insubordinate units, there were 75 regiments of infantry, 23 battalions of *chasseurs,* and only 12 regiments of artillery.[13]

There seemed to be a rough pattern of uniformity in the demonstrations. Usually the outbreaks occurred when infantrymen were ordered to return to the front; or when troops were assigned to tiresome, repetitious training maneuvers, seemingly "to keep them busy"; when leaves were canceled or unduly postponed; or when billeting conditions were bad.[14] In such circumstances the mutineers gathered around their "leaders" (generally noncommissioned officers), listening to their inflammatory harangues. The troops elected these sergeant-orators as "delegates" to transmit their demands to the commanders. The unruly soldiers were ordinarily not lacking in respect for their lieutenants, but they simply refused to obey them.[15] "It was more of a 'strike' than a revolt."[16] Strike, revolt, or conspiracy, a refusal to obey military orders was an offense which no general—and few politicians—would condone.

One of the rare disagreements ever to arise between Painlevé and Pétain was in diagnosing the causes of the mutinies, and even this difference of opinion was without practical consequence since the war minister and the commander in chief concurred in the therapy for the restless army. A civilian such as the Republican Socialist Painlevé would almost certainly place the blame for mutiny upon military errors, even as professional soldier Pétain would be inclined to account for it on the grounds of alleged political delinquencies. According to Painlevé, "the principal cause of the mutinies, that which outweighed all the others, was the weariness of three years of war and of the losses sustained, and especially the disillusionment resulting from the costly and deceptive operations of April."[17] Painlevé pointed out that other belligerents experienced similar disturbances, notably the Austro-Hungarian and Italian armies and the German navy. The war minister listed what he considered to be the subordinate causes of the outbreak: too short rest periods in disregard of promises to the contrary; too wide a breach between officers and enlisted men; refusal to grant leaves; bad billeting; lack of liquor control when the troops received their bonus payments for front-line duty; inadequate rations; the drafting of young, resentful factory workers and of those who had been *embusqués;* and lastly, the example of the Russian Revolution as reflected by some of the French troops.[18]

Pétain may have doubted the wisdom of the army's leadership during Nivelle's command, but—as in the time of *l'affaire Dreyfus*—the army remained above a general's reproach. By tradition loyal to his profession, Pétain, in reporting to the war minister, contended that "in a general manner, these demonstrations do not seem to be directed against the Higher Command.... The men say: 'We have nothing against our officers. It's the government.... The government has refused Germany's peace offer....' What are the causes of this dangerous effervescence?"[19] Pétain enumerated the reasons for the mutinies according to the career soldier's conception of social causation:

1) The corrupting influence of degenerate persons who met the troops on leave at the Parisian railway stations;

2) The actions of *agents provocateurs,* disguised in military uniforms, who frequented the trains and even the army camps;

3) Restrictions upon the severity of the sentences which could be issued by the *conseils de guerre,* with the result that persons of criminal intent could hope to get off with nominal punishment;

4) Drunkenness caused by the ready availability of wine to troops receiving bonuses for trench duty;

5) The reports received by troops at the front, describing the attendance of soldiers and even certain officers at pacifist meetings held in the zone of the interior;

6) Strikes in Paris and other industrial centers;

7) The example of the Russian brigades stationed in France, which formed soviets;

8) The articles in the French press describing in detail the Russian committees of workers and soldiers.[20]

Pétain demanded as correctives the strict policing of railway stations; energetic action against soldiers who had been released to do factory work but who took part in "pacifist agitation"; close supervision of the press; finally, repeal of the law of April 27, 1916 (offering the possibility of pardon to condemned soldiers), which had so seriously hampered the effectiveness of the *conseils de guerre* in court-martialing offenders.[21]

PÉTAIN & PAINLEVÉ

For the sake of keeping the army's record unsullied, General Pétain may have appeared to evade the more basic issues involved in the mutinies, but in actual practice he proved himself as realistic as Painlevé. One of Pétain's first acts as commander in chief was the issuance of "Directive No. 1" in which he ordered his field commanders to avoid unlimited offensives which might create exposed salients, and to base all of their plans upon adequate artillery action, thereby insuring *minimum losses*.[22] Pétain reminded the generals that the confidence of the enlisted men depended upon the "goodwill of the chief."[23] Army commanders were directed on June 2 to correct abuses as follows: majors were to inspect their companies' mess; the commissariat was to improve the quality and variety of fare—under penalty for negligence; camp accommodations and sleeping quarters of the troops must be improved; to avoid tiring the troops unduly, unnecessary exercises must be avoided; troops must be relieved more frequently and front-line duty imposed economically to allow longer service in the rear for those units released.[24] And risky as it might have appeared at first, Pétain boldly restored and regularized furloughs.[25]

Pétain was perceptive enough to realize that the army's morale would not even permit a continuation of the local attacks currently under way. The four small-scaled offensives which General Nivelle had substituted for his abortive "strategic exploitation" were proving disappointing. The most determined efforts of the Fifth Army to capture the crest of Sapigneul-Mont Spin were nullified by a powerful German counterattack on May 31, which all but wiped out the 22d Battalion of *chasseurs*. Pétain readily consented to Colonel de Reynies' request that no immediate command be issued to recover the lost ground.[26] It was the same with the Sixth Army, which had been ordered to attack along the Chemin des Dames sector during the first fortnight of June. But on June 3, General Maistre (the successor to Mangin) requested a postponement of the action, since the morale of his exhausted units was so low that he risked "the men's refusal to leave the trenches." General Pétain, well aware of the fact that "at the moment . . . only two divisions between Soissons and Paris . . . could be absolutely and entirely relied upon," offered no objection to Maistre's request.[27] Fortunately for France, the Germans "heard but little about the mutinies and that only by degrees. Only later on," Ludendorff admitted, "did we learn the whole truth."[28] By that time Pétain's correctives were becoming effective.

Skillfully blending leniency with firmness, Pétain visited in person no less than ninety divisions of the French army,[29] conversing gravely with the officers and frequently with the enlisted men as well.[30] The commander in chief expected his example of personal solicitude to be followed, and to make sure that it was he issued an order on June 5, 1917, requiring the officers to meet informally with their men at least once a week.[31] Furthermore, on June 8, Pétain ordered general officers and even members of the General Staff to "appear frequently in the trenches," and to keep themselves informed about the morale of the troops.[32] Proving that he knew how to brandish the stick as well as offer the carrot, Pétain demanded of his friend Painlevé the reëstablishment of the courts-martial. This system of summary trial for military offenders had been replaced on April 27, 1916, by the much less severe *conseils de guerre,* which had the disadvantage (from the command's point of view) of the rights of appeal and pardon by the president of the republic. These appeals made verdicts of the *conseils de guerre* merely provisional, causing much delay in the entire procedure.

Painlevé agreed with Pétain that the army needed a restoration of the powers of summary judgment, but he knew that the courts-martial could be reëstablished only by legislative enactment, which would undoubtedly stir up heated parliamentary debate over the question of the civil liberties involved.[33] To bypass the whole difficulty, the war minister issued a decree on June 9, retaining the *conseils de guerre,* but canceling the right of appeal in cases of mass disobedience. Legal delays were to be shortened as much as possible. President Poincaré (who had already shown his willingness to coöperate with Pétain in several cases of appeal)[34] expedited the procedure "by ceding his right of pardon to the general in chief." These Draconian measures—added to Pétain's positive efforts to promote the welfare of the troops—had a salutary effect, for "no case of disobedience en masse occurred at the front after June 10...."[85] To prevent discussion of Painlevé's drastic decree, the censorship was ordered to forbid the publication of any "comment on the change in the code of military justice suspending the right of appeal, or even the text of the articles modified."[36] Painlevé admitted in his book that he expected a parliamentary storm over the policy which he and Pétain had adopted, but he declared vehemently: "If they wish, they can shoot me when it is all over, but they must let me restore order."[37]

A great number of generals, according to Painlevé, demanded that the High Command resort to "pitiless executions, in default of which everything would be lost." But the war minister and the commander in chief were not to be turned from a policy of moderation. Every evening during the month of June, 1917, special couriers brought to rue St. Dominique the files on the mutineers who had been sentenced to death. Painlevé would first study the cases, then go by automobile to G.Q.G. at Compiègne, or else telephone Pétain to discuss the advisability of commuting the sentences. "Pétain was not one of those chiefs who [were] surprised at 'quibbling over an execution' when an order for an offensive, depending upon their decision, could put thousands of men in their graves."[38] The result of the relative clemency of Pétain and Painlevé was that of a total of 150 death sentences issued, only 23 were actually carried out.[39] Even so, the question of the justification of these 23 executions was to arouse a strong reaction on the part of the Socialists in Parliament.

The beneficial effects of the policy of Painlevé and Pétain were felt as early as the end of June, 1917. The mutinies were subsiding once the troops became convinced that their lives would not be uselessly squandered. The "sanctions" taken against Generals Nivelle, Mangin, and Micheler were an indication that there would not be a renewal of costly attacks—at least, for the time being. The improvements in the troops' living conditions were increasingly noticeable. The officers, willy-nilly, seemed to be more concerned with the welfare of their men. The troops could look forward to regulated leaves, and they could expect a firm but unobtrusive supervision which would tolerate no further unruliness. The time, therefore, seemed favorable to War Minister Painlevé for a session of a secret committee to allow the government to answer the inevitable parliamentary questioning concerning the Chemin des Dames campaign and the resultant mutinies. President of the Council Ribot was strongly opposed to a secret committee, but Painlevé had promised the army commission on May 22 that such a session would be held as soon as conditions permitted.[40] By the end of June, the most serious objections to the Chemin des Dames strategy had already been anticipated and disposed of. There was no longer much benefit to be derived from the secret committee, but for that very reason the Ribot government could confidently risk interpellation behind closed doors. Further postponement would have been impolitic, since on June 28 some impatient members of the Chamber's army commission—"holding the most diverse political opinions"—pronounced as "insufficient" the sanctions taken by the government against Generals Nivelle and Mangin. The army commission wanted them "broken" once and for all.[41] Thus pressed for a full explanation of its war policy, the government agreed to hold the secret committee on June 29.

The severest critic was not one of the Socialists, but soldier-Deputy Lieutenant Jean Ybarnegaray, a Catholic and Rightist from Basses-Pyrénées, who delivered a scathing indictment of General Nivelle's foolhardiness and overconfidence which had made possible such costly blunders as the attack of the 2d Colonial Division against the undestroyed German positions at Heurtebise on April 16. Ybarnegaray declared that not only

General Nivelle—a man of "petty spirit and immense pride"—but Generals Mangin, Micheler, and Mazel "ought to be broken, without distinction. All four, because all four have lost the confidence of the army! ..."[42] The sanctions must be rigorous, final, and public."[43]

The speaker who followed, Albert Favre, a Left Radical from Charente-Inférieure, went so far as to violate the spirit of the constitution by taking President Poincaré to task for his intervention in Nivelle's behalf at the Compiègne Conference (held in the president's railroad car) at a time when General Nivelle was ready to resign.[44] Favre accused Poincaré of trying to frustrate War Minister Painlevé's efforts to replace Nivelle by General Pétain.[45] President of the Council Alexandre Ribot came to Poincaré's defense by assuring the deputies that he and "the president of the republic had acted in concert in summoning General Pétain to the supreme command...."[46]

The attack upon the governmental war policy was continued by the Socialists (who were bristling with indignation over Ribot's recent refusal to grant them passports to attend their international conference in Stockholm scheduled for the end of June).[47] The Socialist criticism was opened by Aristide Jobert from Yonne, who contrasted the government's lenient treatment of the generals responsible for the Chemin des Dames casualties with the brutal punishment—the "decimation"—which was inflicted upon the insubordinate enlisted men. President Poincaré was accused of having a part in this inhumanity, since he had given up his right of pardon to the commander in chief.[48] Deep sympathy for the mutineers was expressed by Pierre Laval, Socialist deputy from Seine, who defied the conservatives by declaring: "The way to give hope to the troops and confidence to the workers—whether you like it or not—is Stockholm!"[49]

Another denunciation of the government came from a Negro deputy, M. Diagne, a Union Republican representing Sénégal, who called attention to the violation of the promise given by War Minister General Lyautey on March 4, 1917, that the Senegalese troops, then quartered in the south of France, would not be sent into combat until the weather was mild. Yet, on April 16, despite "cold, snow, and rain" which so numbed the Africans that they were "incapable of putting bayonets on their rifles," they were thrown into a "massacre, to no purpose."[50]

The inefficiency of the health service of the army was revealed by a member of the army commission, Deputy Jean Marie Guiraud, a Radical Socialist from Tarn, who gave a harrowing description of the overcrowded evacuation hospitals during the Chemin des Dames offensive.[51] Two members of the army commission of the Chamber, MM. Victor Dalbiez and Abel Ferry, commented upon the mistakes of the command in the April offensive as they had noted them on their inspection missions.[52]

In answering the deputies' criticisms, War Minister Painlevé told how he had tried vainly to call General Nivelle's attention to the effects which the Russian Revolution and the German withdrawal behind the Siegfried Line would have upon the Chemin des Dames strategy. Painlevé described the Compiègne Conference, recounting the opinions expressed there by the commanders of the army groups. He praised Pétain's strategy, the intent of which was "to renounce all kinds of rash and hazardous offensives, and above all, to use matériel methodically before sending in the men, who would go into action only after the [enemy] positions were entirely destroyed."[53] Painlevé explained that upon Pétain's advice he had delayed two weeks in removing Nivelle in order not to disturb the British, whose troops had been expressly entrusted to Nivelle's command. As for sanctions, Painlevé said that Nivelle had been placed at the war minister's disposal, and he promised that a military inquest would be conducted in the former commander's case. The war minister tried to mollify the critics by reminding them that Generals Mangin and Mazel had already been deprived of their armies, and General Micheler's command had been reduced from an army group to an army.[54]

Chiefs ... who could cite glorious records, have been relieved of their commands. The law allows the minister no other sanction without a previous inquest.... This inquest, which will open in a few days, will permit the accused generals to offer their explanations, [thus] apportioning responsibility and enabling the government to make its final decisions in full knowledge....[55]

Painlevé concluded with a general summary of the Ribot government's war policy:

A halt must be called to rash and venturesome schemes, the grandiose appearance of which barely conceals their emptiness and lack of preparation! (Applause on the Socialist benches.) There must be an end to pretentious plans *à la Napoleon,* obstinately inspired by a school of thought at variance with reality, which dares to dash to pieces in a few days armies which are, in fact, the nation in arms. (Hear! Hear!) A reasonable, positive war policy, prudent as well as energetic, which takes into account the resources at hand ... which does not exact the impossible of human beings but utilizes to the utmost all kinds of matériel ... this, gentlemen, is the government's method.[56]

Although this clarification was regarded by the Nivelle sympathizers as a sort of gallant assurance to the Germans that they "had nothing to fear for months to come,"[57] some of the Socialists at least liked its tone of solicitude for the troops. As for the Right, they supported Painlevé because he was considered a faithful champion of that white hope of conservatism, Pétain.[58] The deputies deliberated over thirteen orders of the day before accepting the one drawn up by MM. René Renoult, Louis Klotz, and a score of colleagues. It repeated the customary promise not to "interfere in military operations," but pledged the government to enforce discipline, to administer justice impartially in all ranks of the army, and to reach an agreement with France's allies for a fairer sharing of the war burden which would permit an improvement in the condition of the French soldier. The order of the day expressed satisfaction over the rapidly expanding American army and the new Russian offensive. It was adopted by a vote of 357 to 167.[59] It is surprising that there were as many opposition votes as 167 in view of the absence of any realistic alternative to the Ribot government's policy of restoring the troops' morale, containing the Germans by a vigilant defense, and waiting for the arrival of the Americans. Even so, many of the Socialists were still unreconciled over their failure to obtain passports to Stockholm and over the execution of the twenty-three enlisted men in contrast with the mild punishment apparently in store for the generals disgraced in the April offensive.

Painlevé's promise of an immediate military inquest into the Chemin des Dames failure had to be carried out cautiously, since the campaign was one of the most controversial issues of the war. The war minister decided to appoint an investigating board of three generals who had never served under the command of Nivelle, who had commanded at least an army corps, and who had never "been an object of disgrace."[60] Painlevé was convinced that Generals Brugère, Foch, and Gouraud best met all of the required conditions, so he ordered them to begin the inquest at once. As soon as some of the senatorial army commissioners learned of the board's appointment, they complained privately to President Poincaré that "Nivelle and the other generals... would be exposed to... vulgar prejudice.... The country would be demoralized and an injustice committed."[61] These objections were ignored by the war minister, and the inquest board was allowed to go on with its task of gathering information.

While the military investigation was under way, there came to light the first of a series of political scandals which contributed to the downfall of the Ribot government. It was discovered that at the outset of the war the prolabor minister of interior, Louis Jean Malvy, had given a subvention to a shady journalist, a onetime anarchist turned patriot, Miguel Vigo, alias Almereyda.[62] When Almereyda's journal, *Bonnet Rouge,* began backsliding from its venal patriotism, Malvy suspended the subsidy. Almereyda then turned over the editorship of *Bonnet Rouge* to an assistant, one Duval, who annoyed French patriots with articles of violent Anglophobia. In May, 1917, Duval was arrested at the Swiss border for having German funds in his possession.[63] When the Sûreté Générale negligently released Duval, a Rightist deputy, Maurice Barrès, publicly demanded of the minister of interior on July 7: "... What measures did he intend to take against the canaille of the *Bonnet Rouge?*"[64] The government had to imprison Duval and Almereyda for investigation, but Malvy's lackadaisical attitude toward the issue of defeatism provoked Senator Georges Clemenceau into a bitter attack upon the minister of the interior on July 22. Malvy was accused of unaccountable leniency toward dubious propagandists such as his "friend Almereyda."[65]

Of great embarrassment to the Ribot ministry was Almereyda's suicide in his prison cell at Fresnes on August 14. The charge was made in the Rightist press that "Almereyda has disappeared, the victim of a political assassination!" After a fortnight of indecision, Malvy resigned in an effort to save the threatened Cabinet.[66] Ribot's government lasted only another week, for both the Left and Right were by now deeply suspicious of the aged president of the council—the Left still resentful over their failure to obtain passports for Stockholm, the Right indignant over the revelation of Malvy's apparent indifference to defeatism.[67] Poincaré offered the presidency of the council to former War Minister Painlevé, the paradoxical Republican Socialist friend of Pétain, who alone seemed to inspire the confidence of both extremes.[68]

In view of Painlevé's cordial relations with the general in chief, it was a foregone conclusion that the new executive would keep his old portfolio of war minister, thus assuring a continuation of the harmony between rue St. Dominique and general headquarters. But when Painlevé insisted on appointing Ribot as foreign minister, the Socialist ministers designated for armament and education, Albert Thomas and Alexandre Varenne, brusquely announced that they could not serve. For the first time since August 26, 1914, the French government included no Socialists, a fact which ultimately contributed to the unseating of Painlevé.⁶⁹

In his opening address to the Chamber, Painlevé tried to allay the suspicion of defeatism aroused by *l'affaire du Bonnet Rouge*: "In the policy being followed, as well as in that to come, justice will pursue its course without hesitation, weakness, or regard for personalities. Whoever acts as an accomplice of the enemy must suffer the rigor of the law...."⁷⁰ In its first vote of confidence, the new ministry received 368 ballots, with none in opposition, but with 131 abstentions, of which 86 were Socialists.⁷¹

Although assured of a safe majority of supporters, Painlevé encountered considerable opposition to his government's war policy—chiefly from die-hard proponents of the *offensive à outrance*. Colonel Herbillon reported to him on September 19 that he had heard "criticism...concerning General Pétain, who was reproached for not having undertaken extensive operations." Painlevé related in his book that at the *Comité de guerre* the president of the recently created Economic Council, Senator Paul Doumer, served as "the spokesman for the advocates of an immediate offensive."⁷² Doumer argued that the Allies had on the western front a numerical preponderance over the Germans of 1,800,000 men. "In these conditions, why hesitate?" General Pétain refuted this line of criticism by discussing the strategic situation "in the clearest and most precise fashion, indicating what were [the French] forces...the possibilities, the goal to be reached by the Allies, and the date of the American intervention. He cut blind illusions at the roots...."⁷³ Chief of Staff Foch expressed full agreement with General Pétain. "After the shock of April 16," Foch told the critics, "to imagine that within a few months the French army will be capable of renewing an offensive on the same scale is to show no understanding of the possibilities." Commander in Chief Pétain promised the *Comité de guerre* that at the right time "he would direct against the enemy a succession of hammer blows, powerfully prepared by artillery, as provided in the protocol" signed with the British on May 4. The *Comité de guerre* thereupon unanimously voted its support of Pétain and Foch.[74]

The new strategy of cautious, intensively prepared attacks was first tried out by the British at Paschendaele on July 31, 1917, following an unprecedented artillery barrage lasting eighteen days. The British were supported by the French army of General Anthoine, which had been placed under Haig's orders. But foul weather mired down the offensive, which after three weeks gained only "meager results." The cost was heavy to the British although slight to the French.[75] Much more successful was the two-day attack which General Guillaumat launched on the Verdun sector on August 20. "Mounted carefully and methodically, with small losses," it won 4,000 prisoners and freed Mort-Homme and Hill 304 at a single stroke.[76] The most brilliant of all the little offensives of Pétain was the three-day battle which General Maistre's Sixth Army began along the center of the Chemin des Dames sector on October 20, 1917. Thoroughly rehabilitated after five months of rest, Maistre's forces defied bad weather and on the first day of the attack seized 8,000 prisoners. Colonel Herbillon described the engagement succinctly: "The affair, quite well prepared, succeeded happily. Except upon the extreme right, all of our objectives were reached: Fort Malmaison—Allemant—Vaudesson—Chavignon."[77] The Hindenburg Line was breached to a depth of seven kilometers along a twelve-kilometer front. President of the Council and War Minister Painlevé noted proudly that "these two offensives of Verdun and Malmaison regained for us, in terrain and prisoners, as much as *la grande offensive de rupture* of April 16 to 22."[78]

Painlevé's satisfaction over the success of the policy which he and Pétain were following was soon blighted by further revelations of treason which came in the wake of the *Bonnet Rouge affaire*. These exposés tended to smear Painlevé, who had the ill luck to preside over the government at the time of the disclosures. "During my two months as president of the council," he wrote, "I had a dreary record of arrests and scandals to clear up, almost all of which were the legacy of the distant past...."[79]

It was necessary, first of all, to dispel the effluvium of the *Bonnet Rouge* case by jailing the newspaper's small-fry writers—MM. Goldsky, Landau, Marion, and Joucla—who had assisted Almereyda and Duval in defeatist propaganda.[80] Then on October 7, 1917, Painlevé felt obliged to order the arrest of Radical Socialist Victor Turmel for suspicion of "dealing with the enemy," since the deputy from Côtes-du-Nord was unable to give a satisfactory explanation of a package of 25,000 Swiss francs found in his locker at the Chamber of Deputies.[81] The Turmel scandal was followed by *l'affaire Bolo,* in which a bizarre adventurer, Paul Bolo, was arraigned for using German funds in an effort to bribe such newspapers as *Le Temps, Le Figaro, Le Rappel,* and *Le Journal.* Bolo appeared on the verge of success with *Le Journal* after promising its principal writer, the blatant Senator Charles Humbert, a loan (of German Foreign Office origin) for the purchase of the paper, which was to launch a pacifist campaign.[82] At this juncture Bolo was arrested. In the course of time Charles Humbert also was tried for his part in the case, although the senator from Meuse was acquitted. As if these disgraces were not enough to cause the political welkin to ring with charges and countercharges, Léon Daudet, the editor of the royalist paper, *L'Action Française,* addressed a letter to President Poincaré in which he accused former Minister of Interior Malvy of treacherously delivering to the Germans the battle plans of the Chemin des Dames campaign. Malvy read Daudet's letter aloud to the Chamber and demanded vindication by an official inquest.[83] The Socialist friends of Malvy were so outraged by Daudet's charges that the government feared a disruption of national unity.

In an effort to appease the Left, Painlevé not only appointed a military board of inquest which quickly acquitted Malvy of the imputation of treason,[84] but the president of the council went further by extending parliamentary inspection to the utmost—

as the Socialists had so long desired. In agreement with the High Command, Painlevé issued a circular defining the rights of the parliamentary inspection delegates: equipped with permanent passes, they could now carry their investigations to the most advanced firing posts merely by "notifying the minister of war."[85] The inspection delegates could travel about "without being accompanied by an officer; they might make investigations on the spot and call for papers, and they could take copies of documents given to them. The conception, direction, preparation, and execution of military operations alone remained outside their competence."[86] At last the Socialists had won a sweeping concession, yet it inspired no gratitude toward the president of the council.

Painlevé's political anxieties were increased by the verdict of Generals Brugère, Foch, and Gouraud on the responsibility for the Chemin des Dames disaster. In Painlevé's opinion, the generals' report was "vague, inexact, a 'rose-water' report, whose authors, one felt, wished neither to approve the plans of the offensive, nor to upset their violently attacked comrades."[87] The findings of the inquest were supposed to be secret, remaining in the exclusive possession of the war minister and of the board. Yet Painlevé was convinced that the report would be demanded by the commissions of the Chamber and Senate. He was particularly worried over the misuse which would probably be made of certain "errors" which the verdict contained: censure of the government by Foch for having consented to "so obviously chimerical" a strategy as the one outlined by Nivelle at the Compiègne Conference; a charge that certain newspapers had exaggerated the losses in the offensive, whereas in reality "no journal had published any figure on losses"; an accusation that the undersecretary of state for health, M. Godart, had magnified the number of casualties—the very opposite of the truth. What especially irritated Painlevé was the report's "echoing the groundless legend" that "numbers of parliamentarians, unaccustomed to fighting, [were] present in the battle zone on April

16, thereby spreading alarm to the home front."[88] It appeared that the generals were trying "to have it both ways": after numerous instances in which the command had complained of governmental or parliamentary officiousness in the technical matters of strategy, the inquest board took the Ribot government to task because it had *not* interfered in Nivelle's strategy at the Compiègne Conference. The military gave the impression of wanting a free hand in strategy except when things went awry, in which case they tried to push responsibility for failure upon the civil power.

Painlevé intended to summon the inquest board to protest its findings, but he was distracted by the sudden rout of the Italians at Caporetto toward the end of October, 1917. The reverse on the Piave front proved so serious that the Italian government swallowed its pride and requested French professional advice as well as reinforcements. Chief of Staff General Foch was sent posthaste to the Piave, to be followed shortly by six French divisions under General Duchêne's command.[89]

Italy's distress gave Painlevé the opportunity to sponsor a unification of strategy on the western front—a coördination long overdue. He had begun *pourparlers* with the British upon this ticklish question as far back as August 6, 1917, but Lloyd George and the undersecretary of state for war, Lord Milner, had counseled the greatest patience in trying to obtain the appointment of Foch as chief of an inter-Allied General Staff.[90] The Caporetto disaster clearly demonstrated the urgent need of unification, and in response to a letter from Lloyd George, Painlevé hurried over to London for renewed consultation.[91]

There emerged from the conference a so-called Supreme War Council, a body primarily political, to be made up of the president of the council (wherever possible) and a permanent military councilor from each of the countries to be included (France, Britain, and—it was hoped—Italy and America). The Supreme War Council would hold plenary sessions at Versailles at monthly intervals. The permanent military councilors, with their staffs, would form a secretariat, which would remain in continuous session at Versailles for the purpose of "centralizing all the data, plans, and documents bearing on the war, coördinating the studies and plans, and preparing decisions."[92] Painlevé was greatly disappointed in his determination to have General Foch serve as the presiding officer of the secretariat at Versailles. Lloyd George insisted that Foch resign as chief of the French General Staff before assuming a new post of chief of the inter-Allied General Staff. Lloyd George had to oppose a dual role for Foch because of the jealousy and hostility of Britain's own chief of the Imperial General Staff, Sir William Robertson, who was resolved "to fight the Inter-Allied Council."[93] However, it was a relatively easy matter for Painlevé and Lloyd George to persuade hard-pressed Italy to join the Supreme War Council at a conference held at Rapallo on November 6. There still remained the task of gaining the adherence of America.

The new Supreme War Council was regarded by French parliamentarians as a sham since it had no generalissimo at its head, and the permanent military councilors making up its secretariat depended exclusively upon their respective governments. At a meeting of the *Comité de guerre,* the president of the council acknowledged the imperfections of the Supreme War Council, explaining that "it was only the first step to prepare English public opinion to accept the unified command under General Foch."[94] A serious handicap confronted Painlevé in answering parliamentary questioning about the new body, since he could not state publicly his long-range purpose of appointing General Foch as president of the Supreme War Council, what with Lloyd George already receiving sharp criticism in England for having subordinated the proud British army ever so slightly to a quasi-unified command.[95] The onetime war minister, Alexandre Millerand, greatly embarrassed Painlevé on November 13 by asking him at a public meeting of the Chamber: "When will the Entente entrust the direction of its operations to a generalissimo of the Allies?" The president of the council's reply seemed so evasive that he won only a small vote of confidence, 250 to 192,[96] a narrower margin of safety than Viviani, Briand, or Ribot had been accustomed to receive.

Having barely survived an attack on its war policy, Painlevé's government was almost immediately overthrown for a frivolous reason. Painlevé asked for a fortnight's delay in interpellation on a puerile dispute in which one deputy, a Rightist, Jean Ybarnegaray, attributed cowardice to a colleague, the Radical Socialist Léon Accambray. Both Left and Right were unwilling to postpone debate on whether Accambray had actually "fled before the enemy," and over this trivial issue Painlevé was given a vote of nonconfidence of 277 to 186.[97] The Left, having acted impulsively, protested the vote, while the Right, suspecting Painlevé's negligence in the *Bonnet Rouge,* Bolo, and Turmel *affaires,* were glad to see his defeat.

Painlevé suffered from the defects of his qualities: his leniency was the reverse side of his desire to be fair-minded. Nevertheless, he had rendered a great service to France by aiding Pétain in calming the mutinous army and by assisting Lloyd George in creating the Supreme War Council, which was to have an important evolution in the following ministry. He was denied the credit which was his due because of his inability to explain to Parliament that his ultimate goal was the appointment of Foch as a generalissimo of the Allies, a clarification precluded by British politico-military exigencies. The war minister and president of the council deserved recognition for his earnest efforts to avert class war at a time when France was perilously weak. It was unfortunate for him that there came to light during his conciliatory administration the worst scandals of the war period. The Bolo, Turmel, and *Bonnet Rouge affaires*—not to mention several lesser scandals such as the Mata Hari case—had tainted roots extending much farther back than Painlevé's accession to office. However, the uncovering of corruption was so dismaying that there was a general demand for a thorough house cleaning.

PETAIN & PAINLEVE

Grateful as France may have been to Painlevé the war minister, she wanted a more resolute and determined president of the council. France—except for the Socialists—sought a ruthless and fanatical patriot of the stripe of some of the Jacobins or of Gambetta. That she was to receive in dour old Clemenceau.

The Painlevé-Pétain love feast represented a lull in the relations between the command and the government in marked contrast to the previous period of Nivelle's bitter difficulties with the ministry, and different in spirit from the subsequent epoch of Clemenceau's Jacobin bravura which was reminiscent of the time of the representatives on mission. Painlevé attempted—and in vain—to keep in harness the extreme Left and Right. Clemenceau, of bolder temperament, disregarded the Socialists and set out upon a course of his own choosing which won conservative and moderate support.

9

Clemenceau's Jacobin Rule

FRANCE, WHICH HAD ENTERED THE WAR IN THE circumstances of parliamentary deference to the military, emerged from the conflict with a strong-minded president of the council in the ascendant over both command and Parliament. The nation had groped its way from the initial military dictatorship through a gradual recovery of parliamentary authority until it came out with virtually a civilian dictatorship in the hands of the chief of the executive power. The reason for this backing and filling lay principally in the failure of Joffre to win a quick and decisive victory, and in Parliament's inability to do any better when it and the government narrowly circumscribed the command during the Nivelle epoch. The loss of face by the military was soon equaled by the tarnished prestige of civilian politicians when it transpired during the lenient Painlevé administration that traitors, near traitors, and defeatists were in the very midst of Parliament, if not of the government itself. Through default, therefore, power shifted from Joffre to Parliament until it finally resided with a figure whose name symbolized the will to victory, Georges Clemenceau.

The keynote to Clemenceau's character and administration was given in an address to the Chamber soon after he assumed the presidency of the council: "My formula is the same in every respect. Domestic policy? I wage war. Foreign policy? I wage war. I always wage war."[1] Fighting was the breath of life to the indestructible old duelist who for forty-seven years had been the bogey of French politics.

---

[1] For notes to chap. 9, see pages 268–271.

CLEMENCEAU'S JACOBIN RULE

Beginning public life as a physician-mayor of Montmartre at the very time of the overthrow of the Second Empire, Clemenceau followed a career which was a miniature history of the Third Republic. He was elected to the Chamber of Deputies in 1876, becoming known as the "destroyer of ministries" because of his role in overthrowing the cabinets of Gambetta in 1882, Ferry in 1885, and Brisson in 1886. An early supporter of General Boulanger[2] (because of the general's rare republicanism), as well as a friend of Cornelius Herz, one of the most rascally promoters involved in the Panama Canal scandal,[3] Clemenceau made amends for these lapses by repudiating pinchbeck Boulanger and by championing the cause of justice in the Dreyfus affair, courageously publishing Zola's *J'Accuse* in the pages of his newspaper *L'Aurore*.[4] Having entered political life as a Radical, Clemenceau irrevocably alienated the Socialists in 1906 when as minister of interior he used troops against striking miners.[5] During his own ministry, lasting from 1906 to 1909, he acquired an anglophile label by trying to cement the entente with England.

Upon the outbreak of the war Clemenceau used his journal *L'Homme Libre* (after many bouts with the censor, renamed *L'Homme Enchaîné*)[6] as a means of exposing inertia, incompetence, red tape, and the shortages of matériel. As one of the most active members of the senatorial army commission, he made a much-discussed attack upon the slackness of Interior Minister Malvy before the Senate on July 22, 1917, a denunciation which won him the reputation of being the embodiment of France's will to victory. President Poincaré, despite recollections of many unpleasant encounters, managed to put aside his personal antipathy to Clemenceau on the grounds that "the devil of a fellow has the support of patriots, and if I do not call him, his legendary power will kill any other ministry."[7] Accordingly, he invited him to succeed Painlevé.

As the Tiger prepared to take over the second ministry in his long career, he reviewed the strategic situation with General

Jean Mordacq, commander of the 24th Division, whom he asked to serve as his military adviser. The general state of affairs, as sketched by Clemenceau, appeared as follows: Russia and Rumania were out of the war; Italy was reduced to the defensive for a long time by the rout at Caporetto; Britain was having difficulty in filling the gaps left in her ranks by the loss of from 700,000 to 800,000 men in 1917; the French army was deficient in reserves, tanks, planes, long-range heavy artillery, and machine guns, and the Army of the Orient had a defective command, since Sarrail was not sufficiently bold.[8] The Germans could now move westward nearly all of the divisions which they had used on the eastern front. "The Allies were reduced to the defensive until the Americans could be transported to France in sufficient numbers. Would they arrive in time, and what would be the quality of their troops?" After speculating upon these factors, General Mordacq outlined for Clemenceau what, in his opinion, should be the procedure for conducting the war:

... In order to win this war, a coalition war, and consequently one very difficult to conduct, there must be a close alliance between policy and strategy, the latter being the continuation and the result of the former. Hence the necessity of a first-rate, energetic policy. I visualize the supreme direction entrusted to three men, a prerequisite to success. For policy, you, Clemenceau; for strategy, General Foch, commander in chief of the Allied armies, and General Pétain, commander in chief of the French army. Consequently, it is necessary to bring about the unified command as soon as possible, and to retain General Pétain at the head of the French army, although he will be very much attacked, especially by the parliamentarians.[9]

Clemenceau expressed full agreement with General Mordacq on this program which seemed so simple and yet was to prove so difficult of realization, since unifying the Allied command was probably the most arduous political task of the war. But indicative of the nebulousness—not to say meaninglessness—of the Mordacq victory formula was the fact that immediately

CLEMENCEAU'S JACOBIN RULE

after Clemenceau and the general had agreed upon the theoretical distinction between policy and strategy, the new president of the council boldly invaded the sphere of Pétain's strategy, telling Mordacq that he was going to visit the front in person more frequently than ever before; that he would have three lines of trenches prepared for defense; that he would rejuvenate the officer cadre; round up *embusqués;* put the fear of God in troops on leave; decorate combat officers more often than staff officers.[10] Had Pétain been informed at once of these intentions (especially the trench digging), he might have wondered just what Clemenceau was going to leave to him as commander in chief of the French army.

There was no longer any question about France having at its head a man of sweeping ambition, firm resolution, and stubborn independence. His very decision to appoint Mordacq as his personal "military adviser" was a revelation that Clemenceau would not follow the course marked out by his more easygoing predecessors, Viviani, Briand, Ribot, and Painlevé. Clemenceau was obviously resolved to extend the scope of policy until it practically coincided with strategy. Nor was the Tiger planning to neglect purely political affairs. Reserving the War Ministry for himself, he appointed a Cabinet of thirteen members comprising, apart from its chief, not "a single man of the first rank"[11] but instead such "disciplined lieutenants" as Minister of Foreign Affairs Stephen Pichon.

Parliament knew what to expect when it heard Clemenceau's ministerial statement of November 20, 1917:

... To triumph through justice—that has been the keynote of all our governments since the beginning of the war. We shall carry on with this program.... [We have] a single, simple duty: to be one with the soldier, to live, suffer, fight with him.... The duties of the front and the obligations of the interior are henceforth the same.... All zones are to be the zone of the army.... It is ... the dynamic of the French soul ... which makes our people work as if they were waging a battle.... Justice will be meted out with all the rigor of the law.

Neither consideration of persons, nor partisan passions (applause on the Left, Center, and Right—interruptions on the Socialist benches) will turn us aside from our duty.... No more pacifist campaigns, no more German intrigues. Neither treason, nor half treason, but war. Nothing but war. Our armies will not be caught between two fires.... The nation will know that it is defended....[12]

This stirring declaration of general policy was approved by a vote of 418 to 65. A discordant note was at once sounded by the Socialist deputy from Puy-de-Dôme, Alexandre Varenne, who reminded the Tiger that in 1906 his previous ministry had been well received at first. But having "arrived in office full of promise, preceded by a great reputation for courage and liberalism, [Clemenceau had] veered within several months toward a policy of repression and resistance which had placed [him] in violent conflict with the most firmly democratic group."[13] The Socialists had a long memory, and they were serving notice to that effect upon the onetime Radical turned strikebreaker. Even so, Clemenceau could discount their opposition, since he commanded such a large majority that the success of any reasonable domestic policy was practically a certainty.

Vastly more difficult for Clemenceau was the external aspect of the "victory program"—the formation of the unified command. To dominate France was easily within his power, but to control the Allies was an altogether different matter. Before General Foch could be appointed commander in chief of the Allied armies, it would be necessary to prevail upon the British, Italians, Belgians, and Americans to revolutionize their thinking and to submit their forces to the control of one of the most Gallic of all Frenchmen. Only the gravest danger (which the Germans conveniently supplied through their offensive of March 21, 1918) would ever induce sovereign nations to entrust their security to the representative of a foreign power. Yet an Allied generalissimo was urgently needed, since the Supreme War Council, which had been created by Painlevé and Lloyd George (and which Italy had joined on November 6 at the

CLEMENCEAU'S JACOBIN RULE

Rapallo Conference), was not so much an Allied General Staff as a political body.[14] "The Supreme War Council did not supersede the Commanders-in-Chief but gave them for their guidance an expression of the definite policy of the Allied Governments. It was not to act as a Commander-in-Chief, but as an agency for the adoption and maintenance of a general policy for the Allies in the prosecution of the war, consistent with the total resources available and the most effective distribution of those resources among the various theatres of operations."[15]

Clemenceau was fully aware of the limitations of the Supreme War Council, but no one understood better the difficulty of unifying the command of all the Western Allies. He illustrated with the following anecdote the ticklishness of this problem: "The day I first broached the subject to General Sir Douglas Haig, as I was breakfasting at his Headquarters, the soldier jumped up like a jack-in-the-box, and, with both hands shot up to heaven, exclaimed: '*Monsieur* Clemenceau, I have only one chief and I can have no other. My King.'" Clemenceau concluded his account of the incident with the wry remark, "A bad beginning."[16]

Of all the Western Allies, the British were the most unwilling to subordinate their armies to a foreigner, and especially to a Frenchman. Not only was there vivid recollection of the numerous wars between Britain and France, but there still rankled in English memories the calamitous events of the spring of 1917, when Lloyd George had so readily entrusted the British armies on French soil to the temporary command of General Nivelle.[17] Lloyd George recognized the unwillingness of British public opinion to incur such a risk twice within the same year. "At that time," he explained, "I could [not] have agreed to making Foch Generalissimo without encountering formidable opposition in...the Services, and without facing a risk of repudiation at home which would have had a chilling effect on our relations with the French army and the French people."[18] Clemenceau was of the opinion that "resistance in England came not so much from the army as from Parliament, and, most of all, from the 'man in the street.' "[19] Lloyd George was willing to humor British nationalism while working deviously for a unified command. With a politician's elasticity, he declared to the House of Commons on November 19, 1917, that the appointment of a generalissimo "would produce real friction...not merely... between the armies, but friction between the nations and the Government."[20] He went so far in seemingly truckling to popular prejudice as to express opposition even to a coördination of the British and French Chiefs of Staff.[21]

Clemenceau recognized that with the lag of nationalism being what it was, the Rapallo agreement was the present extent of his tether. The old president of the council wanted a French generalissimo of the Allies, although he believed that others would have to take the lead in the appointment. Strong support was to come to him from the Americans, Colonel Edward M. House and General Tasker H. Bliss,[22] the former President Wilson's adviser, the latter the American representative on the Secretariat of the Supreme War Council. It was easier for the Americans than for the British to subordinate their army to a foreigner, since their forces existed largely on paper as yet, and they did not have commanders like Haig who had already been exercising authority in the field for several years. On November 23, 1917, Colonel House had an interview with Clemenceau, which was summarized in a cable to President Wilson. The French president of the council, according to Colonel House, "is earnestly in favor of unity of plan and action, but he... has nothing in mind and says that he dares not formulate a plan because it might be looked upon with suspicion. He wants us to take the initiative and he promises that we can count upon him to back to a finish any reasonable suggestion that we make...."[23]

House and Bliss were convinced that "unity of military control was essential to success, and, in default of a generalissimo, that it could be achieved only through a purely military council

CLEMENCEAU'S JACOBIN RULE

with executive powers."[24] With this in view, Colonel House and General Bliss drafted a memorandum for President Wilson on November 25, 1917, in which they proposed a drastically revised Supreme War Council "composed of the Commanders-in-Chief of the principal national forces in the field... together with the Chiefs of Staff... or officers designated by these Chiefs of Staff.... To ensure the prompt execution of the will of this Supreme War Council, there must be one man to carry this will into effect. This man must be the President of the Supreme War Council, chosen by the other members and having power to execute their will."[25] This proposal met with the full approval of Clemenceau and General Pétain.[26] The House-Bliss memorandum of November 25, 1917, anticipated by nearly five months the general outline of the authority which was to be conferred upon General Foch at Doullens. Clemenceau could nowhere have found stauncher supporters than the Americans.

When Lloyd George caught wind of the conversations between the Americans and the French concerning the revision of the Rapallo agreements, he lost no time in telling Colonel House that British nationalism would oppose the American plan of a president of the Supreme War Council.[27] The British prime minister also considered infeasible the American suggestion of including Chiefs of Staff on the military council. He sent Colonel House to Clemenceau with the message that "if Clemenceau looked on the agreement come to at Rapallo as a personal agreement, and therefore not binding on the French Government, then Lloyd George had nothing further to do and he would return to London this afternoon."[28]

Colonel House and the Tiger discussed Lloyd George's seemingly contradictory attitude toward the unified command. Clemenceau acquiesced in the Welshman's objection to having the Chiefs of Staff serve on the Supreme War Council. With a "sardonic smile," the Tiger said to Colonel House: "What I shall do is to put on a second or third rate man instead of Foch, and let the thing drift where it will...."[29] Clemenceau proceeded to appoint Foch's adjutant, Maxime Weygand (promoted from colonel to general for the purpose), as the French military representative on the Supreme War Council.[30] Fully aware of all the obstructions in the path of the unified command, Clemenceau consoled himself with the belief that patience on his part and the logic of events would eventually furnish a remedy. "I remained very moderate in conversations on the matter," he wrote, "knowing in any case... that the problem was moving slowly but surely toward the happy solution."[31]

Clemenceau understood that the members of the Chamber's army commission could not follow day by day the vicissitudes of such an intricate undertaking by the executive power, and, consequently, they were due at least an interim report. He agreed to bring the commissioners *au courant* on December 12, addressing them as follows:

M. Lloyd George declared in the House of Commons several days ago that he was absolutely opposed to the unity of command. M. Sonnino [the Italian foreign minister] informed us in a dispatch that it would be the hardest blow, the most painful injury, to Italian honor and pride. I will be candid and tell you everything: at present, unity of command is unattainable. The question of national sensibilities increases the complexity of the problem. So it is necessary for the present to rest content with a unity of direction, which, I recognize, is a most complicated arrangement.[32]

The day after Clemenceau's meeting with the army commission, he gave another review of his war policy, this time before the *Comité de guerre*. Clemenceau described in detail the nature of the organization completed at Rapallo and explained his inability to form a unified command, as yet. There ensued a somewhat desultory discussion over the soundness of Pétain's strategy of partial offensives. Antonin Dubost, the president of the Senate (who was much influenced by General Micheler, a critic of Pétain's "inertia"), told the president of the council: "I cannot hide from you the fact that I am entirely opposed to

CLEMENCEAU'S JACOBIN RULE

your methods." M. Paul Deschanel, the president of the Chamber, added that the deputies were concerned with the problem of having the British take over more of the front.[33]

General Pétain assumed that the criticisms of Dubost and Deschanel were aimed primarily at himself as general in chief. He gravely assured the *Comité de guerre:* "I must say that if some other method is preferred to mine, I am ready to step down and return in silence to the ranks."[34] Pétain's piqued remark brought forth an immediate reminder from Clemenceau as to who was in charge of France: "There can be no question [of resignation]. I alone am responsible here. I am not for the offensive, because we do not have the means. We must hold on, we must endure.... I do not wish at this time to risk the outcome of the war on an offensive. General Pétain is under my orders; I cover him fully. I am confident that he knows it. That said, I thank the president of the Senate for having so clearly posed the question...."[35] The civilian president of the council was not merely laying down the general lines of policy but emphasizing that the commander in chief was his docile executant, and that he, Clemenceau, had the last word in strategy as well. The pendelum had swung to the opposite extreme from Viviani's and Briand's deference to Joffre.

Fully aware of his own powers and confident of broad popular support, the Tiger showed magnanimity toward most of his domestic "enemies"—labor leaders and their politician friends who were regarded in Rightist circles as "defeatist" or "pro-German." Clemenceau irritated many conservatives by his refusal to arrest Adolphe Merrheim,[36] the pacifistic director of the metal workers union, and by his release from the army of the union secretary, Landrieu, whose draft order had set off a strike of 100,000 workers in the Loire basin.[37] Clemenceau later explained to an assistant his refusal to become greatly excited over "defeatism" during his administration: "Your revolutionaries are as gifted with ideas as my boot.... I didn't have to engage in a struggle with them. They melted away like pale shadows.

I've had less trouble with anarchists than with Poincaré and Foch...."[38]

The Tiger's geniality was unexpected in view of the vehemence of his attack upon former Minister of Interior Malvy in a Senate speech on July 22, 1917. Malvy, apparently unable to believe that Clemenceau might not renew the campaign against him, decided to take the initiative from the president of the council. On November 22, 1917, Malvy demanded of the Chamber that a commission be named for the purpose of examining "grounds for indicting ... the former minister of interior for crimes committed in his exercise of office."[39] The Senate was given the responsibility of trying Malvy on the flimsy charges of treason contained in Léon Daudet's letter of October 4, 1917, addressed to President Poincaré.[40] There began a historic trial which dragged on for nine months (during most of which time Malvy remained at liberty), until the High Court quashed the treason charges on August 6, 1918. However, the Senate did not let Malvy off scot free, judging him guilty of culpable negligence in the performance of his duties as minister of interior from 1914 to 1917. For this malfeasance he was banished from France for a period of five years.

Having discreetly handled *l'affaire* Malvy, Clemenceau decided to take up the equally delicate problem posed by the activities of Joseph Caillaux, Radical Socialist deputy from Mamers, and allegedly the pro-German leader of the "peace party" in France. Caillaux's name had been linked by rumor with that of the German ambassador to Argentina, Count Luxburg, whom he allegedly consulted while on a purchasing mission in Argentina as paymaster general of the French army.[41] In addition, there were persistent reports that the notorious German agent, Bolo Pasha, was a friend of Caillaux's, and that anarchist Almereyda had been his former bodyguard.[42] Although Clemenceau had no conclusive evidence of treason on the part of Caillaux, he believed nonetheless that light should be thrown upon the politician whose name had become synonymous with Ger-

CLEMENCEAU'S JACOBIN RULE

manophilia. To begin proceedings, Clemenceau had the military governor of Paris, General Dubail, draw up an indictment of Caillaux for "intelligence with the enemy." The Chamber was asked to drop Caillaux's parliamentary immunity, and the deputy from Mamers was arrested on January 17, 1918, and imprisoned for two years until the Senate, sitting as High Court in February, 1920, finally cleared him of the charge of "seconding the efforts of the enemy."[43]

Albeit surprisingly diplomatic, Clemenceau was quite willing to take measures attended with political risk such as trying Malvy and Caillaux, both favorites of the Left. He was no less willing to reopen—and to settle once and for all—the ticklish *affaire* Sarrail. The Tiger viewed askance the republican general who was hated by Greek royalists, and who had irritated the Venizelists as well as British General Milne at Salonika, not to mention the courts of Savoy, Windsor, and Romanoff." At a meeting of the *Comité de guerre* on December 6, 1917, Clemenceau announced that he was putting General Sarrail at the disposal of General in Chief Pétain because the commander of the Army of the Orient had been lax, and had "given an accounting of nothing." Pétain preferred to side-step the nice problem of removing Sarrail, probably because the general in chief was already sufficiently aware of his own unpopularity with the Left.[45] Inasmuch as Sarrail had received orders directly from the minister of war rather than from the general in chief since December, 1916 (when Joffre was removed as generalissimo), Pétain had justification in declining the case. Clemenceau was more contemptuous of criticism than Pétain, and he readily agreed to shelter the general in chief. "Rest assured," he told Pétain, "I alone will assume this responsibility, if you wish."[46] He accepted Pétain's recommendation of General Guillaumat for the Salonika command,[47] and on December 10, 1917, telegraphed to General Sarrail the following terse message: "I have the honor to inform you that the government, acting in the general interest, has decided to order your recall to France."[48]

In view of what the Germans were holding in store for the Allies, it was unfortunate that Clemenceau could not direct inter-Allied war policy with the ease and dispatch which characterized his administration of strictly French affairs. Had he been able at once to unify the Allied command, the threatened German break-through of March 21, 1918, might have been met with an immediate riposte. But taking into account the nationalistic objections to the appointment of Foch as generalissimo of the Allies, the best alternative was the creation of an inter-Allied or a General Reserve, composed of Allied units which could be rushed to any seriously threatened sector. Even this substitute plan contained a hidden problem of inter-Allied unity, since "the control of a General Reserve, the ability to order it hither and yon ... is the supreme function of a Commander-in-Chief."[49] The crux of the matter was whether the stubborn field commanders, Pétain and Haig, could be made to coöperate with a superior placed over them. When the question of a General Reserve was broached at a gathering of Western Allied generals at Compiègne, January 24, 1918, Haig and Pétain uttered "lamentations about the poverty of their effectives.... Pétain and Haig were determined to fight the Germans with separate armies, operating separately...."[50]

Clemenceau could easily have disregarded any pique which Pétain might have displayed over being subjected to an executive of a General Reserve, since on several previous occasions he had shown no tender concern for Pétain's feelings. The president of the council was fully aware of the urgent necessity of a General Reserve under a commander. At a session of the Supreme War Council at Versailles on January 30, 1918, he readily conceded that "when the question of creating an Interallied Reserve was raised it was with the idea that, *as we could not have a single Commander-in-Chief* ... we might at least have a Commander of Reserves."[51] The dubious role which Clemenceau played with regard to the General Reserve was at least partially explicable in the light of his ambivalent feelings toward

CLEMENCEAU'S JACOBIN RULE

General Foch, the likeliest candidate for commander of the General Reserve. Clemenceau was an inveterate anticlericalist who had the greatest difficulty in overcoming his suspicion and hostility toward pious General Foch, whose education had been in the hands of the Society of Jesus. The Tiger's attitude toward Foch fluctuated between begrudging respect for the general's indisputable professional ability, and personal antipathy for a commander who had an aura of sanctity. Clemenceau was ready to admit that "popular feeling in France ... placed the hope of success in unity of command; and when once experience and the logic of theory were both agreed on this point, nothing was left but to agree upon the choice of a Generalissimo.... There were no competitors. Only the name of Foch was uttered. The main point was that Foch had displayed qualities of the highest kind...."[52] Clemenceau had long appreciated Foch's military talents, having appointed him *commandant* of the Ecole de Guerre in 1908, "without taking any notice of his relations with the Society of Jesus." The Tiger contended in his memoirs that he had again supported Foch in the autumn of 1916, when the general had been *"Limoged"* because of the meager results of the Somme offensive. On this occasion he had advised him to "lie low,"[53] which Foch had done as an obscure inspector of French troops on the Swiss border until he became Pétain's chief of staff. With the greatest of inconsistency, Clemenceau, who had repeatedly demonstrated his confidence in Foch and was to do so again in recommending him as a commander of Reserves, swung around and supported Pétain and Haig in their determination to undermine Foch's actual authority once the general was given that post.

The question of commanding a General Reserve came up for consideration at the February 1 session of the Supreme War Council. There was proposed an executive committee of a General Reserve for the entirety of the western, Italian, and Balkan fronts. The executive committee was to be composed of the permanent military representatives of the Supreme War Council. This body of directors was to have the right of determining the strength of the Reserve in arms and troops, the national contributions to it, the location of the Reserve, and its means of transport. The executive committee was to draw up a plan for a possible counteroffensive, determining its time, place, and strength, but the various field commanders were to have charge of the execution of strategy. Until the movement of the General Reserve actually got under way, its discipline and administration were to remain in the hands of the respective commanders in chief.[54]

Everyone understood that the greatest influence in the executive committee would be exerted by its president. Lloyd George was the one who officially nominated General Foch for this station, a gesture which several years later elicited from the general a grateful note: "I am deeply touched. I have not forgotten that it is to your firmness that I owe the position which I occupy today." In view of the difficulties which Foch was to have with Clemenceau, this attitude was understandable although not wholly just, since the Tiger had all the while been quite willing for Foch to become the Allied commander, as General Mordacq[55] and André Tardieu testified.[56] Moreover, in conformity with diplomatic procedure, an Allied military executive was not to be nominated by a citizen of his own country.

Foch may have felt gratitude toward the British prime minister for his nomination, but Lloyd George's part in creating the new office aroused deep distrust in Field Marshal Haig,[57] and "fury" in General Robertson, the chief of the Imperial General Staff.[58] Their disgruntlement over a supposed derogation of their authority was shared by the British Army Council, which protested to Lloyd George on February 4 that the "Executive Committee had been given such powers that it could disregard the [members of the Army] Council and interpose between them and the Commanders-in-Chief."[59]

In a determination to circumvent General Foch, Haig was abetted by the French commander in chief. General Pétain tried

CLEMENCEAU'S JACOBIN RULE

to give the impression to the Supreme War Council that Foch's new functions would be largely superfluous, since "the whole of the plans, both for the defensive and for the preparation of sectors for local attacks, have been completed between Sir Douglas Haig and myself. I will have an army ready to support Sir Douglas Haig in an emergency, and I know Sir Douglas will assist me in the same manner."[60]

The authority supposedly vested in Foch as president of the executive committee was quickly rendered illusory by Haig and Pétain, who opposed the General Reserve all along the line. On February 6, 1918, the executive committee addressed a letter to the British, French, and Italian armies, requesting an allotment of sufficient troops from their forces to constitute a General Reserve of thirty divisions.[61] It was proposed that France contribute thirteen or fourteen divisions, Britain nine or ten, and Italy seven.[62] General Foch drew up a plan which called for the stationing of the earmarked divisions behind their own fronts, with the French contributions held in a triangular zone between Paris, Château-Thierry, and Troyes. The British contingents were to be massed around Amiens. "They were to be so stationed at the outset that when the crisis did demand it either could go to the assistance of another with the minimum delay."[63] Had Foch been permitted to carry out his plan, it would probably have precluded any split of the Anglo-French forces such as the Germans undertook in their drive of March 21.[64] But Haig and, to a lesser extent, Pétain, clung obstinately to their divisions, refusing to turn them over to the Reserve.

The newly appointed successor to Robertson as chief of the Imperial General Staff, the ardently Francophile Sir Henry Wilson, encountered repeated refusals from Haig when the British commander in chief was asked to turn over some of his divisions to Foch's Reserve. On February 25, Sir Henry recorded in his diary: "A talk with Haig about his earmarking some divisions for the Versailles Reserve. He flatly refuses, says he won't be responsible for his line, and rather than do it he would resign. He is quite prepared to agree to any divisions we have in Italy being treated as General Reserve, but no others."[65] On the following day, Wilson wrote: "At 6 o'clock I went up to Paris to see M. Clemenceau.... Haig [had] told [Clemenceau] flatly he would not hand over any of his divisions to the General Reserve, and Clemenceau thinks Haig would rather resign than do so. Clemenceau thinks this would be a disaster at this juncture. Then, in addition, the Tiger finds Pétain much in the same mood and does not want to quarrel with him, and he told me that he had not discussed this with Foch at all."[66]

General Foch was indignant over the uncoöperative behavior of Haig and Pétain. When Wilson and General Henry Rawlinson (the new British military representative on the executive committee) visited Foch on February 27, the fiery French general took what Wilson conceded was "a perfectly legitimate stand as regards Haig and the General Reserve. He said that the Governments had ordered the Executive Board to form and command a General Reserve,"[67] but contrary to agreement he was not receiving the necessary troops. As late as March 13, a little more than a week before one of the greatest German drives of the war, Haig was still protesting to C.I.G.S. Wilson that "he [could not] and he [would not] give any divisions to the General Reserves. He explained that he had not enough for G.H.Q. Reserve, so the thing was impossible, and he said that, if I wanted a General Reserve, I must make some more divisions and I must get more man power.... I impressed on him the fact that by refusing to contribute to the General Reserve he was killing that body, and he would have to live on Pétain's charity, and he would find that very cold charity."[68] Prophetic warning! But in vain.

Clemenceau's indulgent attitude toward the sabotaging of the General Reserve by Haig and Pétain was due in part to an unwonted desire to maintain amity with Commanders in Chief Haig and Pétain. Again it must be said that "Clemenceau had a deep distrust of all Catholic Generals," and devout Foch was

CLEMENCEAU'S JACOBIN RULE

guilty of being the brother of a bishop.[69] But for a veteran so long inured to every type of opposition, Clemenceau showed in regard to the General Reserve a disappointingly passive attitude which hardly bespoke "victory at any price." English testimony seems conclusive on this point. Sir Henry Wilson wrote in his diary on February 26, following a conversation with Clemenceau: "On the whole ... the Tiger favours the General Reserve being composed only of those troops which we can withdraw from Italy, and then let it grow later. I confess I don't agree, and said so bluntly, but I am not in a position to overcome the Tiger, Pétain and Haig."[70]

Field Marshal Haig perceived that Clemenceau was his staunch ally against the "unreasonable" demands of Foch for building up the General Reserve. The British commander in chief wrote in his diary the following account of a conference with Clemenceau in late February:

He [Clemenceau] spoke quite frankly.... Friction had arisen between Foch and Pétain, and he was uncertain how to act over the question of Reserves.... I said that I had told my Prime Minister that I could not earmark any divisions at the present time as an Inter-Allied Reserve without upsetting my plans for defense. I only had six divisions under my own hand at the present moment. And that rather than change my plans at a time when, at any moment, the enemy might attack in force, I would prefer to resign my command. M. Clemenceau at once said that my statements indicated his line of action. He would arrange to *écarter* (set aside) Foch gradually. He personally looked upon a close agreement between Pétain and myself as the surest guarantee of success.... Clemenceau and I parted great friends.[71]

General Foch regarded the stubbornness of Haig and Pétain as the undoing of the work of his executive committee. Completely balked by the two commanders in chief who were being obligingly covered by Clemenceau,[72] Foch's executive committee drew up a resolution of protest on March 4, 1918: "... The executive committee does not believe that it can continue its task, and is therefore unable to organize the General Inter-Allied Reserve, as the Supreme War Council had instructed it to do at the session of February 2. The executive committee decides that each military representative shall so inform his own government and ask for instructions."[73]

The question of the nullification of the General Reserve was debated at the session of the Supreme War Council which was held in London on March 14, 1918. Lloyd George, in broaching the topic, supported the stand of Haig in order "to make the best of an unsatisfactory situation."[74] Clemenceau likewise palliated Haig's actions by conceding that "because of imminent attack, it is impossible to withdraw the divisions either from Marshal Haig or General Pétain. However, there existed a complete agreement, endorsed by the two governments, between Marshal Haig and General Pétain who have taken all the preparedness measures for mutual support, in case of necessity."[75] The American delegation to the Supreme War Council acknowledged that it might "be found impracticable to furnish British divisions for the Reserve," but nevertheless, they hoped that "there [would] be no abandonment of the principle established for the creation of the General Reserve. . . ."[76] The upshot of the debate was the adoption of the American position, that is, the retention of the mere *principle* of the General Reserve. It was agreed that the five British and six French divisions stationed in Italy, together with a "certain number of Italian divisions . . . to be determined by the executive committee . . . and the commander in chief of the Italian army," would henceforth constitute the General Reserve.[77]

This travesty of the original plan so carefully drawn up by the executive committee angered General Foch, who arose and "objected to the whole resolution." There ensued a heated exchange of words between Foch and Clemenceau—to the fatuous enjoyment of Haig, who did not seem to object to the trouncing of a French military rival by a French civilian. General Foch was at last silenced by the president of the council who waved

CLEMENCEAU'S JACOBIN RULE

his hand and rudely shouted at him: "Shut up! It is I who represent France here!"[78] Jacobin Clemenceau had no grounds for pride in thus defeating Foch on so vital an issue as the Reserve, as he himself soon realized. Three days after this unseemly altercation, Chief of the Imperial General Staff Wilson recorded in his diary: "I had a talk with the Tiger and told him that the real difficulty was that Foch and I were right [about the Reserve], whilst he [Tiger], Haig and Pétain were wrong, and yet Foch and I had to give way, Foch with a bad grace and I with a good one. The Tiger agreed absolutely."[79] Before Clemenceau could rectify his grave mistake, the Germans released their long-awaited spring offensive which underscored the soundness of Foch's views, but threatened to destroy Allied hopes of victory in the process.

"All the world, including the Entente, knew we were going to attack in the West," wrote General Ludendorff.[80] The reasons for a German attack were self-evident. Italy had been rendered incapable of taking the offensive by the defeat at Caporetto. France had to be finished off quickly, since Germany was feeling the pinch of hunger, and it was necessary to split the Anglo-French armies and to reduce them piecemeal before the Americans arrived in the promised numbers.[81] It was obviously impossible to conceal traces of the extensive preparations which the great German offensive called for, but the French and British commands were thrown into confusion by adroit feinting on the part of the Germans. The army groups of Crown Prince Wilhelm, Crown Prince Rupprecht, and Gallwitz engaged in "dummy works on the fronts remote from attack, which, as a matter of fact, served as the basis of attack later on."[82] The main German onslaught was to be delivered "between Croisilles, south-east of Arras, and Moeuvres, and... between Villers-Guislain and the Oise, south of St. Quentin." The direction of the German thrust was toward the Channel coast. "If this blow succeeded," wrote Ludendorff, "the strategic result might indeed be enormous, as we could separate the bulk of the English army from the French and crowd it up with its back to the sea."[83] From 40 to 50 German divisions were marched by night into the Arras–La Fère zone of attack, unobserved by the Allies, who were distracted by heavy rail traffic behind the entirety of the enemy lines.[84] Along the western front, from 182 to 200 German divisions confronted 175 of the Allies.[85]

At four o'clock on the morning of March 21, 1918, the German artillery began a short but violent bombardment along a seventy-kilometer front between Croisilles and La Fère, flattening the British lines under thousands of explosive and gas shells. The army group of Crown Prince Rupprecht and the Eighteenth Army of Crown Prince Wilhelm's group were hurled upon seventeen divisions of the British Third Army of General Byng and the Fifth Army of General Gough.[86] The Allied front began to give way, first, in the region of St. Quentin, and soon along the entire zone of attack. Gough's Fifth Army was in grave danger of losing contact on its right wing with the French Sixth Army of General Duchêne. On March 22, Pétain ordered General Humbert to lead the Third French Army of reserves into line next to Gough's battered Fifth.[87] Gough had to be reinforced by the French, since Haig had massed his own reserves on the British left wing, too far to the north to be of immediate usefulness at the point of impending break-through. It took four critical days for the meager French reinforcements of six divisions (three without artillery) to join the southern end of the British line.[88]

Meanwhile, Commander in Chief Pétain acknowledged to Colonel Herbillon his gnawing anxiety as to whether the British would hold along the Somme, as "Douglas Haig had promised him."[89] Colonel Herbillon notified Poincaré and Clemenceau on March 23 that in Pétain's opinion, "the situation was not only serious but grave; the English were falling back too quickly.... If the enemy advance were not promptly checked, the road to Paris might be menaced."[90] Belatedly aware of this very danger was bullheaded Haig himself, who, with

CLEMENCEAU'S JACOBIN RULE

touching hindsight, telegraphed to London on March 24, "asking Mr. Lloyd George to come over and arrange for a single Supreme Commander."[91] Unable to leave at that time, Lloyd George sent to Paris Lord Milner, the new secretary for war, "to restore the broken Versailles Front by conferring on Foch the necessary authority to organize a reserve and to control its disposition."[92]

A conference was hastily convoked at General Pétain's headquarters at Compiègne on March 25. Present, in addition to Lord Milner, were Clemenceau, Poincaré, Pétain, Foch, and Louis Loucheur, French minister of armament and aviation. Poincaré presided. General Pétain depressed Milner with his "very pessimistic view of the conditions of the Fifth Army... now... placed by Haig under his [Pétain's] orders." To meet the German push toward Montdidier and Moreuil, Pétain was bringing up from the west and south nine more divisions—"all that he could possibly spare"—to supplement the six French reserve divisions already heavily engaged in the vicinity of Noyon, Roye, and Nesle.[93] The grim admission by Pétain that he could "not neglect either the danger of the Germans pushing down the Oise from about Noyon, nor a threatened attack in the region of Reims," signified one thing to Milner: "... [if] the rupture of the armies ... [took] place, each commander had to think of his own defensive objective—the one Paris, the other the Channel ports."[94] Was there to occur, then, the predictable calamity of Haig's racing for the coast while Pétain's sundered forces fell back toward Paris? Such an eventuality would allow the pursuing Germans to destroy both forces in detail—a decided probability if the pivot of Amiens fell.

General Foch expressed an opinion that contradicted Pétain's ingrained pessimism. While conceding the possibility that Amiens might fall, and that a rupture of the Anglo-French line might result therefrom, Foch nevertheless advocated "risk-taking"—employing still more reserve divisions, "even if the relieving forces were thrown in in less complete formation than under conditions of less extreme urgency would be desirable."[95] This was the sort of spirited talk that Poincaré, Clemenceau, and Lord Milner wanted to hear, but the new British war secretary said that before he could commit himself, he would have to consult with field commander Haig and C.I.G.S. Wilson.[96]

Upon Milner's return to Paris the night of March 25, he spoke with Sir Henry Wilson about the urgent need to "keep in touch with the French, and [to] fill up the gap...south of the Somme." Both Milner and Wilson recognized the necessity of "the greatest promptitude in bringing up reserves and [in] complete coöperation between the armies...."[97] Sir Henry Wilson thereupon "made the suggestion—which seemed a good one [to Milner]—that both countries might agree to leave it to Clemenceau, in whom the British Generals had confidence as well as the French, to take any decisions necessary to bring about the better coöperation of the armies and the best use of all available reserves."[98]

According to the jaundiced testimony of President Poincaré, Clemenceau had entertained this very idea of making himself a "generalissimo" of sorts as far back as February 22, 1918, when the president of the council spoke with Poincaré about the alarming quarrels between Foch and Pétain over the use of the General Reserves. "I will arrange all that," Poincaré quoted Clemenceau as saying. "The organization of the army of maneuver [the General Reserve] is scarcely defensible in itself. But I will be there. At the moment of attack, I will be there. If there should be a dispute, it is I who will settle it if I am still in power—and I hope not to be forced out sooner, for I alone know what to do. What I say is not very modest, but circumstances compel me to say it."[99] When Clemenceau was questioned a decade later about his alleged ambitions to be a generalissimo, the witty cynic gave the following retort, quoted by his private secretary: "I'd even had a uniform made—and the most gorgeous cap!"[100]

CLEMENCEAU'S JACOBIN RULE

Judging by the Tiger's long public record, it seems improbable that the aged statesman seriously considered trying to be a Caesar or a Napoleon. It should be recalled that Clemenceau, as a well-known champion of the primacy of civilian power over the military, had decided during his first ministry in 1908 "to modify the decree of Thermidor regulating the prescribed order of precedence in public ceremonies... demand[ing] that generals should come after prefects and many other functionaries."[101] Although Clemenceau's Jacobinism may have prompted him to extend policy to the point of encroachment upon strategy, the Tiger doubtless intended to assert his authority as president of the council and minister of war rather than as a military commander.

In contrast to Clemenceau's humorous view on the subject, Lord Milner seriously advocated making the Tiger the titular "generalissimo." The British war secretary sent C.I.G.S. Wilson on the night of March 25, 1918, to speak with Foch about this plan. Clemenceau, under the proposed scheme, would have both the *political and strategic* direction of the war, and would be authorized "to make all the decisions which seemed to him necessary to assure the closest coöperation of the armies and the best use of all available reserves." Foch would serve as Clemenceau's technical counselor. According to General Mordacq, this "bad solution... [which] I am able to affirm M. Clemenceau would never have accepted," was inspired by Lord Milner's desire for a diplomatic formula which would enable Field Marshal Haig to save face, since the proud British cavalryman might be more inclined to take orders from M. Clemenceau, a civilian, than from a French general.[102] General Foch quickly indicated to Sir Henry Wilson the defects in this scheme: "... Clemenceau, placed in the ... [position of 'generalissimo' with Foch as counselor], might be drawn in opposite directions by Pétain and [Foch] himself, and if he agreed [first] with one and [then] with the other there would be no unity of control."[103] C.I.G.S. Wilson reported Foch's opinion to Lord Milner, and

GENERALS & POLITICIANS

then, according to General Mordacq, "the two men swung over to the...solution [of] entrust[ing] the control of the Allied armies to General Foch."[104]

The urgent need of concerted action to prevent an irreparable breach in the line caused the French and British to hold a conference at Doullens on March 26, 1918. Clemenceau and Poincaré strolled about the garden of the Doullens town hall, whiling away the time before the meeting with the British began. Taking the president of the republic to one side, the Tiger said to him: "Pétain is annoying with his pessimism. You can't imagine what he said to me, and which I shall confide to no one but you. This is the phrase: 'The Germans will beat the English in open country; after that, they will beat us also.' Should a general speak or even think in that fashion?"[105]

At this moment there drove up to the town hall a little gamecock of a general whose every word and gesture bristled with vivacity. Clemenceau has described the celebrated scene as follows: "There was a bustle, and Foch arrived, surrounded by officers, and dominating everything with his cutting voice. 'You aren't fighting? I would fight without a break. I would fight in front of Amiens. I would fight in Amiens. I would fight behind Amiens. I would fight all the time.'"[106] This sort of speech dispelled the mood of disgust engendered by Pétain's pessimism. Clemenceau, complex character that he was, admitted that he could hardly refrain from embracing this admirable chief "in the name of France in deadly peril," but instead he grunted his begrudging approval: *"C'est un bougre!"*[107]

At noon, on March 26, the joint Anglo-French conference at Doullens got formally under way, with Poincaré, Clemenceau, Loucheur, Pétain, and Foch representing the French, and Haig, Milner, and Wilson the British.[108] The foreseeable rout of his forces had made Haig a chastened man who now sadly confided to War Secretary Milner that "far from resenting...the thought of Foch's interference, [he] rather welcomed the idea of working with the latter...."[109] Lord Milner thereupon took

CLEMENCEAU'S JACOBIN RULE

Clemenceau to one side and "without preamble" said to him: "The British generals accept the command of General Foch." Clemenceau asked: "Is that a proposal from your government?" Milner replied: "The British government, whose authority I possess, will ratify whatever we agree upon. Are we in agreement?"[110] Clemenceau readily accepted the proposal, but he asked for a few minutes to speak with Foch about it. Clemenceau and Foch drew up a formula which would save face for Haig and Pétain, and yet would give Foch effective supervision of their armies. The Tiger showed the formula to Pétain and after a minor change in wording the general declared it acceptable.[111] The amended formula, leaving open the possibility of including the Belgian, American, and conceivably the Italian armies which might some day be used on the Franco-British front, was phrased as follows:

General Foch is entrusted by the British and French Governments with the coördination of the action of the Allied armies on the Western front. In fulfillment of this task, he will consult with the Generals-in-Chief who are requested to furnish him all necessary information.[112]

Then "the conference ... rose with every appearance of general satisfaction," and the participants set out for the *Hôtel des Quatre-Fils Aymon* where a luncheon had been prepared for them. But the new spirit of harmony was shattered as soon as they reached the dining salon. As Clemenceau was taking his seat, he greeted Foch with a sarcastic jibe which fully revealed the pettiness which often offset the Tiger's greatness. Forgetting his impulse to embrace Foch scarcely an hour before, he growled at him, *"Eh bien,* now you have got the position you wanted so much!"[113] Foch, fully aware of Clemenceau's unworthy part in the weakening of the General Reserve, gave a furious retort which forecast the stormy scenes which were to become commonplace in their relations as the war drew to a close. "What do you mean ... ? You give me a lost battle and you ask me to win it. I consent, and you think you are making me a present. I am disregarding myself entirely when I accept it."[114] For once, Clemenceau was shamed into silence.

The Doullens agreement, important milestone that it was, did not make Foch Allied commander in chief. Foch's "functions were limited to the British and French armies. They did not extend to the American army. No American was summoned to the Conference at Doullens. No control was given over the Belgian nor the Italian armies. Moreover, there was given [Foch] no power of command. He could only consult and advise."[115] But the door had been left open for these necessary revisions and amendments to Foch's authority. At Beauvais on April 3, his powers were broadened further to include the "brevet" command of "the strategic direction of military operation." The various commanders in chief still retained "the tactical conduct of their armies," with the right to appeal to their own governments.[116] It was only at Abbeville on May 1-2, 1918, that the term *le front ouest* was expressly extended to Italy, but in actual practice Foch could only "beg" the compliance of the Italian commanders.[117]

For all the limitations, unified command was materially achieved at Doullens. According to a judicious observer, General Tasker H. Bliss, "unified command came in 1918 at the first moment it could possibly come. Opposition gave way only when it was manifest that every other course had been tried—and had failed. Unified command was then accepted, not for the purpose of winning victory but to prevent irretrievable defeat."[118] Clemenceau could undoubtedly have played a more helpful role earlier in the struggle by sincerely assisting Foch in the building up of the General Reserve. When the Tiger realized his mistake after the predictable German drive, he was anxious to make amends at Doullens—although penance was a rite which the fierce old freethinker performed with a singularly bad grace.

10

Foch and Clemenceau

"Do you know," Foch commented to Clemenceau, "that I am not your subordinate?" "No, I don't," Clemenceau replied. "I don't even want to know who put that notion into your head. You know that I am your friend. I strongly advise you not to try to act on this idea, for it would never do."[1] Clausewitz observed that friction between strategists and policy makers arose from "imperfect knowledge," an interpretation which largely explains the bittersweet relations between Foch and Clemenceau in the last months of the war, since the general's status and powers were left in considerable doubt.

Foch's title expanded haphazardly with the course of events. As "coördinator of the action" of the Anglo-French forces (the position conferred upon him at Doullens) he checked the German offensive which had threatened to split the two Allied armies. He ordered the First French Army to aid the British Fifth under its new commander, Rawlinson. By April 3 both armies were inactive, having successfully closed the breach which the Germans had tried to drive between them. Foch's functions thereupon became nugatory, since he could only "coördinate" armies already on the move.[2] When the Germans brought on another crisis by renewing the offensive on April 9, hammering at the British First Army in an effort to reach the Channel, Foch was elevated to the more impressive rank of commander in chief of the Allied armies operating in France. On this occasion American forces were entrusted by President Wilson to General Foch's strategic (but not tactical) command, this being done with General Pershing's concurrence. Assured of the right

---

[1] For notes to chap. 10, see pages 271–274.

of passing upon Foch's orders, the Italian government, on May 3, likewise accepted the general as Allied commander in chief[8]—upon the assumption that Allied forces might fight in Italy some day. Although the Belgian commander, General Gillain, refused to subordinate himself formally to Foch, military exigencies in July forced him to accept a coördinated Allied strategy.[4]

Five nations in practice were to acknowledge Foch's strategic direction of the war. But doubts arose over what Foch should or should not do in the exercise of his command. Nor had it been made clear just what Foch could or could not do, if he so desired. As an Allied commander, was he now free from Clemenceau's supervision? Was he answerable directly to the Supreme War Council rather than to Clemenceau who was only one of its ex officio members? He seemed to think so, judging by the conversation with the Tiger quoted above. Endless conflict resulted from Foch's assumption that he could by-pass Clemenceau because his rank had been conferred upon him by the Allies rather than by France's president of the council and war minister.

Clemenceau, with his Jacobin peremptoriness, expected Foch to order the various national commanders about with the same forthrightness which a commander in chief of the French army customarily showed toward his subordinates. Such directness seemed essential to Clemenceau for the coördination of Allied strategy. When Foch proved reluctant to give blunt orders to Haig and Pershing, the Tiger looked for motives of expediency in the Jesuit-trained general. Clemenceau expressed his suspicions as follows:

For many reasons I am not convinced that [the Allied command] actually played the decisive part public opinion is inclined to attribute to it.... We must be told what amount of obedience was *asked for and obtained,* and in what circumstances, and for what results.... It must indeed be said that in his exercise of the single command [General Foch] at times gave way to hesitancies, to temperings of authority calculated to leave the desired and expected results in uncertainty. On the other hand, I think I can say that the commander of the British army never submitted wholly to the instructions of General Foch, who was perhaps overanxious to have no difficulty with the two great chiefs theoretically his subordinates.[5]

Foch never denied the charge of "leniency" toward Haig and Pershing, although he felt entirely justified in his policy.

When several armies are in the field together [he explained to his friend Raymond Recouly] it is absolutely impossible to evolve any unity of command save by... moral influence. In other words, force is useless, whereas persuasion is all-powerful. The armies may differ in formation, even in value; their leaders have characters, customs and temperaments peculiar to themselves; each one is dependent upon his own government. Each instinctively tends to believe that he is doing far more than his neighbor.... When allied armies are under one command, categorical imperatives are useless. The commander must be able to inspire confidence and the spirit of coöperation in his followers, so that his orders may be accepted in all willingness. That must be his only method.[6]

The first instance of friction between Clemenceau and Foch over the latter's leniency arose from the general's refusal to order Pershing "to send into action, in [French] ranks, the first American regiments that were considered sufficiently trained, so as to relieve... a crisis of manpower [such as the French] armies had never known before."[7] Clemenceau held a number of conversations with Pershing on this question of American man power. The Tiger related that "General Pershing, in a friendly but obstinate fashion, was asking me to wait until he was in possession of an army complete in every part...." Clemenceau, "in a state of nervous exasperation," importuned Pershing for immediate American reinforcements. "And the more I insisted the more the American General resisted. So much so that we often parted with smiles that on both sides concealed gnashings of teeth. Is it very astonishing that I began to wonder how much assistance... Commander-in-Chief

[Foch] was to me in this matter? In principle... General [Foch] could not possibly hold any opinion different from mine."[8]

Foch did agree, *in principle,* with the urgent need of American troops. In his *Mémoires* he readily conceded that by the end of April, 1918, there was an immediate requirement of 70,000 American infantry, which, if sent over "to the exclusion of all other forces," could free French and British infantry to reinforce the weak spots in the line. At the time, the Americans had only five combat divisions in France—one fighting with the French First Army, three others stationed in quiet sectors, and the fifth in training with French units.

Clemenceau did not see how Foch and Poincaré could fail to share his opinion that

we were in urgent need of effectives to replace the men who were falling day by day on the battlefield. But General Foch and M. Poincaré wished the opinion to remain merely an opinion, whereas I was trying to transform it into action in some form. My two opponents did not care to be brought up against the stubbornness of General Pershing, which might easily cause a rupture. In other words, they would have it that I wanted too much, to which I replied that they did not want enough. Foch refused to give an order to his subordinate, alleging always that his authority as Commander-in-Chief amounted to the power, not to give commands, but simply to suggest.[9]

Clemenceau did not misstate Foch's conception of his role. The general's aide-de-camp, Major Charles Bugnet, recorded a conversation which fully revealed Foch's attitude toward his functions as commander in chief of the Allied armies:

You see, the unified command is only a word. It was tried in 1917 under Nivelle, and it did not work. One must know how to lead the allies—one does not command them. Some must be treated differently from the others. The English are English, the Americans are another matter, and similarly with the Belgians and Italians. I could not deal with the Allied generals as I did with our own men.... I could not give them orders in an imperative manner.... One talks, one discusses, one persuades, one does not give orders.... One says "That is what should be done; it is simple; it is only necessary to will it." That cannot be done on paper; a man is needed! Don't say that it is a difficult problem; it is hardly a problem at all."[10]

In the opinion of Clemenceau, Foch "managed" to remain on friendly terms with Pershing by refusing to command him to do what the circumstances required.[11] This appeared to be a high price for amity between generals. The greatest urgency, according to Clemenceau, "lay in the single fact that we had already been fighting for a long time when the first American contingents, which were of necessity inexperienced, joined us. The true function of the American Allies was first and foremost to help us make up for lost time by joining the fray as they arrived, whereas the natural vanity of the great democracy inclined her to throw in her full power for the supreme victory on the last battlefield."[12]

Foch was equally convinced that he was right in being conciliatory toward Pershing. With what appeared an easy conscience, he told his friend Raymond Recouly: "I ... succeeded in obtaining the utmost efforts out of the various foreign armies under my orders. The effect was remarkable in the case of the young American army, which was excellent and full of enthusiasm, but, naturally, inexperienced and immature; it had to learn in a few months—a few weeks even—what the rest of us had taken several years to learn. It seemed to me unjust and unreasonable not to take into account its lack of experience; I could not treat it as though it had been fighting with us for years past."[13] Foch seemed to take pride in his finesse as a diplomat.[14] A decade after the war, he commented to Recouly: "Thanks to the plan to which I was determined to adhere, I succeed[ed] in winning the confidence, good-will and enthusiasm of General Pershing and his subordinates, which steadily increased. In the end, they acted entirely on my instructions and did exactly what I wanted—and did it with pleasure. When the War was over I was gratified to find myself the personal friend of all the American generals, beginning with Pershing, with whom I had been in contact."[115]

The urgent need of American reserves could not be exaggerated, since on May 27, 1918, the Germans began one of the greatest offensives of the war, the Second Battle of Chemin des Dames. The objective was largely the same as in the attack of March 21, which had been broken up by Foch. Von Hindenburg explained the general strategy as follows: "In May, 1918, it was our immediate business to attempt to separate the two friends in Flanders once more. England was easier to beat when France was far away. If we faced the French with a crisis on their own front, they would withdraw the divisions which were now in line on the English front in Flanders. . . . The sensitive point of the French front was the direction of Paris."[16] The attack was to begin with a heavy bombardment of the region between Vauxaillon and Brimont. The earlier offensive of March 21 had won for the Germans a potentially valuable salient east of Amiens, between La Fère and Montdidier, only forty kilometers from Paris. Before this base could be used as a springboard against the French capital, the Germans would have to drive Foch's troops from the wooded *massif* between Compiègne and Villers-Cotterets. To avoid being outflanked from this sector, it was necessary for the Germans to storm the Chemin des Dames.[17]

The French were badly prepared to withstand the assault. Their military intelligence had been deceived by prisoners' "romantic" reports of defeatism in the German army.[18] Consequently, the bridges across the Aisne had not been blown up, and the Germans were able to cross the river with ease. French infantry divisions were badly depleted by four years of attrition, and the surviving units were dangerously overextended as a result of the relief sent north to the British following the German attacks of March 21 and April 9.[19]

The spearhead of the attack of May 27, led by von Boehn's Seventh Army, was directed against the French Sixth Army of

General Duchêne who could resist it with only seven divisions in the front lines of Chemin des Dames, and with three divisions in reserve. Once von Boehn's shock force (outnumbering Duchêne's troops by nearly four to one) had breached the first line of the Sixth Army, it quickly overran the plateau of Chemin des Dames and pushed on five miles to the Aisne, occupying the north bank of the river from Vailly to Oeuilly.[20]

The immediate success of the attack astonished the Germans almost as much as the French. The entire maneuver had been intended merely as a diversion to draw Allied reserves away from the Flanders front, which was supposed to be broken later by a German thrust toward the sea.[21] Ludendorff observed with elation that by the third day even Soissons and Fismes "had in places been left far behind."[22]

The rumors concerning the German success caused "a veritable panic" in the corridors of Parliament, according to General Mordacq.[23] To learn the true state of affairs, Clemenceau and his military adviser traveled to Foch's headquarters at Sarcus early on the morning of May 28. With sound intuition, General Foch explained to Clemenceau and Mordacq that "this business of the Chemin des Dames could only be a feint. Consequently, for the time being, [Foch] saw no necessity of removing most of his strategic reserves"[24] which were concentrated chiefly in Flanders and in the Somme region. Clemenceau was astounded at this interpretation of enemy strategy,[25] especially at the hesitation to call down practically all of the reserves from the north. In contrast to his previous officiousness toward Pétain and despite his deepest misgivings, Clemenceau wisely refrained from interfering with Foch in this dangerous crisis. "I had made it a fixed rule," the Tiger declared with remarkable forgetfulness, "to abstain from all discussions of a purely military nature, but I had the right—it was even my duty—to make inquiries to discover whether the Supreme Command was functioning properly."[26] This was an instance in which the president of the council quite properly confined his activities to his proper sphere, for technician Foch was right and the civilian wrong in guessing the German strategic design. The postwar testimony of von Hindenburg[27] and Crown Prince Wilhelm[28] confirmed Foch's surmise that the Germans had begun the Second Battle of Chemin des Dames as a ruse to divert attention from Flanders, where the British and French armies were to be split later on. The initial success of this German stratagem led Clemenceau rather naturally to the false assumption that Paris must have been the enemy's chief goal all the time. "Three rivers crossed within five days...," he gloomily observed, "will anyone maintain that that is not an important result?"[29]

The enemy pushed on, capturing Soissons on May 29, crossing the Ailette the following day, and reaching the Marne at Jaulgonne. Foch thereupon decided to throw in all the French reserves which could possibly be spared from Flanders.[30] Still aware of the ultimate danger in the north, he warned Haig to remain on the qui vive, and to try to replace with British reserves the French forces (almost all of the Fifth Army) sent south of the Oise to bolster the line. General Foch likewise notified the commander of the French Tenth Army that he must be ready for eventual intervention on the British front.[31] When Clemenceau, the civilian amateur, learned of the arrival of the French reserves along the Marne, he expressed exasperated relief. "And high time!" was his comment. The news that the Germans had made the Paris-Châlons railway unusable through the seizure of the north bank of the Marne from Château-Thierry to Dormans elicited from the Tiger the surly observation: "If the operation was on such a small scale as... Foch had declared, why all that elaborate and formidable organization at this particular place?... There are altogether too many *whys* about this curious business."[32]

Foreseeing the inevitable parliamentary furor which would be created by the German drive, Clemenceau made another tour of the command posts. Upon his return, he reported to President Poincaré that as yet he could hold no one responsible for the

German break-through—not even General Duchêne, who should not be removed during the height of action, despite what had happened to his Sixth Army.[33] Clemenceau said that he feared the possible loss of Reims and Dormans, but Pétain was preparing a strong defense. The Tiger then upbraided Poincaré for what he had allegedly been doing in his absence—receiving malcontents at the Elysée and listening to criticisms of the generals, such as those being circulated against Pétain by Aristide Briand.[34] Poincaré admitted that he and his visitors had discussed the failure to cut Aisne bridges, although he attributed the responsibility not so much to Pétain as to Foch, who seemed "to be hypnotized by the north."[35] Poincaré denied that he had criticized either Clemenceau or Pétain. The two statesmen thereupon agreed that "it would be necessary not to disturb either Foch or Pétain."[36]

Foch and Clemenceau displayed their best qualities during the Second Battle of Chemin des Dames. Despite all the clamor raised against Foch, he refused to meet the immediate threat to Paris by bringing down all of his reserves from Flanders, the point of real (albeit delayed) danger. Technician Foch thereby demonstrated superlative insight. At the same time Clemenceau displayed his statesmanship by resolutely defending Foch, notwithstanding his misgivings that the general might possibly be in error in regard to the German strategy. In a military crisis such as this, the civilian had to place implicit faith in the judgment of the technician until the soldier could be proved wrong—and in this case Foch was right. The president of the council and war minister prepared for interpellation with the same degree of calculation which Foch was showing in his military operations. He tried, first of all, to obviate as much criticism as possible by inviting the president of the Chamber's army commission, Deputy René Renoult (the successor to General Pédoya) to accompany him to the front for an inspection. Renoult, the Tiger, and General Mordacq were pleased to see great columns of tractor and truck-drawn heavy artillery rolling up to the front in the Trilport sector.[87] Assured thereby of at least Renoult's support, Clemenceau "complied unhesitatingly with all the demands for information that came from Parliament." The Tiger described his actions as follows: "I appeared before the Commissions, where I met the keenest hostility.... It was necessary to hold one's own against currents of public opinion clamoring for penalties without knowing on whom they were to fall...."[38]

When a delegation of the Tiger's old enemies, the Socialists, visited him at his office on May 31 to demand the dismissal of General Pétain, he "roused himself and ... scattered his questioners." General Mordacq described the scene as "most violent."[89] The Socialists had also wanted another secret committee—something to which Clemenceau would never consent, according to what he had told Poincaré.[40] The deputies were hardly in a position to insist upon a secret committee, since the embarrassing Turmel, Malvy, Caillaux, and Charles Humbert *affaires* had placed Parliament at a serious disadvantage vis-à-vis so awesome a patriot as Georges Clemenceau. "The secret committee had disappeared, and with it the means of exacting from the government ticklish discussions which might weaken its authority."[41]

Clemenceau next defended the command before France's allies—whose attitude was not without malice as they contemplated France's setback.[42] At the close of the June 1–2 session of the Supreme War Council, Clemenceau, Lloyd George, and Orlando drafted a cablegram for President Wilson, in which General Foch's statement of man-power requirements was corroborated.[43] President Wilson was informed that Foch had a pressing need of American machine gunners and infantrymen in June and July to meet a crisis in which 162 Allied divisions were opposed by 200 German divisions."[44] Clemenceau declared in his memoirs that "to confirm General Foch's authority I had the following sentence inserted into the message sent by the heads of the Allied Governments to Mr. Wilson: 'We consider that General Foch, who is conducting the present campaign with consummate skill, and whose military judgment inspires us with the utmost confidence, does not exaggerate the necessities of the moment.' "[45]

Foch's career was never in greater danger than at the beginning of June, 1918, when the Germans stormed into Château-Thierry, the gateway to Paris. No one knew this better than Clemenceau. "I had to make things right with Parliament...," he wrote. "All the conversations... were full to bursting with evil auguries for the High Command.... I took everybody under my shield, to the great astonishment of those who had told me that by throwing all the responsibility on the Commander-in-Chief I should regain the authority belonging to my position."[46] One reason for the steadfastness of the Tiger's defense of Foch, as he admitted to Poincaré, was that he saw at last that "Foch was right" in having massed the reserves in the north, "because the north was menaced."[47]

Although the German drive was actually being halted at the Marne (in part due to Pershing's rescue with the 2d and 3d American Infantry divisions at Château-Thierry),[48] parliamentary unrest reached its climax at the session of June 4. Clemenceau informed the Chamber of Deputies that he "had received several demands for interpellations on the military situation." He explained that there were three courses of action: direct interpellation, conferences with the parliamentary commissions, and the secret committee. The second course had already been tried, for only the day before he had addressed the army commission, replying "to all the questions asked." As for the secret committee, Clemenceau expressed the opinion that although it had served a good purpose earlier in the war, its usefulness was past. It encouraged all sorts of rumors which were seized upon and twisted beyond recognition by the press, especially the foreign journals, which tried thereby to elicit revealing denials or corrections from the French government. Moreover, it lent itself to domestic political intrigue.[49]

GENERALS & POLITICIANS

After a brief passage at arms with some of the Socialists who raised objections to being members of a "chained assembly," Clemenceau went on with his speech, asserting that the army commission could bear witness to the fact that he had already begun inquiries into recent military actions. The investigations, so far, would not warrant his taking action "against anyone at all."[50] The president of the council defied the Socialist opposition by declaring: "If winning the favor of certain persons who make snap judgments calls for abandoning chiefs who have deserved well of their country, then I am not capable of such meanness."[51]

The president of the council paid tribute to the French soldiers who, in "the terrible battle" still raging, had fought without sleep for three or four days, against odds of five to one. The Chamber rose to applaud the troops. Clemenceau praised the High Command as well as the enlisted men.

I was prejudiced against some of [the chiefs] who have lately filled me with admiration.... Is this the same as saying that no faults have been committed? I could not maintain that. I know it very well, for it is my duty to find out and correct faults.... I have been aided in this by two great chiefs... General Foch and General Pétain. General Foch has the confidence of our Allies, who only yesterday at the Versailles Conference testified... to the trust which they have in him.... These men at this very moment wage the hardest battle of the war, and they wage it with a heroism which I am incapable of describing.... And are we... to demand explanations before we know the facts, while the battle is still raging, from a man worn out with fatigue, whose head droops over his maps in hours of terrible stress, as I have seen with my own eyes? Is this the man we are going to have tell us whether on such and such a day he did thus or so! Drive me from the tribune, if that is what you wish, for I will never do it....[52]

The Tiger was upheld by a vote of 377 to 110.[53] He was fully aware of his service to Foch, self-effacing modesty not being conspicuous among Clemenceau's virtues. "I won a signal victory," he wrote, "and at the same time shielded all my subordinates; but nobody can seriously doubt that, had I faltered for a single moment, the High Command would have been swept away. Foch never said a word to me about this sitting, at which it is no mere boast for me to say that I saved him."[54]

Clemenceau's loyalty to Foch did not signify any intention of condoning the faults of the command, but it did mean that sanctions would be imposed only by the imperious president of the council and war minister and by the Allied commander in chief, with no interference from the parliamentarians. Clemenceau appeared uncertain as to Foch's own degree of responsibility for the reverse. "This lamentable rout," according to the Tiger, "... was no doubt attributable in the first place to the High Command, which was not sufficiently in touch with the actual fighting units. But had the secondary commands been strongly welded together, we should have been able to hold out, in spite of the absence of the reserves which Foch was keeping up in Flanders...."[55]

Resolved upon a house cleaning, the statesman went to see the commander in chief several days after the vote of confidence. "... I told the General," wrote Clemenceau, "that new duties had been imposed upon us by reason of our victory in Parliament, and I appealed to him on his military conscience as supreme commander to tell me if he had no urgent reforms in the personnel to suggest."[56] Clemenceau and Foch went over a list of older generals whom the Tiger believed should be replaced. Foch winced at some of the names on Clemenceau's list. "An old friend!" Foch would murmur. With a few exceptions, he acquiesced in the changes demanded, although he asked the president of the council and war minister "to spare those of his 'old comrades' who were on parts of the front where there was no fighting...." "I took that chance," explained Clemenceau, "to win my way into the good graces of the General... who himself only retained his post thanks to my intervention in the Chamber."[57]

GENERALS & POLITICIANS

Of the chiefs dismissed because of the reverses in the offensive of May 27, the best known were Generals Duchêne, Franchet d'Esperey, and Micheler, although such lesser lights as Generals Putz, Bazelaire, and Maud'huy were also removed from their commands. The reconstituted command was henceforth made up of leaders who had withstood the test of four years of war.

It soon became apparent that Foch had been correct in his assumption that the Chemin des Dames attack of May 27 was to be preliminary to an enemy thrust in Flanders—the Hagen movement, as the Germans called it. But the Hagen operation had to be postponed by the Germans because their gains in the Second Battle of Chemin des Dames had placed them in an exposed salient which could be safeguarded and widened only by the capture of Reims, which was planned for July. This unexpected delay gave the British invaluable time to strengthen their endangered front, and meanwhile a flood of Americans was pouring into France—24 complete divisions by the end of June. Arriving at the rate of 250,000 a month,[58] the Americans soon provided Foch with the forces needed for counterattacks, such as the one against Soissons for the purpose of cutting off the Germans in the Château-Thierry salient.[59]

Foch won a brilliant victory in the Second Battle of the Marne in July, 1918. Instructed by prisoners as to the German plan of enveloping Reims,[60] he released his own counteroffensive. On July 18, three days after the opening of the ineffectual German campaign against Reims, Foch directed against Soissons the Tenth Army of General Mangin (augmented by the American 1st and 2d Infantry divisions),[61] while the Sixth Army of Degoutte was sent toward La Fère-en-Tardenois. Two days later, General Berthelot's Fifth Army pushed northward from Epernay in a converging movement to close the ring, if possible. These counterdrives were designed to throw off balance the German offensive against Reims, and to level out the Marne salient. The eastward thrust of Mangin and Degoutte began promisingly, but the two-day defensive wait of Berthelot's Fifth

Army enabled the Germans to pull back the bulk of their forces from the endangered Marne salient, although 30,000 were left behind as prisoners.[62] The hard-pressed enemy had to fall back hastily to a shortened line along the Vesle.[63] These victories won for Foch a marshal's baton.

Foch had wrested the initiative from the enemy, and he was determined to keep it. If ever the *offensive à outrance* had validity since the beginning of the war, it was during the last five months when the Allied commander was able to swamp the exhausted enemy with waves of American troops and with the French and British survivors of four years of struggle. At a conference of commanders held at Foch's headquarters at Bombon on July 24, 1918, Pershing was instructed to make ready an American army which was to obtain "the release of the Paris-Avricourt railroad in the region of Commercy by the reduction of the St. Mihiel salient.... By thus reducing the front, it would bring the Allies within reach of the Briey [iron] region and permit action on a larger scale between the Meuse and Moselle."[64] The British and French would attempt simultaneously to free the Paris-Amiens railway.[65] Pershing issued an order creating the American First Army, "to take effect on August 10th, with Headquarters at La Ferté-sous-Jouarre."[66]

Victory for the Allies was finally in sight. While the Americans were preparing their attack upon the St. Mihiel salient, the British on August 8 released a surprise offensive along the Amiens–St. Quentin road, obtaining a deep penetration of the German line through the employment of large squadrons of tanks.[67] The Allies struck the enemy with a rapid succession of blows: the French, on August 20, drove between the Oise and the Aisne in the direction of Chauny; on August 21, the British extended their attack of August 8 to the north side of Bapaume and, maintaining their momentum, pushed on toward Cambrai on August 26. Temporarily checked, the British renewed the assault on the Arras-Cambrai road on September 2, forcing the Germans back to the Siegfried Line.[68] On September 12 the

American First Army went into action at last, undertaking the reduction of the St. Mihiel salient.[69] Flushed with success, the confident Americans were soon transferred to the Meuse-Argonne sector where, on September 26, they began a powerful drive on the west bank of the Meuse, in the general direction of Mézières, to outflank the enemy positions south of the Aisne.[70]

"From September 26 to October 14 the Americans [fought] a continuous battle; they [drove] the enemy through the Argonne forest, captured the first three of the four lines constituting the Hindenburg system, crossed the Aire, joined hands with the French [Fourth] Army at Grandpré, cleared the Meuse as far as Sivry and brought the main line of German supply under long-range bombardment."[71] Then the Americans slackened their pace because of the tremendous and sustained efforts which had been exerted by a relatively unseasoned army. The slowing down of the American drive deeply perturbed Clemenceau, who was impatient to deliver the knockout blow at almost any cost. This loss of momentum brought a renewal of the bitter wrangling between Clemenceau and the marshal.

Foch later described the conflict to Raymond Recouly:

... M. Clemenceau deemed that the American army was not putting forth all possible effort. He attributed this to ... General Pershing. According to M. Clemenceau, the American General was ... acting on his own account without paying sufficient attention to the operations of the other forces. ... My patience with Pershing was causing, he alleged, a considerable loss of strength. ... The efforts that the Americans did not put forth had to be supplied by the English and above all by the French, he said. It was his belief that as persuasion provoked no response, it was time to resort to force and energy. ... M. Clemenceau upbraided me for showing [Pershing] too much patience and indulgence. "You will answer to France for it," he told me. ... I replied that I was ready to answer for it to anyone, and I continued, as though nothing had happened, to act upon my method, which seemed to me the only practicable one because it alone was reasonable.[72]

FOCH & CLEMENCEAU

The antagonism between the president of the council and Foch was brought to a head on October 11, when Field Marshal Haig visited "his friend Clemenceau" to urge him "to intervene with the Americans to obtain from them ... two or three divisions."[73] The British troops needed relief, since they were "very tired from ceaseless combat." Clemenceau sent General Mordacq to discuss the matter with Foch, but as Mordacq reported in his own words: "... From the first mention of the subject, I encountered in [the marshal] a characteristic resistance, the reason for which I vainly sought." Foch answered the request with the vague promise that "he would study the question, but he saw certain difficulties in solving it."[74]

Clemenceau was greatly incensed when he learned of Foch's latest evasion. He drew up a blistering letter and, accompanied by M. Jules Jeanneney, undersecretary of state, he "betook [him]self to the Elysée to show the President of the Republic the draft of the letter [which he] intended to send Foch...."[75] Clemenceau conceded that "the letter was certainly pretty strongly worded ... it was 'harsh' both to Pershing, who did not want to obey, and to Foch, who did not want to command."[76] When President Poincaré read Clemenceau's letter, he advised him not to send it.

Clemenceau took back his letter, "toned it down," and submitted it once again to M. Poincaré. The president of the republic gave his opinion in writing to M. Jeanneney, the intermediary:

I maintain my point of view. This letter ... is still too harsh with regard to the Americans and ... to Foch.... M. Clemenceau says to the Marshal, "It's our country's command that you shall command." If that was said to me I should resign.

And, furthermore, is it M. Clemenceau's business to concern himself with what Marshal Foch does as Commander-in-Chief of the American army? In that capacity is not Marshal Foch responsible rather to the American Government?[77]

Once again, the amorphousness of Marshal Foch's status made it appear that he could by-pass Clemenceau if he wished. The Tiger was furious over Poincaré's siding with Foch in this stratagem. He leapt to the conclusion that Poincaré and Foch were in collusion against him.

At the height of the War [declared Clemenceau] the President of the Republic actually furnishes the Commander of the Allied armies with arguments to encourage him to resist his immediate chief, the Prime Minister and Minister of War. He explains to the simple mind of the soldier, unversed in legal intricacies, that the Allied Governments, when they gave him powers over their troops, partly withdrew him from the authority of the Prime Minister and Minister of War. The dispute turned simply on what action ought to follow from the establishment of the sole command. General Pershing would not alter his way of working. Marshal Foch, from whom Poincaré could not take away a jot of his definite right to command Pershing, and M. Poincaré, who would not admit any right to command Foch to command, would have it that we must all three remain eyeing one another in helpless deadlock....[78]

To try to break the impasse, Clemenceau on October 21 had General Mordacq repeat Haig's request for the two American divisions. Foch "replied once more that before he could reach a definite decision on the subject ... he would have to know the precise facts about the American army, information which had been impossible to obtain...."[79] This quibble caused the president of the council and war minister to write Foch a famous letter:

I have put off from day to day writing you about the crisis in the American army....

You have watched at close range the development of General Pershing's wilfullness, which, thanks to his invincible obstinacy, has unfortunately triumphed over you and your immediate subordinates....

I am constitutionally the head of the French army.... I would be criminal if I allowed [it] to wear itself out indefinitely in battle.... The French army and the British army, without once letting up, have been fighting daily for the past three months.... But our worthy American allies, who thirst to get into action and who are unanimously acknowledged to be great soldiers, have been marking time since their first jump.... Nobody can maintain that these fine troops are unusable; they are merely unused.... I know all of the efforts which you have made to overcome the resistance of General Pershing ... but I ... ask myself whether ... the time has not come for changing methods. When General Pershing refused to obey your orders, you could have appealed to President Wilson. For reasons which you considered more important, you put off this solution of the conflict....

If General Pershing finally resigns himself to obedience ... I shall be wholly delighted. But if this new attempt to reconcile two contrary points of view should not bring the advantageous results you anticipate, I must say to you that in my opinion ... it would be high time to tell President Wilson the truth and the whole truth concerning the situation of the American troops.... The President of the United States has frequently declared that he was ready to conform to your judgment in all military questions. He will undoubtedly appraise ... the patience you have so long shown and the decision to which you have finally been led....[80]

Foch was completely unruffled by Clemenceau's letter. The marshal later remarked to his friend Raymond Recouly that Clemenceau was like Don Quixote tilting against a windmill in his jousting with Pershing. Foch, in retrospect, doubted whether President Wilson would have yielded to a request to remove Pershing, and if Pershing had stayed on, he would probably have learned of the French effort to have him sacked and he would have been all the more recalcitrant.[81] Even if Pershing had been dismissed, reasoned Foch, "his successor would [have] need[ed] a long time to take up all the threads. We would then have gained nothing by the change, and probably would [have been] in a worse plight.... Therefore, M. Clemenceau's letter, despite its urgency, did not cause me to vary my plans. Convinced as I was that my method of command, based on persuasion rather than harshness, was a good one—in fact, the only good one—I was determined to apply it to the very end."[82]

In Foch's formal answer to Clemenceau's letter, he furnished a chart showing the distribution of the thirty American divisions fit for service. Ten of these divisions, Foch explained, were shared among the Allies. The remaining twenty divisions made up General Pershing's autonomous American army. He intended to maintain this arrangement.[83] Foch concluded his letter by tactfully reminding Clemenceau of something which he seemed to underestimate: the heroic sacrifices of the young American army. "The efforts made by the American army cannot be denied. After having attacked at St. Mihiel on September 12, it took the offensive in the Argonne on September 26. It has lost under fire, from September 26 to October 20, 54,158 men, and although it is true that the front was narrow, it made some slight gains over a particularly rough terrain in the face of serious resistance from the enemy."[84]

Although Foch seemed to be trying to outwit Clemenceau again, the marshal in reality capitulated. He lost no time in ordering the American commander "to prepare and carry out, *without any delay,*[85] a powerful attack in the direction of Boultaux-Bois, Buzancy, the wood of La Folie...."[86] Clemenceau's letter to Foch thus had the desired effect of making the marshal apprehensive of an international crisis, thereby compelling him to order the renewal of the American drive.

As the war drew to a close, the French policy maker and the strategist had a brief moment of harmony. Clemenceau and Foch were in basic agreement upon granting the Germans an armistice.[87] On this question they were opposed by President Poincaré[88] and by the Americans, Generals Pershing[89] and Tasker H. Bliss,[90] who wanted to impose unconditional surrender upon the enemy.

When the Tiger asked Foch what he thought of the proposal to fight all the way to Berlin, the marshal replied: "To continue the struggle longer would incur great risk. It would mean that perhaps fifty or a hundred thousand more Frenchmen would be killed, not counting the Allies, and for quite problematic results.... Enough blood, alas! has already been shed, and that should suffice." Clemenceau emphatically agreed: "Marshal, I am entirely of this same opinion."[91]

The statesman quite properly left to Foch the technical tasks of drawing up the armistice terms. Foch acknowledged that he was given virtually a free hand in such preliminary armistice matters as the evacuation of Belgium, France, Alsace-Lorraine, Luxembourg; the seizure of bridgeheads on the Rhine; the occupation of the left bank of the Rhine, and the restoration of French and Belgian railway equipment. "As regards the armistice," he said to Recouly, "being first judge of the situation, I succeeded, after some difficulty, in imposing my views on the others."[92]

Encouraged by this success, Foch was hopeful of sketching the peace conditions as well. He contended in his *Mémoires* that he was convinced "it was necessary to have a careful, preliminary study of the political terms to be included in the armistice as a precaution against future surprises. The armistice ought to contain the gist of the principal conditions of the... treaty of peace, in such a form that future decisions could involve no serious change in the situation established at the time hostilities ended."[93] With this ambitious plan in mind, Foch addressed a letter to Clemenceau on October 16, 1918, asking him what were the government's ultimate intentions with regard to the occupation of the left bank of the Rhine. "Will such a pledge be a sufficient guarantee of the reparations required by France and her allies, notably Belgium? If the answer is in the affirmative, and assuming that reparations will be forthcoming, what, then, will be the future of this [occupied] territory? Will our occupation continue? Are we to annex a part of this region, or are we to have there a neutral, autonomous, independent buffer state? Will the armistice specifically safeguard the status of this region... ?" Foch concluded his letter with a request that a "high official of the Ministry of Foreign Affairs" be authorized to maintain "close and continuous relations" with him so that he "could be kept informed of [Clemenceau's] views and of those of the Allied governments."[94]

Foch insisted to his friend Raymond Recouly that his letter of October 16 "had been carefully pondered; it was eminently reasonable; but what answer did I receive from M. Clemenceau... and from his colleague for Foreign Affairs, M. [Stephen] Pichon? Their answer was: 'Your business is war; but everything pertaining to peace, our Rhineland policy... concerns ourselves exclusively. We will not suffer you to interfere in those matters.'"[95] The marshal related that Clemenceau's reply of October 23 "began by stating specifically that I was merely military adviser to the Government. Such an official... was consulted only on technical matters, and the Government was free to act on his advice, to reject it, or to modify it in any way. Diplomatic and political discussions bearing on matters of pledges and the Rhineland were outside his province. [Clemenceau] dwelt on the distinction between political and diplomatic matters and military affairs. He intimated that I should be kept informed of matters only as and when they had a military bearing."[96]

Foch and Recouly tried to imagine how Clemenceau, "the old Jacobin, must have been filled with glee as he pored over his own letter and dictated that of Pichon. He must have been delighted to put a mere military man in his place, and make him feel the unquestionable supremacy of the civilian."[97]

The marshal regarded the letter from Foreign Affairs Minister Pichon as being even more offensive than Clemenceau's. Pichon flatly rejected Foch's request for a liaison official with the Quai d'Orsay to keep him informed of the government's intentions.[98] "Only the Minister can give you such information," Pichon wrote. Foch explained that Pichon "straightway proceeded to say that he would do no such thing [as keep him informed of peace negotiations, since] soldiers [had] nothing to do with politics and diplomacy. Not content with refusing my request, [Pichon] resolved to teach me a lesson. 'Everyone has his own task to perform.... It is advisable that the work of each be clearly defined in scope, so as to avoid any confusion of power.' "[99]

The rebukes of Clemenceau and Pichon deeply offended Foch. "... I had no need of such a pedantic lecture on constitutional law and the limitation of power—especially pedantic on the part of the Quai d'Orsay. I had simply taken my stand on the level ground of reason and common sense. Peace is the logical finish of a war, and as it was nearly upon us, I wanted to know the Government's policy on the vital question of the Rhine, so as to turn my own steps in the same direction." But Foch contended that from the time Clemenceau received his letter of October 16, the president of the council and war minister "was...extremely jealous of his prerogatives and power. As victory drew nearer he became increasingly dictatorial, and would suffer proportionately little questioning of his views."[100]

After Foch had been thus admonished not to dabble with peace terms, the problem nevertheless turned up again on November 8, 1918. The German armistice delegation, in its conference with the marshal at Rethondes, insisted on bringing up the question of peace terms. Foch's staff officer, General Weygand, informed General Mordacq by telephone that "the Germans, instead of confining their discussion to questions concerning the armistice, were trying to feel out the peace terms which would be imposed upon them."[101] When Mordacq delivered this message to Clemenceau, the Tiger sent word to Marshal Foch "that under no pretext whatsoever must he speak of peace terms with the Germans."[102] The marshal was further instructed by the president of the council that if the German negotiators returned to the subject, he would have "to make them comprehend that he, as a soldier, could concern himself only with the armistice, and that the conditions of the peace were the affairs of the government."[103]

GENERALS & POLITICIANS

France thus emerged from the four-year struggle with her civilian government and democratic institutions intact, notwithstanding the great prestige of Marshal Foch. Seldom was the nation in less danger of a "man on horseback" than on November 11, 1918. The military hero was overshadowed by the civilian, the "father of victory."

That France had been no better equipped to meet the problems of a democracy at war was due to a complex of historic circumstances. The great prestige which the military had enjoyed for centuries gave them an advantage over the civilians at the outset of the war. The very idea of the "sacred union" was chiefly to the benefit of conservatives, of which the military were a most important part. Criticizing the command would have been considered disloyal—if not downright treasonable—during the crucial weeks of August and September, 1914. The government and Parliament deferred to the command, thus carrying out popular expectation. A short war was anticipated, and only a temporary overshadowing of the civilian power. The inconclusive victory on the Marne, the exhaustion of supplies, and the belated awareness that the war was one of attrition caused Parliament to reconsider its role and to resume the functions of army supervision, chiefly through the agency of the army commissions.

The Sarrail affair emboldened Parliament to pass judgment upon army appointments. Furthermore, it embittered the Left, and foreshadowed the eventual rupture of the "sacred union." Verdun greatly discredited the command, endangering as well the Briand government which was suspected by Parliament of having condoned the command's negligence in the city's defenses. The secret committees represented the recovery of parliamentary power, which reached its peak with the sporadic efforts of parliamentarians to interfere directly with the command during the Chemin des Dames campaign. The government frustrated the meddlesomeness of the individual deputies, but it had to respond to the parliamentary demand for an end to Napoleonic offenses until the Americans arrived on the battlefield in full force. Even as the prolonged stalemate and the costly battles of Verdun, the Somme, and Chemin des Dames impaired the prestige of the command, so the political scandals of the *Bonnet Rouge,* Malvy, Caillaux, Turmel, and Charles Humbert *affaires* discredited parliamentarians in the eyes of the public. By November, 1917, France was ready to acquiesce in a Jacobin quasi dictatorship. Having gone into the war under the "dictatorship" of Joffre, the exhausted nation emerged under the rigorous rule of Clemenceau, who not only embodied the "will to victory" but was known as the champion of civilian primacy over the military.

The a priori method of regulating policy and strategy by assigning the political ends of the war to the civilian power, and the forcible achievement of those aims to the military, had been abandoned in actual practice. The military at first invaded the government's sphere. Then Parliament encroached upon the power of the government and the command, and finally the government, under Clemenceau, became the dominant factor. This shift of power from the command to Parliament to the government was quite unforeseen, but almost inescapable in the circumstances. Pragmatic testing, blind groping, and trial and error took the place of any rule of thumb formula laid down for separate spheres of authority.

If any lesson is to be drawn from France's experience, it would probably be the counsel of perfection for a nation to "have a good history"—a set of conditions in which an able civilian government maintained national interests by effective diplomacy, closely supported by a capable military who were willing to remain in their proper place. If war proved unavoidable, the government would clearly understand the political ends to be reached, the military the means of their achievement. If a nation should be so blessed, and possessed in addition to this model government and command great material resources, vast reserves of man power, room for maneuver—and strong allies—

then the prospect of an immediate victory could reasonably guarantee an absence of friction between policy makers and strategists. That France was not favored with all of these advantages was hardly her own fault. The nation, in any case, was fortunate in having toward the end of the war so competent an executive as Clemenceau and so able a soldier as Foch, and the French deserve credit for placing in posts of authority these two preëminent men.

NOTES

Notes

NOTES TO CHAPTER 2

[1] France, Assemblée nationale. *Annales de la Chambre des Députés, débats parlementaires* (Paris, 1915) ... Séance de 4 août 1914, II, 907. Hereafter cited as *Annales de la Chambre.*
[2] Raymond Recouly, *Joffre* (New York, 1931), p. 56. Hereafter cited as Recouly, *Joffre.*
[3] Joseph J. C. Joffre, *Mémoires du maréchal Joffre* (Paris, 1932), I, 11.
[4] Adolphe Messimy, *Mes souvenirs* (Paris, 1937), pp. 76–77.
[5] Recouly, *Joffre*, p. 60.
[6] Aulard, et al., *Histoire politique de la grande guerre* (Paris, 1924), p. 51.
[7] Basil Henry Liddell Hart, *Reputations Ten Years After* (Boston, 1928), p. 10. Hereafter cited as Liddell Hart, *Reputations.*
[8] *Ibid.,* p. 8.
[9] Recouly, *Joffre*, p. 55.
[10] Jean de Pierrefeu, *Plutarque a menti* (Paris, 1923), p. 40.
[11] Liddell Hart, *Reputations*, p. 7.
[12] *Ibid.,* p. 32.
[13] Joffre, *op. cit.*, I, 208.
[14] *Ibid.,* p. 207.
[15] It was a matter of capital importance that Joffre should not allow the war minister to do his work for him. Joseph Barthélemy discusses this general problem in his book, *The Government of France* (New York, 1919), p. 109. "... The Ministers are the representatives of the nation charged with controlling the specialists in their work of ... management and upkeep of the national [organization]; and thus while representing the sovereign will, which controls the administration, the Ministers themselves must be strangers to that administration; otherwise the nation would fall into a state of uncontrolled bureaucracy ... inefficiency, red tape and stagnation."
[16] France, Ministère de la Guerre, Etat-Major de l'armée, service historique. *Les armées françaises dans la grande guerre* (Paris, 1922), I, 72. Hereafter cited as *Les armées françaises.*
[17] Joffre, *op. cit.*, I, 208. Cf. Messimy, *op. cit.*, pp. 131–132.
[18] *Ibid.,* p. 209.
[19] *Ibid.,* p. 213.
[20] *Les armées françaises*, I, 75–76.

NOTES

[21] Joffre, *op. cit.*, I, 213.
[22] *Ibid.*, p. 218. Cf. Messimy, *op. cit.*, pp. 131–132.
[23] *Ibid.*, pp. 220–221.
[24] *Ibid.*, p. 222.
[25] *Les armées françaises*, I, Annex 21, p. 63.
[26] Raymond Poincaré, *Au service de la France* (Paris, 1927), IV, 500.
[27] *Les armées françaises*, I, Annex 27, p. 67.
[28] *Ibid.*, Annex 31, pp. 69–70.
[29] *Annales de la Chambre* ... Séance du 4 août 1914, II, 909.
[30] Gabriel Terrail [Mermeix, *pseud.*], *Au sein des commissions* (Paris, 1924), p. 1. Hereafter cited as Terrail, *Au sein*.
[31] Messimy *op. cit.*, p. 232.
[32] Joseph Barthélemy, "Le contrôle parlementaire en temps de guerre," in *Problèmes de politique et finances de guerre*, by Gaston Jezé, Joseph Barthélemy, and Charles Rist (Paris, 1915), pp. 132–133. Hereafter cited as Barthélemy, "Le contrôle parlementaire."
[33] Terrail, *Au sein*, p. 3.
[34] Pierre Renouvin, *Les formes du gouvernement de guerre* (New Haven, Conn., 1925), p. 28.
[35] Barthélemy, "Le contrôle parlementaire," p. 153.
[36] Terrail, *Au sein*, p. 8.
[37] Aulard, *op. cit.*, p. 45. Cf. Messimy, *op. cit.*, p. 231.
[38] Jean Marie Gustave Pédoya, *La commission de l'armée pendant la grande guerre* (Paris, 1921), p. 399.
[39] Aulard, *op. cit.*, p. 37.
[40] Alexandre Zévaès, *Le parti socialiste de 1904 à 1923* (Paris, 1923), pp. 65–66.
[41] Aulard, *op. cit.*, p. 37.
[42] *Annales de la chambre* ... Séance du 4 août 1914, II, 906–907.
[43] France, Assemblée nationale. *Journal officiel de la république française*, août 8, 1914, p. 7126. Hereafter cited as *Journal officiel*.
[44] All of France was included by an executive decree of September 3, in order to expedite court-martial procedure in the interior. See Renouvin, *op. cit.*, p. 29.
[45] *Journal officiel*, août 6, 1914, p. 7127.
[46] *Ibid.*
[47] *Ibid.*
[48] Aulard, *op. cit.*, p. 46.
[49] *Journal officiel*, août 6, 1914, p. 7131.
[50] Aulard, *op. cit.*, p. 49.
[51] Georges Weill, "Les gouvernements et la presse pendant la guerre," *Revue d'histoire de la guerre mondiale* (avril, 1933), p. 103.
[52] Renouvin, *op. cit.*, p. 39.
[53] *Ibid.*
[54] Weill, *loc. cit.*, p. 103.
[55] *Ibid.*

NOTES

[56] Aulard, *op. cit.*, p. 44.
[57] Terrail, *Au sein*, p. 8.
[58] Joffre's staff officers, the "Young Turks," included Generals Belin, Berthelot, Pellé, Colonels Gamelin, Alexandre, and Lieutenant Colonels Buat, Bel, and Renouard. See Terrail, *Au sein*, pp. 54–55.
[59] Aulard, *op. cit.*, p. 55. Cf. Messimy's admission to Gallieni in Joseph Simon Gallieni, *Les carnets de Gallieni* (Paris, 1932), pp. 179–180. Hereafter cited as Gallieni, *Les carnets*.
[60] Paul Coblentz, *The Silence of Sarrail* (London, 1930), pp. 41, 42.
[61] Aulard, *op. cit.*, p. 55.
[62] Messimy, *op. cit.*, pp. 206–207.
[63] Liddell Hart, *Reputations*, p. 12.
[64] Joffre, *op. cit.*, I, 267. Cf. Pierrefeu, *Plutarque a menti*, pp. 59–60.
[65] *Ibid.*, p. 266.
[66] *Ibid.*, p. 268.
[67] Poincaré, *op. cit.*, V, 98.
[68] Liddell Hart, *Reputations*, p. 79.
[69] Joffre, *op. cit.*, I, 267. Cf. Messimy, *op. cit.*, p. 210.
[70] Messimy, *op. cit.*, p. 230.
[71] Terrail, *Au sein*, p. 27.
[72] Renouvin, *op. cit.*, p. 34.
[73] *Ibid.*, pp. 34–35.
[74] Terrail, *Au sein*, pp. 27–28.
[75] *Ibid.*, p. 28.
[76] *Ibid.*, p. 29.
[77] *Ibid.*
[78] *Ibid.*, p. 31.
[79] *Ibid.*, p. 32. Cf. Messimy, *op. cit.*, pp. 238–239. Cf. also Joseph Barthélemy, *La démocratie et politique étrangère* (Paris, 1917), p. 361. Hereafter cited as Barthélemy, *Démocratie*.
[80] Léopold Marcellin, *Politique et politiciens pendant la guerre* (Paris, 1923), I, 20.
[81] *Ibid.*, p. 21.
[82] *Ibid.*
[83] *Ibid.*
[84] *Ibid.*, p. 23.
[85] Joffre, *op. cit.*, I, 293. Cf. Poincaré's complaint given in Messimy, *op. cit.*, pp. 246–247.
[86] *Ibid.*
[87] Liddell Hart, *Reputations*, p. 20.
[88] Joffre, *op. cit.*, p. 303.
[89] *Ibid.*, p. 314. Cf. Messimy, *op. cit.*, pp. 217–218.
[90] *Ibid.*
[91] Aulard, *op. cit.*, p. 76. Cf. Zévaès, *op. cit.*, pp. 144–145. Sembat was made minister of public works, Guesde minister without portfolio. Viviani also called Aristide Briand to the vice-presidency of the council and Gaston Doumergue to the Ministry of Colonies.

NOTES

[92] Emile Herbillon, *Souvenirs d'un officier de liaison pendant la guerre mondiale* (Paris, 1930), I, 13.
[93] Joseph-Simon Gallieni, *Mémoires du général Gallieni* (Paris, 1920), p. 23. Hereafter cited as Gallieni, *Mémoires*.
[94] René Samuel, *Le parlement et la guerre 1914–1915* (Paris, 1918), p. 150.
[95] Herbillon, *op. cit.*, I, 17.
[96] Poincaré, *op. cit.*, V, 215.
[97] *Ibid.*, p. 217
[98] *Ibid.*, p. 220.
[99] Aulard, *op. cit.*, p. 60.
[100] Marcellin, *op. cit.*, I, 34.
[101] *Ibid.*, p. 41.
[102] *Ibid.*, p. 32.
[103] Samuel, *op. cit.*, pp. 30–31.
[104] Messimy, *op. cit.*, p. 235.
[105] Gallieni, *Mémoires*, p. 65.
[106] Frederick Maurice, "Joffre, Gallieni and the Marne," *The Contemporary Review*, June, 1927, p. 684.
[107] Herbillon, *op. cit.*, I, 81.
[108] Gallieni, *Mémoires*, p. 116.
[109] Herbillon, *op. cit.*, I, 81.
[110] Maurice, *loc. cit.*, p. 687.
[111] Liddell Hart, *Reputations*, p. 86.
[112] *Ibid.*, p. 87.
[113] Herbillon, *op. cit.*, I, 82.
[114] *Ibid.*
[115] *Ibid.*
[116] Gallieni, *Mémoires*, p. 229.
[117] *Ibid.*, p. 145.
[118] *Ibid.*, p. 172.
[119] *Ibid.*, p. 256.
[120] *Ibid.*, p. 14.
[121] *Ibid.*, p. 194. Cf. Gallieni, *Les carnets*, pp. 88–89.
[122] *Ibid.*, p. 198.
[123] Herbillon, *op. cit.*, I, 35.
[124] Barthélemy, *The Government of France*, pp. 85–86.
[125] Terrail, *Au sein*, p. 32. Cf. Herbillon, *op. cit.*, I, 152.
[126] Herbillon, *op. cit.*, I, 51. Cf. Poincaré, *op. cit.*, V, 353–356.
[127] Poincaré, *op. cit.*, V, 356.
[128] Herbillon, *op. cit.*, I, 41.
[129] *Ibid.*, p. 56.
[130] Terrail, *Au sein*, p. 34.
[131] *Ibid.*
[132] Quoted in Gabriel Terrail [Mermeix, *pseud.*], *Sarrail et les armées d'Orient* (Paris, 1920), p. 238. Hereafter cited as Terrail, *Sarrail*.

NOTES

[133] Herbillon, *op. cit.*, I, 80.
[134] Marcellin, *op. cit.*, I, 50.
[135] Herbillon, *op. cit.*, I, 80.

NOTES TO CHAPTER 3

[1] Renouvin, *op. cit.*, pp. 96–97.
[2] *Annales de la Chambre* ... Séance du 18 juillet 1916, II, 1495. Cf. also Renouvin, *op. cit.*, p. 118.
[3] *Ibid.*, p. 1496.
[4] Terrail, *Au sein*, pp. 40–41.
[5] Barthélemy, *Démocratie*, p. 325. Cf. Renouvin, *op. cit.*, pp. 117–118.
[6] Herbillon, *op. cit.*, I, 131.
[7] Barthélemy, *Démocratie*, p. 325.
[8] *Annales du Sénat* ... Séance du 13 juillet 1914, p. 1429.
[9] *Ibid.*, pp. 1429–1434.
[10] Charles Humbert, *Chacun son tour* (Paris, 1925), p. 406.
[11] Francis Martel, *Pétain: Verdun to Vichy* (New York, 1943), p. 70.
[12] Pédoya, *op. cit.*, p. 7.
[13] Terrail, *Au sein*, p. 36.
[14] Pédoya, *op. cit.*, p. 7.
[15] *Ibid.*, p. 8.
[16] *Ibid.*
[17] *Ibid.*, p. 9. Cf. Renouvin, *op. cit.*, p. 118.
[18] *Ibid.*
[19] *Ibid.*
[20] Terrail, *Au sein*, p. 37.
[21] Jean Marie Bourget, *Gouvernement et commandement: les leçons de la guerre mondiale* (Paris, 1930), p. 200.
[22] Poincaré, *op. cit.*, V, 523.
[23] *Ibid.*
[24] *Ibid.* Cf. Renouvin, *op. cit.*, pp. 94–95.
[25] Renouvin, *op. cit.*, pp. 95–98.
[26] *Annales du Sénat* ... Séance du 14 janvier 1915, p. 6.
[27] Quoted in Renouvin, *op. cit.*, p. 95.
[28] *Ibid.*
[29] Marcellin, *op. cit.*, I, 62.
[30] Poincaré, *op. cit.*, VI, 7.
[31] *Ibid.*, pp. 7–8.
[32] *Ibid.*, p. 8.
[33] Herbillon, *op. cit.*, I, 90.
[34] *Ibid.*
[35] Gabriel Terrail [Mermeix, *pseud.*], *Joffre: première crise du commandement* (Paris, 1919), p. 13. Hereafter cited as Terrail, *Joffre*.
[36] *Ibid.*, p. 16.
[37] *Ibid.*

NOTES

[38] Jean de Pierrefeu, *G.Q.G. secteur I: trois ans au grand quartier général par le rédacteur du "communiqué"* (Paris, 1920), I, 100. Hereafter cited as Pierrefeu, *G.Q.G.* Cf. Poincaré, *op. cit.*, VI, 332.
[39] Joffre, *op. cit.*, II, 105.
[40] Pierrefeu, *G.Q.G.*, I, 52.
[41] *Ibid.*
[42] *Ibid.*, p. 54. Cf. Edward Louis Spears, *Liaison, 1914: A Narrative of the Great Retreat* (London, 1930), p. 29.
[43] Quoted by Pierrefeu, *G.Q.G.*, I, 100.
[44] *Ibid.*
[45] *Annales de la Chambre* ... Séance du 14 janvier 1915, I, 6.
[46] Poincaré, *op. cit.*, VI, 19.
[47] Pédoya, *op. cit.*, p. 10.
[48] *Ibid.* Cf. Renouvin, *op. cit.*, pp. 118–119.
[49] *Ibid.*
[50] Aulard, *op. cit.*, pp. 131–132. Cf. Renouvin, *op. cit.*, p. 117.
[51] Terrail, *Au sein*, pp. 250–251.
[52] *Ibid.*, p. 253.
[53] *Ibid.*, p. 252.
[54] Poincaré, *op. cit.*, VI, 23.
[55] *Ibid.*
[56] Charles Bugnet, *Rue St. Dominique et G.Q.G. ou les trois dictatures de la guerre* (Paris, 1937), p. 71. Hereafter cited as Bugnet, *Rue St. Dominique*.
[57] Pédoya, *op. cit.*, p. 11.
[58] *Ibid.*
[59] *Ibid.*, p. 12.
[60] *Ibid.*
[61] *Ibid.*
[62] Marcellin, *op. cit.*, I, 67.
[63] Pédoya, *op. cit.*, p. 12.
[64] *Ibid.*
[65] *Ibid.*, p. 13.
[66] *Ibid.*
[67] *Ibid.*
[68] *Ibid.*, p. 14.
[69] *Ibid.*
[70] Poincaré, *op. cit.*, VI, 33. Cf. Renouvin, *op. cit.*, p. 94.
[71] Herbillon, *op. cit.*, I, 105.
[72] Terrail, *Au sein*, p. 255.
[73] Poincaré, *op. cit.*, VI, 59–60.
[74] Gordon Wright, *Raymond Poincaré and the French Presidency* (Stanford University, Calif., 1942), p. 149. Hereafter cited as Wright, *Poincaré*.
[75] Poincaré, *op. cit.*, p. 62.
[76] *Ibid.*, p. 63.
[77] *Ibid.*
[78] *Ibid.*, p. 71.

NOTES

[79] *Ibid.*, pp. 77–78.
[80] Marcellin, *op. cit.*, I, 79.
[81] Pédoya, *op. cit.*, p. 16.
[82] *Ibid.* See also Terrail, *Au sein*, pp. 64–65. Cf. Renouvin, *op. cit.*, p. 122.
[83] *Ibid.* Cf. Terrail, *Au sein*, p. 65.
[84] *Ibid.*, p. 17.
[85] *Ibid.* Cf. Terrail, *Au sein*, p. 68.
[86] *Ibid.*
[87] Terrail, *Au sein*, p. 68.
[88] Pédoya, *op. cit.*, p. 18.
[89] *Ibid.* Cf. Terrail, *Au sein*, p. 66.
[90] *Ibid.*
[91] *Ibid.*, pp. 18–19. Cf. Terrail, *Au sein*, p. 67.
[92] Poincaré, *op. cit.*, VI, 196–197.
[93] Terrail, *Au sein*, p. 67.
[94] Pédoya, *op. cit.*, p. 19.
[95] Herbillon, *op. cit.*, I, 139.
[96] Poincaré, *op. cit.*, VI, 197.
[97] Herbillon, *op. cit.*, I, 133.
[98] *Ibid.*, p. 151.
[99] *Ibid.*, p. 139.
[100] *Ibid.*, pp. 151–152.
[101] *Ibid.*, p. 152. Italics the author's.
[102] Abel Ferry, *La guerre vue d'en bas et d'en haut* (Paris, 1920), pp. 9–10.
[103] Herbillon, *op. cit.*, I, 143.
[104] Ferry, *op. cit.*, pp. 17–18.
[105] *Ibid.*, p. 28.
[106] *Ibid.*, p. 29.
[107] *Ibid.*, p. 31. Cf. Herbillon, *op. cit.*, I, 143.
[108] Terrail, *Au sein*, p. 44.
[109] Ferry, *op. cit.*, p. 38. See also Pierrefeu, *G.Q.G.*, I, 145.
[110] Terrail, *Au sein*, p. 45.
[111] *Ibid.*, p. 40.
[112] Ferry, *op. cit.*, p. 40.
[113] Liddell Hart, *Reputations*, pp. 30–31.
[114] Joffre, *op. cit.*, II, 105.
[115] *Ibid.*, p. 106.
[116] Poincaré, *op. cit.*, VI, 257.
[117] Pédoya, *op. cit.*, pp. 20–21. Cf. Renouvin, *op. cit.*, p. 122. See also Terrail, *Au sein*, p. 67.
[118] *Ibid.*, p. 22. Cf. Terrail, *Au sein*, p. 68.
[119] Marcellin, *op. cit.*, I, 85.
[120] See Poincaré, *op. cit.*, VI, 258.
[121] Pédoya, *op. cit.*, pp. 22–23. See Terrail, *Au sein*, p. 68.
[122] *Ibid.*, p. 23. Cf. Terrail, *Au sein*, p. 69.
[123] *Ibid.*

NOTES

[124] Terrail, *Au sein*, p. 69.
[125] Pédoya, *op. cit.*, p. 24. Cf. Terrail, *Au sein*, p. 69.
[126] Terrail, *Au sein*, p. 52.
[127] *Ibid.*, p. 53.
[128] *Ibid.*
[129] *Ibid.*, p. 54.
[130] *Ibid.*
[131] *Annales de la Chambre* ... Séance du 17 juin 1915, I, 833.
[132] Poincaré, *op. cit.*, VI, 211.
[133] *Ibid.*, p. 306.
[134] *Ibid.*, p. 211.
[135] Aulard, *op. cit.*, p. 148.
[136] Poincaré, *op. cit.*, VII, 99.
[137] *Annales de la Chambre* ... Séance du 13 janvier 1916, I, 6–7.
[138] Poincaré, *op. cit.*, VI, 277.
[139] Marcellin, *op. cit.*, I, 79.

NOTES TO CHAPTER 4

[1] Herbillon, *op. cit.*, I, 171.
[2] Coblentz, *op. cit.*, p. 30.
[3] *Ibid.*, p. 32. Cf. Jean-José Frappa, *Makédonia: souvenirs d'un officier de liaison en Orient* (Paris, 1921), pp. 28–29.
[4] *Ibid.*, p. 33.
[5] *La Guerre Sociale*, août 7, 1915.
[6] Emile Mayer, *Nos chefs de 1914* (Paris, 1930), p. 269.
[7] Gallieni, *Les carnets*, p. 201. Cf. Mayer, *op. cit.*, p. 269.
[8] Mayer, *op. cit.*, p. 269.
[9] *La Guerre Sociale*, août 7, 1915.
[10] Terrail, *Sarrail*, p. 192.
[11] *Ibid.*, p. 178.
[12] Joffre, *op. cit.*, II, 104–105. The general in chief was especially bitter toward Senator Paul Doumer, Gallieni's devoted former secretary of civil affairs, who, according to Joffre, made the rounds of the army commanders, telling them that Gallieni, "who had won the battle of the Marne," would soon replace Joffre. See Gallieni, *Les carnets*, p. 131.
[13] *Ibid.*, p. 106.
[14] Yvon Edmond Dubail, *Quatre années de commandement, 1914–1918* (Paris, 1921), II, 360.
[15] Joffre, *op. cit.*, II, 117. Cf. Mayer, *op. cit.*, p. 269.
[16] *Ibid.*, p. 118.
[17] Poincaré, *op. cit.*, VI, 336.
[18] Mayer, *op. cit.*, p. 278. Cf. Terrail, *Joffre*, p. 344.
[19] *Ibid.*, pp. 278–279.
[20] Jean Martet, *Georges Clemenceau* (New York, 1930), p. 281. English translation.

NOTES

[21] Mayer, *op. cit.* See also Michel Corday, *The Paris Front* (London, 1933), p. 14.
[22] Maurice Paul Sarrail, *Mon commandement en Orient* (Paris, 1920), p. vii.
[23] *Ibid.*, p. xv.
[24] *Ibid.*, p. viii.
[25] Poincaré, *op. cit.*, VI, 336.
[26] *Ibid.*
[27] *Ibid.*, pp. 336–337.
[28] Georges Suarez, *Briand: sa vie–son oeuvre* (Paris, 1939), III, 197. Hereafter cited as Suarez, *Briand*.
[29] Sarrail, *op. cit.*, p. viii.
[30] Poincaré, *op. cit.*, VI, 340.
[31] *Ibid.*
[32] *Ibid.*
[33] Gallieni, *Les carnets*, p. 208.
[34] Poincaré, *op. cit.*, VI, 341.
[35] *Ibid.*
[36] *Ibid.*, p. 340.
[37] Sarrail, *op. cit.*, p. viii.
[38] Poincaré, *op. cit.*, VI, 344.
[39] Terrail, *Joffre*, pp. 82–83. See footnote.
[40] Winston S. Churchill, *The World Crisis: 1915* (New York, 1923), p. 86.
[41] Poincaré, *op. cit.*, VI, 29–30.
[42] Joffre, *op. cit.*, II, 100.
[43] *Ibid.*, p. 101.
[44] *Ibid.*, p. 102.
[45] Sarrail, *op. cit.*, p. viii.
[46] Mayer, *op. cit.*, p. 279.
[47] Sarrail, *op. cit.*, p. viii.
[48] *Ibid.*, pp. viii–ix.
[49] *Ibid.*
[50] *Ibid.*
[51] *Ibid.*, p. ix. Cf. Mayer, *op. cit.*, p. 279.
[52] *Ibid.* Cf. Coblentz, *op. cit.*, p. 103.
[53] Poincaré, *op. cit.*, VII, 11.
[54] Sarrail, *op. cit.*, p. ix.
[55] Coblentz, *op. cit.*, p. 103. Cf. Herbillon, *op. cit.*, I, 183.
[56] Pédoya, *op. cit.*, p. 353.
[57] Poincaré, *op. cit.*, VII, 30. Cf. Samuel, *op. cit.*, p. 327.
[58] Pédoya, *op. cit.*, p. 354.
[59] *Ibid.*, pp. 354–355. See also Renouvin, *op. cit.*, p. 119.
[60] Poincaré, *op. cit.*, VII, 37.
[61] *Ibid.*, p. 38.
[62] Sarrail, *op. cit.*, p. 298.
[63] *Ibid.*, p. 301. Cf. Herbillon, *op. cit.*, I, 182–183.
[64] Poincaré, *op. cit.*, VII, 76.

NOTES

[65] Sarrail, *op. cit.*, p. x.
[66] *Annales de la Chambre* ... Séance du 20 août 1915, II, 1270. Cf. Herbillon, *op. cit.*, I, 179.
[67] *Ibid.*
[68] Poincaré, *op. cit.*, VII, 46–47.
[69] Albert Pingaud, *Histoire diplomatique de la France pendant la grande guerre* (Paris, 1938), II, 56.
[70] *Ibid.*, p. 60.
[71] *Ibid.*, p. 64.
[72] William Robertson, *Soldiers and Statesmen, 1914–1918* (New York, 1926), II, 89.
[73] Pingaud, *op. cit.*, p. 86.
[74] Robertson, *op. cit.*, II, 90.
[75] Sarrail, *op. cit.*, p. xiv. Cf. Poincaré, *op. cit.*, VII, 155.
[76] *Ibid.*, p. xv.
[77] *Ibid.*
[78] Coblentz, *op. cit.*, p. 108.
[79] *Ibid.*
[80] Sarrail, *op. cit.*, p. xv.
[81] *Ibid.*
[82] Robertson, *op. cit.*, II, 91.
[83] David Lloyd George, *War Memoirs* (London, 1933), I, 527–528.
[84] Robertson, *op. cit.*, II, 92–93.
[85] Poincaré, *op. cit.*, VII, 209. Cf. Suarez, *Briand*, III, 172. The new Briand Cabinet was formed on a broad base: the Rightist minister of state, Denys Cochin, offset the radical Emile Combes, with Charles de Freycinet, Léon Bourgeois, and Jules Guesde keeping a fair balance. René Viviani was given the portfolio of justice; Admiral Lucien Lacaze, navy; Alexandre Ribot, finances; Louis Jean Malvy, interior; Paul Painlevé, public instruction; Etienne Clementel, commerce; Jules Meline, agriculture; Marcel Sembat, public works; and Gaston Doumergue, colonies. The four undersecretaries of state (munitions, supply, health, and aviation) remained in the hands of Albert Thomas, Joseph Thierry, Justin Godart, and René Besnard.
[86] Marius-Ary Leblond, *Gallieni parle* ... (Paris, 1920), p. 88.
[87] Gallieni, *Les carnets*, p. 210.
[88] *Ibid.*, pp. 207–208. Cf. Suarez, *Briand*, III, 166.
[89] Robertson, *op. cit.*, II, 94.
[90] Gallieni, *Les carnets*, p. 228.
[91] Robert David, *Le drame ignoré de l'armée d'Orient* (Paris, 1927), p. 116.
[92] *Ibid.*, p. 124.
[93] Terrail, *Sarrail*, pp. 12–13.
[94] Erich von Falkenhayn, *General Headquarters 1914–1916 and Its Critical Decisions* (London, 1919), pp. 190–192. English translation.
[95] Pédoya, *op. cit.*, p. 364.
[96] Joffre, *op. cit.*, II, 135. Cf. Terrail, *Sarrail*, p. 11.
[97] Terrail, *Joffre*, p. 87.

NOTES

[98] Joffre, *op. cit.*, II, 156–157. Cf. Terrail, *Joffre*, pp. 87–88.
[99] Pédoya, *op. cit.*, p. 365.
[100] *Ibid.*, p. 366.
[101] Victor Giraud, *Le Général de Castelnau* (Paris, 1921), p. 77.
[102] Suarez, *Briand*, III, 221.
[103] Frappa, *op. cit.*, p. 121.
[104] Suarez, *Briand*, III, 224.
[105] *Ibid.* Cf. Sarrail, *op. cit.*, pp. 71–72.
[106] Coblentz, *op. cit.*, pp. 170–171.
[107] Terrail, *Joffre*, p. 197.

NOTES TO CHAPTER 5

[1] Herbillon, *op. cit.*, I, 227.
[2] Joffre, *op. cit.*, II, 203–206.
[3] Falkenhayn, *op. cit.*, pp. 217–218.
[4] Liddell Hart, *Reputations*, p. 34.
[5] Terrail, *Joffre*, p. 122.
[6] *Ibid.*
[7] *Ibid.*, p. 123.
[8] *Ibid.*
[9] *Ibid.*, p. 124. Cf. Liddell Hart, *Reputations*, p. 34.
[10] Quoted in Gallieni, *Les carnets*, pp. 233–234, footnote.
[11] Ferry, *op. cit.*, pp. 67–70.
[12] Pédoya, *op. cit.*, p. 230.
[13] Terrail, *Joffre*, p. 128. See also Charles à Court Repington, *The First World War, 1914–1918* (London, 1920), I, 216.
[14] Ferry, *op. cit.*, p. 70.
[15] Pédoya, *op. cit.*, p. 328.
[16] Terrail, *Au sein*, p. 49.
[17] Suarez, *Briand*, III, 239.
[18] Pédoya, *op. cit.*, p. 328.
[19] *Ibid.*, p. 26.
[20] *Ibid.*, pp. 328–329.
[21] Poincaré, *op. cit.*, VII, 336.
[22] *Ibid.*
[23] Suarez, *Briand*, III, 239.
[24] Terrail, *Joffre*, p. 128.
[25] Suarez, *Briand*, III, 239–240.
[26] *Ibid.* Cf. Bugnet, *Rue St. Dominique*, pp. 89–92.
[27] Gallieni, *Les carnets*, p. 234.
[28] Joffre, *op. cit.*, II, 201.
[29] *Ibid.*, p. 202.
[30] Liddell Hart, *Reputations*, p. 35.
[31] Joffre, *op. cit.*, II, 202.
[32] Suarez, *Briand*, III, 241–242. Cf. Liddell Hart, *Reputations*, p. 96.

NOTES

[33] *Ibid.*, p. 242. Cf. Gallieni, *Les carnets*, pp. 238–239.
[34] Gallieni, *Les carnets*, p. 238, footnote.
[35] Suarez, *Briand*, III, 242. Cf. Joffre, *op. cit.*, II, 203.
[36] Giraud, *op. cit.*, p. 80.
[37] Suarez, *Briand*, III, 242.
[38] Liddell Hart, *Reputations*, p. 36.
[39] Henri Joseph Pétain, *Verdun* (New York, 1930), pp. 58–59.
[40] *Ibid.*, pp. 59–60.
[41] Suarez, *Briand*, III, 246–247.
[42] Winston S. Churchill, *The Unknown War* (New York, 1931), pp. 354–355. See also Falkenhayn, *op. cit.*, pp. 217–218.
[43] Suarez, *Briand*, III, 248.
[44] Joffre, *op. cit.*, II, 208.
[45] Corday, *op. cit.*, p. 151.
[46] Suarez, *Briand*, III, 249–250.
[47] *Ibid.*, p. 250.
[48] Pierrefeu, *G.Q.G.*, I, 125.
[49] Corday, *op. cit.*, p. 149.
[50] Auguste Bréal, *Philippe Berthelot* (Paris, 1937), p. 145.
[51] Suarez, *Briand*, III, 251.
[52] *Ibid.*
[53] Corday, *op. cit.*, p. 149. Cf. Renouvin, *op. cit.*, pp. 15–17. See also Barthélemy, *Démocratie*, pp. 357–359.
[54] Suarez, *Briand*, III, 251.
[55] Joffre, *op. cit.*, II, 212. Cf. Repington, *op. cit.*, I, 153. See also Herbillon, *op. cit.*, I, 248.
[56] Philip Guedalla, *Two Marshals: Bazaine–Pétain* (New York, 1943), p. 243.
[57] Martel, *op. cit.*, p. 33.
[58] Paul Heuzé, *La voie sacrée* (Paris, 1919), p. 6.
[59] Pétain, *op. cit.*, p. 93.
[60] Guedalla, *op. cit.*, p .267.
[61] Joffre, *op. cit.*, II, 233.
[62] Poincaré, *op. cit.*, VIII, 220.
[63] *Ibid.*
[64] Terrail, *Joffre*, pp. 62–68.
[65] *Ibid.*, p. 61.
[66] *Annales de la Chambre* ... Séance du 15 decembre 1915, II, 1867.
[67] Terrail, *Joffre*, pp. 111–112.
[68] *Ibid.*, pp. 73–74. Cf. Renouvin, *op. cit.*, pp. 78–79.
[69] *Annales de la Chambre* ... Séance du 18 fevrier 1916, I, 278.
[70] *Ibid.*, p. 279. Cf. Barthélemy, *Démocratie*, pp. 354, 361.
[71] Terrail, *Sarrail*, pp. 231–232. See also Renouvin, *op. cit.*, pp. 15–16.
[72] *Ibid.*, pp. 233–234.
[73] *Ibid.*, p. 234. Cf. Renouvin, *op. cit.*, pp. 15–16.
[74] *Ibid.*, p. 235.
[75] *Ibid.*, pp. 236–237.

NOTES

[76] *Ibid.*, p. 239.
[77] *Ibid.*, p. 240.
[78] *Ibid.*, pp. 242–243.
[79] *Ibid.*, p. 246.
[80] Gallieni, *Les carnets*, p. 278.
[81] *Ibid.*, p. 280.
[82] Poincaré, *op. cit.*, VIII, 122.
[83] Joffre, *op. cit.*, II, 386, footnote.
[84] *Ibid.*, p. 387.
[85] Bugnet, *Rue St. Dominique*, p. 134.
[86] *Ibid.*, p. 135.
[87] Herbillon, *op. cit.*, I, 263. See also Repington, *op. cit.*, I, 170.
[88] *Ibid.*, p. 266.
[89] *Ibid.*, pp. 266–267.
[90] Bugnet, *Rue St. Dominique*, p. 138. Cf. Renouvin, *op. cit.*, p. 80.
[91] *Ibid.*
[92] Churchill, *The Unknown War*, p. 363.
[93] *Le Petit Parisien*, mai 8, 1916.
[94] *Le Matin*, mai 10, 1916.
[95] Herbillon, *op. cit.*, I, 277.
[96] Suarez, *Briand*, III, 266.
[97] Poincaré, *op. cit.*, VIII, 213.
[98] Suarez, *Briand*, III, 295.
[99] Poincaré, *op. cit.*, VIII, 213.
[100] Suarez, *Briand*, III, 295.
[101] Poincaré, *op. cit.*, VIII, 216.
[102] *Ibid.*
[103] Bugnet, *Rue St. Dominique*, pp. 138–139.
[104] Herbillon, *op. cit.*, I, 278.
[105] Suarez, *Briand*, III, 266. Cf. Herbillon, *op. cit.*, I, 281.

NOTES TO CHAPTER 6

[1] Renouvin, *op. cit.*, p. 115.
[2] *Ibid.*, p. 114. Cf. Terrail, *Joffre*, p. 176. See also Terrail, *Au sein*, p. 82.
[3] Paul Allard, *Les dessous de la guerre révélés par les comités secrets* (Paris, 1932), p. 7.
[4] *Ibid.*, pp. 6–7.
[5] Poincaré, *op. cit.*, VIII, 241.
[6] Suarez, *Briand*, III, 301.
[7] Allard, *op. cit.*, p. 13.
[8] *Ibid.*, p. 14.
[9] *Ibid.*, pp. 15–16.
[10] Allard, *op. cit.*, p. 17.
[11] Herbillon, *op. cit.*, I, 293.
[12] Terrail, *Au sein*, pp. 82–84.

NOTES

[13] Corday, *op. cit.*, p. 174.
[14] Renouvin, *op. cit.*, p. 69.
[15] Poincaré, *op. cit.*, VIII, 269–270.
[16] Allard, *op. cit.*, pp. 31–32.
[17] *Ibid.*, p. 34.
[18] *Ibid.*, pp. 42–43. Cf. Terrail, *Joffre*, p. 175.
[19] Suarez, *Briand*, III, 312–313.
[20] *Ibid.*, p. 315.
[21] Marcellin, *op. cit.*, I, 284–286.
[22] *Ibid.*, I, 285.
[23] Suarez, *Briand*, III, 319.
[24] Terrail, *Au sein*, p. 57.
[25] Suarez, *Briand*, III, 323.
[26] *Ibid.*
[27] Terrail, *Au sein*, p. 59.
[28] Suarez, *Briand*, III, 325.
[29] *Ibid.*, pp. 327–328.
[30] *Ibid.*, p. 329.
[31] *Annales de la Chambre* ... Séance du 22 juin 1916, II, 1295–1296.
[32] Allard, *op. cit.*, p. 53.
[33] *Annales du Sénat* ... Séance du 9 juillet 1916, p. 736.
[34] Poincaré, *op. cit.*, VIII, 276. Cf. Terrail, *Au sein*, pp. 85–88.
[35] Renouvin, *op. cit.*, p. 123.
[36] *Annales de la Chambre* ... Séance du 26 juillet 1916, II, 1642.
[37] *Ibid.* ... Séance du 18 juillet, 1916, II, 1491.
[38] Charles Benoist, "Chronique de la quinzaine," *Revue des Deux Mondes*, 1 août, 1916, p. 715.
[39] *Ibid.*, p. 714. Cf. Barthélemy, *Démocratie*, pp. 331–333.
[40] Renouvin, *op. cit.*, p. 125.
[41] *Ibid.* The army commission of the Senate unanimously accepted Chaumet's procedure on August 1.
[42] *Annales de la Chambre* ... Séance du 27 juillet 1916, II, 1647.
[43] *Ibid.* Cf. Terrail, *Joffre*, pp. 185–186.
[44] Barthélemy, *Democratie*, p. 328.
[45] Pédoya, *op. cit.*, p. 32.
[46] *Ibid.*, p. 33.
[47] *Ibid.*
[48] Renouvin, *op. cit.*, pp. 125–126.
[49] Repington, *op. cit.*, I, 256. Cf. Joffre, *op. cit.*, II, 237.
[50] Falkenhayn, *op. cit.*, p. 267.
[51] Poincaré, *op. cit.*, VIII, 305.
[52] Joffre, *op. cit.*, II, 249–250.
[53] Allard, *op. cit.*, p. 55.
[54] Herbillon, *op. cit.*, I, 309.
[55] Joffre, *op. cit.*, II, 245.
[56] Poincaré, *op. cit.*, VIII, 294–296.

NOTES

[57] Joffre, *op. cit.*, II, 245–246.
[58] Herbillon, *op. cit.*, I, 310.
[59] Joffre, *op. cit.*, II, 246.
[60] Herbillon, *op. cit.*, I, 310–311.
[61] *Ibid.* Cf. Allard, *op. cit.*, pp. 56–57.
[62] Herbillon, *op. cit.*, I, 312.
[63] *Ibid.*, p. 313.
[64] *Ibid.*, p. 314–315. Cf. Allard, *op. cit.*, pp. 57–58.
[65] *Ibid.*, p. 315.
[66] Poincaré, *op. cit.*, VIII, 298.
[67] Joffre, *op. cit.*, II, 395–396.
[68] Herbillon, *op. cit.*, I, 323.
[69] *Ibid.*
[70] Joffre, *op. cit.*, p. 399.
[71] Herbillon, *op. cit.*, I, 323.
[72] *Ibid.*
[73] Pingaud, *op. cit.*, II, 185. Cf. Joffre, *Mémoires*, II, 309.
[74] Sarrail, *op. cit.*, pp. 367–368.
[75] *Ibid.*, p. 142.
[76] *Ibid.*, p. 144–145.
[77] *Ibid.*, pp. 156–157.
[78] Edouard Driault, *Histoire diplomatique de la Grèce de 1821 à nos jours* (Paris, 1925), V, 254.
[79] Pingaud, *op. cit.*, p. 204.
[80] Terrail, *Joffre*, p. 190.
[81] *Ibid.*, pp. 191–192.
[82] *Ibid.*, p. 203. Cf. Sarrail, *op. cit.*, p. 153.
[83] Poincaré, *op. cit.*, VIII, 324–325.
[84] Terrail, *Joffre*, p. 207.
[85] *Ibid.*
[86] Poincaré, *op. cit.*, VIII, 325.
[87] Terrail, *Joffre*, p. 208.
[88] Poincaré, *op. cit.*, VIII, 330.
[89] Terrail, *Joffre*, p. 220. Cf. Herbillon, *op. cit.*, I, 339, 354.
[90] Poincaré, *op. cit.*, VIII, 330.
[91] Sarrail, *op. cit.*, p. 179.
[92] *Ibid.*, pp. 161–162.
[93] Herbillon, *op. cit.*, I, 359.
[94] *Ibid.*
[95] Suarez, *Briand*, IV, 15.
[96] Joffre, *op. cit.*, II, 403.
[97] Suarez, *Briand*, IV, 13.
[98] Joffre, *op. cit.*, II, 404. Cf. Bugnet, *Rue St. Dominique*, p. 155.
[99] Suarez, *Briand*, IV, 16.
[100] *Ibid.*
[101] Allard, *op. cit.*, p. 59.

NOTES

[102] *Ibid.*
[103] Renouvin, *op. cit.*, p. 82.
[104] Allard, *op. cit.*, p. 63.
[105] *Ibid.*
[106] Renouvin, *op. cit.*, p. 82.
[107] Allard, *op. cit.*, p. 62.
[108] *Ibid.*, p. 63.
[109] Renouvin, *op. cit.*, p. 82.
[110] Joffre, *op. cit.*, II, 407.
[111] Suarez, *Briand*, IV, 51.
[112] Poincaré, *op. cit.*, IX, 30–31.
[113] Suarez, *Briand*, IV, 67.
[114] André Maurois, *Marshal Lyautey* (London, 1931), pp. 214–215.
[115] Suarez, *Briand*, IV, 68–69.
[116] *Ibid.*, p. 89.
[117] Joffre, *op. cit.*, II, 425.
[118] *Ibid.*, p. 427.
[119] Suarez, *Briand*, IV, 96.
[120] Poincaré, *op. cit.*, IX, 41.
[121] Allard, *op. cit.*, p. 81.

NOTES TO CHAPTER 7

[1] Pierrefeu, *G.Q.G.*, I, 213.
[2] Herbillon, *op. cit.*, II, 25.
[3] Gabriel Terrail [Mermeix, *pseud.*], *Nivelle et Painlevé: la deuxième crise du commandement* (Paris, 1919), p. 54. Hereafter cited as Terrail, *Nivelle*.
[4] Suarez, *Briand*, IV, 69.
[5] Terrail, *Nivelle*, pp. 13–14.
[6] Pierrefeu, *G.Q.G.*, I, 230.
[7] *Ibid.*
[8] *Ibid.*, p. 235.
[9] *Ibid.*, pp. 240–241.
[10] Renouvin, *op. cit.*, p. 83.
[11] Terrail, *Nivelle*, p. 14.
[12] Poincaré, *op. cit.*, IX, 47.
[13] Renouvin, *op. cit.*, p. 83. Cf. Terrail, *Nivelle*, pp. 25–26.
[14] Herbillon, *op. cit.*, II, 14.
[15] Terrail, *Nivelle*, p. 29. See also Herbillon, *op. cit.*, II, 15. Cf. Renouvin, *op. cit.*, p. 83.
[16] Commandant de Civrieux, *L'offensive de 1917 et le commandement du Général Nivelle* (Paris, 1919), p. 3.
[17] Alfred Duff Cooper, *Haig* (London, 1935), II, 40.
[18] Ferry, *op. cit.*, pp. 191–192. Cf. Robertson, *op. cit.*, II, 204.
[19] De Civrieux, *op. cit.*, p. 43.
[20] Charles Edward Callwell, *Field-Marshal Sir Henry Wilson* (New York, 1927), I, 328–329.

NOTES

[21] De Civrieux, *op. cit.*, p. 43.
[22] Paul Painlevé, *Commend j'ai nommé Foch et Pétain* (Paris, 1923), p. 32.
[23] Maurois, *op. cit.*, p. 237. Cf. Painlevé, *op. cit.*, p. 32.
[24] *Ibid.*
[25] Painlevé, *op. cit.*, p. 33.
[26] Maurois, *op. cit.*, p. 238.
[27] *Ibid.*, pp. 238–239.
[28] Herbillon, *op. cit.*, II, 22.
[29] *Ibid.*, p. 25. Cf. Terrail, *Nivelle*, pp. 19–20.
[30] Poincaré, *op. cit.*, IX, 67.
[31] Robertson, *op. cit.*, II, 208.
[32] Lloyd George, *op. cit.*, III, 1510. Cf. Pierrefeu, *G.Q.G.*, I, 262.
[33] De Civrieux, *op. cit.*, p. 60. Cf. Suarez, *Briand*, IV, 182.
[34] Louis Hubert Lyautey, *Paroles d'action* (Paris, 1927), p. 216.
[35] *Annales de la Chambre* ... Séance du 14 mars 1917, I, 703.
[36] Terrail, *Nivelle*, p. 34. Terrail says that Lyautey's suspicion was justified, what with Deputy Victor Turmel, Radical Socialist from Côtes-du-Nord, present in the Chamber. Turmel later committed suicide while in prison awaiting trial for treasonable possession of German funds.
[37] Allard, *op. cit.*, p. 100.
[38] *Annales de la Chambre* ... Séance du 14 mars 1917, I, 703.
[39] *Ibid.*
[40] *Ibid.*
[41] Maurois, *op. cit.*, p. 244.
[42] Cooper, *op. cit.*, II, 94. Ribot was actually seventy-five years old in 1917.
[43] Wright, *Poincaré*, p. 168. Cf. Terrail, *Nivelle*, p. 40.
[44] Terrail, *Nivelle*, pp. 50–53.
[45] Suarez, *Briand*, IV, 69–70. Cf. Bourget, *op. cit.*, p. 215.
[46] Poincaré, *op. cit.*, IX, 77.
[47] Terrail, *Nivelle*, p. 46.
[48] Alexander Ribot, *Journal d'Alexandre Ribot et correspondances inédites, 1914–1922* (Paris, 1936), p. 45. Hereafter cited as Ribot, *Journal*.
[49] Jean Ernest-Charles, *Painlevé* (Paris, 1925), pp. 13–14.
[50] Terrail, *Nivelle*, p. 44.
[51] *Ibid.*, p. 49.
[52] Painlevé, *op. cit.*, p. 39.
[53] Erich Ludendorff, *My War Memories, 1914–1918* (London, 1919), II, 410. English translation.
[54] Painlevé, *op. cit.*, pp. 40–41. Cf. Bourget, *op. cit.*, p. 215.
[55] Ludendorff, *op. cit.*, II, 405–407.
[56] Painlevé, *op. cit.*, p. 41.
[57] Bourget, *op. cit.*, pp. 215–216.
[58] Ribot, *Journal*, p. 48, footnote.
[59] Quoted in Bourget, *op. cit.*, p. 215.
[60] Painlevé, *op. cit.*, p. 42.
[61] *Ibid.*

NOTES

[62] Charles M. Mangin, *Comment finit la guerre* (Paris, 1920), p. 122. Cf. De Civrieux, *op. cit.*, p. 69.
[63] Painlevé, *op. cit.*, pp. 44-45.
[64] *Ibid.*
[65] Terrail, *Nivelle*, pp. 65-66.
[66] Painlevé, *op. cit.*, p. 47.
[67] *Ibid.*, p. 46.
[68] *Ibid.*, p. 49.
[69] Mangin, *op. cit.*, p. 123.
[70] Painlevé, *op. cit.*, pp. 49-50.
[71] *Ibid.*, p. 50.
[72] Ribot, *Journal*, p. 76.
[73] Painlevé, *op. cit.*, p. 51.
[74] *Ibid.*
[75] Poincaré, *op. cit.*, IX, 101.
[76] *Ibid.* Cf. Herbillon, *op. cit.*, II, 50.
[77] *Ibid.*
[78] *Les armées françaises*, V:I, 562. Cf. Aulard, *op. cit.*, p. 254.
[79] Poincaré, *op. cit.*, IX, 101.
[80] See de Civrieux, *op. cit.*, pp. 67, 70-72.
[81] Bourget, *op. cit.*, pp. 217-218.
[82] Mangin, *op. cit.*, p. 124.
[83] *Les armées françaises*, V:I, 563.
[84] Mangin, *op. cit.*, p. 124.
[85] De Civrieux, *op. cit.*, p. 75.
[86] *Ibid.*, p. 76.
[87] *Ibid.*, pp. 76-77.
[88] *Les armées françaises*, V:I, 564-565.
[89] Mangin, *op. cit.*, p. 124.
[90] *Les armées françaises*, V:I, 565.
[91] Terrail, *Nivelle*, p. 72.
[92] Mangin, *op. cit.*, p. 24.
[93] *Les armées françaises*, V:I, 565-566.
[94] Mangin, *op. cit.*, pp. 124-125.
[95] Herbillon, *op. cit.*, II, 53.
[96] Wright, *Poincaré*, p. 201. Cf. Herbillon, *op. cit.*, II, 55.
[97] *Les armées françaises*, V:I, 566.
[98] Alexandre Ribot, *Lettres à un ami* (Paris, 1924), p. 190. See also version of de Civrieux, *op. cit.*, pp. 90-91.
[99] Ludendorff, *op. cit.*, II, 419. Cf. Cooper, *op. cit.*, II, 82.
[100] Pierrefeu, *G.Q.G.*, I, 264.
[101] Poincaré, *op. cit.*, IX, 117.
[102] Ludendorff, *op. cit.*, II, 424-425.
[103] Ribot, *Lettres*, p. 191. Cf. Ferry, *op. cit.*, p. 239.
[104] Allard, *op. cit.*, p. 118.
[105] De Civrieux, *op. cit.*, pp. 148-149. Cf. Painlevé, *op. cit.*, p. 62.

NOTES

[106] Painlevé, *op. cit.*, p. 62.
[107] De Civrieux, *op. cit.*, p. 149.
[108] Wright, *Poincaré*, pp. 200–201.
[109] Poincaré, *op. cit.*, IX, 114. Cf. Mangin, *op. cit.*, p. 134. See also Herbillon, *op. cit.*, II, 65–66.
[110] *Ibid.*, p. 115.
[111] Allard, *op. cit.*, p. 127. Cf. Mangin, *op. cit.*, p. 134.
[112] *Ibid.*, pp. 126–127.
[113] Painlevé, *op. cit.*, pp. 62–63.
[114] Herbillon, *op. cit.*, II, 64.
[115] Painlevé, *op. cit.*, p. 63.
[116] De Civrieux, *op. cit.*, p. 151.
[117] Cooper, *op. cit.*, II, 88–89.
[118] Painlevé, *op. cit.*, pp. 380–382.
[119] On this point see also Mangin, *op. cit.*, p. 135.
[120] Painlevé, *op. cit.*, p. 65. Cf. de Civrieux, *op. cit.*, p. 152.
[121] *Ibid.* Cf. Terrail, *Nivelle*, pp. 98–99.
[122] *Ibid.*, pp. 65–66.
[123] De Civrieux, *op. cit.*, p. 153.
[124] Herbillon, *op. cit.*, II, 68–69.
[125] *Ibid.*, p. 69.
[126] Terrail, *Nivelle*, p. 94.
[127] De Civrieux, *op. cit.*, p. 165.
[128] Herbillon, *op. cit.*, II, 69.
[129] De Civrieux, *op. cit.*, p. 166.
[130] *Ibid.*, p. 165.
[131] Herbillon, *op. cit.*, II, 69.
[132] Terrail, *Nivelle*, p. 96.
[133] Ribot, *Journal*, p. 82.
[134] *Ibid.*, p. 80. See also Repington, *op. cit.*, I, 540-541.
[135] Cooper, *op. cit.*, II, 94.
[136] *Ibid.*, p. 95. Cf. Ribot, *Journal*, p. 80.
[137] Painlevé, *op. cit.*, pp. 86–87.
[138] Cooper, *op. cit.*, II, 95.
[139] Painlevé, *op. cit.*, p. 87.
[140] Ribot, *Journal*, pp. 82–83.
[141] Poincaré, *op. cit.*, IX, 123.
[142] Terrail, *Nivelle*, p. 119.
[143] Poincaré, *op. cit.*, IX, 123. Cf. Ribot, *Journal*, p. 84.
[144] Herbillon, *op. cit.*, II, 73. Cf. Terrail, *Nivelle*, p. 103.
[145] *Ibid.*, pp. 73–74.
[146] *Ibid.*, p. 75. Cf. Terrail, *Nivelle*, pp. 103–104.
[147] *Ibid.*
[148] Terrail, *Nivelle*, pp. 101, 106. Cf. Mangin, *op. cit.*, p. 136.
[149] *Ibid.*, p. 108.
[150] Painlevé, *op. cit.*, p. 97. Cf. Pierrefeu, *G.Q.G.*, I, 272.

NOTES

[151] *Ibid.*, p. 72.
[152] Mangin, *op. cit.*, p. 147.
[153] Ribot, *Journal*, p. 85.
[154] Herbillon, *op. cit.*, II, 81. Cf. Pierrefeu, *G.Q.G.*, I, 273.
[155] Quoted in Poincaré, *op. cit.*, IX, 130.
[156] De Civrieux, *op. cit.*, p. 192.
[157] Painlevé, *op. cit.*, p. 113.
[158] Aulard, *op. cit.*, p. 213.
[159] Herbillon, *op. cit.*, II, 84.
[160] Terrail, *Nivelle*, p. 140.
[161] Edward Louis Spears, *Prelude to Victory* (London, 1939), p. 376.

NOTES TO CHAPTER 8

[1] Callwell, *op. cit.*, I, 342.
[2] Painlevé, *op. cit.*, p. 133. Cf. Cooper, *op. cit.*, II, 95.
[3] *Ibid.*, p. 206.
[4] *Ibid.*, p. 208.
[5] *Ibid.*, pp. 126–127. Cf. Repington, *op. cit.*, II, 58. See also Gabriel Terrail [Mermeix, *pseud.*], *Le commandement unique: Foch et les armées d'occident* (Paris, 1920), pp. 185–186. Hereafter cited as Terrail, *Le commandement unique*.
[6] Terrail, *Nivelle*, p. 170.
[7] Allard, *op. cit.*, p. 175.
[8] Terrail, *Nivelle*, p. 171.
[9] George Adam, *Treason and Tragedy: An Account of French War Trials* (London, 1929), p. 96.
[10] Allard, *op. cit.*, p. 175. Cf. Terrail, *Nivelle*, p. 172.
[11] Aulard, *op. cit.*, p. 260.
[12] Terrail, *Nivelle*, p. 174.
[13] Allard, *op. cit.*, p. 170.
[14] *Ibid.*, p. 260. Cf. Painlevé, *op. cit.*, pp. 153–156.
[15] See Poincaré, *op. cit.*, IX, 148–149.
[16] Aulard, *op. cit.*, p. 260. Cf. Pierrefeu, *G.Q.G.*, II, 17–18.
[17] Painlevé, *op. cit.*, p. 153. Cf. Pierrefeu, *G.Q.G.*, II, 17.
[18] *Ibid.*, pp. 154–156. Cf. General Staff report quoted in Louis Jean Malvy, *Mon crime* (Paris, 1921), p. 135. See also the corroboration in the 17 prefectural reports quoted by Malvy in pages 137–143 of his book.
[19] Adam, *op. cit.*, p. 96.
[20] Terrail, *Nivelle*, pp. 186–187.
[21] *Ibid.*, pp. 187–188. See also Pétain's letter to Foch, abstracted in Herbillon, *op. cit.*, II, 98.
[22] Auguste M. Laure, *Au 3ème bureau du troisième G.Q.G.* (Paris, 1921), p. 22.
[23] Aulard, *op. cit.*, p. 261.
[24] *Ibid.*, p. 262. Cf. Pierrefeu, *G.Q.G.*, II, 36.
[25] Painlevé, *op. cit.*, p. 158.
[26] *Ibid.*, pp. 131–132.

NOTES

[27] *Ibid.*, p. 143.
[28] Ludendorff, *op. cit.*, II, 426.
[29] Pierrefeu, *G.Q.G.*, II, 33.
[30] André Geraud [Pertinax, *pseud.*], *Les fossoyeurs: Pétain* (New York, 1943), II, 17.
[31] Aulard, *op. cit.*, p. 262.
[32] *Ibid.*
[33] Painlevé, *op. cit.*, p. 145.
[34] For an example, see Poincaré, *op. cit.*, IX, 156.
[35] Painlevé, *op. cit.*, p. 145.
[36] Allard, *op. cit.*, p. 200.
[37] Painlevé, *op. cit.*, p. 146.
[38] Painlevé, *op. cit.*, pp. 146–147.
[39] *Ibid.*, p. 147. Cf. Adam, *op. cit.*, p. 99.
[40] Ribot, *Lettres*, pp. 215–216.
[41] Painlevé, *op. cit.*, p. 177.
[42] Allard, *op. cit.*, pp. 114–115.
[43] *Ibid.*, p. 120.
[44] *Ibid.*, pp. 123–124. Cf. Marcellin, *op. cit.*, II, 124.
[45] *Ibid.*, p. 131.
[46] *Ibid.*, p. 132. For a different version, see Wright, *Poincaré*, p. 204.
[47] Poincaré, *op. cit.*, IX, 149. General Pétain steeled the nerve of the government in making such a refusal by testifying at a *Comité de guerre* on May 31, 1917, that if French delegates attended the Socialist Conference at Stockholm, it would be construed by the French army as "the equivalent of an armistice, and it would be impossible to obtain from the troops the vigorous effort and support which the circumstances required." See Ribot, *Journal*, p. 139, footnote.
[48] Allard, *op. cit.*, pp. 133–134.
[49] *Ibid.*, pp. 168–171.
[50] *Ibid.*, pp. 135–136.
[51] *Ibid.*, pp. 145–147.
[52] *Ibid.*, pp. 182–190.
[53] *Ibid.*, p. 142.
[54] *Ibid.*, pp. 142–143. Cf. Poincaré, *op. cit.*, IX, 183.
[55] *Annales de la Chambre* ... Séance du 7 juillet 1917, II, 1724.
[56] *Ibid.*
[57] Terrail, *Nivelle*, p. 221.
[58] Painlevé, *op. cit.*, pp. 179–180.
[59] *Annales de la Chambre* ... Séance du 7 juillet 1917, II, 1744–1745.
[60] Painlevé, *op. cit.*, p. 181.
[61] Poincaré, *op. cit.*, IX, 191.
[62] Malvy, *op. cit.*, p. 148.
[63] C. Paget, ed., *Revue des causes célèbres: Les procès de trahison* (Paris, 1918), p. 176.
[64] *Annales de la Chambre* ... Séance du 7 juillet 1917, II, 1736.
[65] Georges Clemenceau, *L'antipatriotisme devant le Sénat* (Paris, 1917), p. 23.

NOTES

[66] Poincaré, *op. cit.*, IX, 263.
[67] Aulard, *op. cit.*, p. 278.
[68] *Ibid.*
[69] *Ibid.*
[70] *Annales de la Chambre* ... Séance du 18 septembre 1917, II, 2409.
[71] Aulard, *op. cit.*, p. 279.
[72] Painlevé, *op. cit.*, p. 213.
[73] Herbillon, *op. cit.*, II, 140.
[74] Painlevé, *op. cit.*, p. 194.
[75] *Ibid.*, p. 201.
[76] *Ibid.*, p. 202.
[77] Herbillon, *op. cit.*, II, 154. Cf. Pierrefeu, *G.Q.G.*, II, 58.
[78] Painlevé, *op. cit.*, p. 202. Cf. Pierrefeu, *G.Q.G.*, II, 57.
[79] *Ibid.*, pp. 220–221.
[80] Paget, *op. cit.*, p. 170.
[81] Aulard, *op. cit.*, p. 279. Cf. Poincaré, *op. cit.*, IX, 281.
[82] Adam, *op. cit.*, p. 43.
[83] *Annales de la Chambre* ... Séance du 4 octobre 1917, II, 2681–2682.
[84] Painlevé, *op. cit.*, pp. 169–170.
[85] Renouvin, *op. cit.*, p. 126. Cf. Pédoya, *op. cit.*, pp. 37–38.
[86] *Ibid.*
[87] Painlevé, *op. cit.*, pp. 182–183. Cf. Marcellin, *op. cit.*, II, 204–205.
[88] *Ibid.*, p. 184. Cf. Repington, *op. cit.*, II, 206.
[89] *Ibid.*, p. 185.
[90] *Ibid.*, p. 241. Cf. Robertson, *op. cit.*, I, 219.
[91] Lloyd George, *op. cit.*, IV, 2385–2389.
[92] Painlevé, *op. cit.*, p. 254.
[93] Lloyd George, *op. cit.*, IV, 2395. Cf. Robertson, *op. cit.*, I, 218–219.
[94] Painlevé, *op. cit.*, p. 254.
[95] Lloyd George, *op. cit.*, IV, 2402.
[96] *Annales de la Chambre* ... Séance du 13 novembre 1917, III, 3038.
[97] *Ibid.*, p. 3044.

NOTES TO CHAPTER 9

[1] Jean Jules Mordacq, *Le ministère Clemenceau: journal d'un témoin* (Paris, 1930), I, 205. Hereafter cited as Mordacq, *Le ministère Clemenceau*.
[2] Léon Daudet, *Clemenceau qui sauva la patrie* (Paris, 1930), p. 66.
[3] Georges Suarez, *La vie orgueilleuse de Clemenceau* (Paris, 1930), p. 16. Hereafter cited as Suarez, *Clemenceau*.
[4] *Ibid.*, pp. 298–299.
[5] *Ibid.*, p. 348.
[6] Geoffrey Bruun, *Clemenceau* (Cambridge, Mass., 1943), p. 122.
[7] Poincaré, *op. cit.*, IX, 367.
[8] Mordacq, *Le ministère Clemenceau*, I, 2–3.
[9] *Ibid.*, p. 6.
[10] *Ibid.*, pp. 9–11. Cf. Bruun, *op. cit.*, p. 135.

NOTES

[11] Aulard, *op. cit.*, p. 288.
[12] *Annales de la Chambre* ... Séance du 20 novembre 1917, III, 3053–3054.
[13] *Ibid.*, p. 3057.
[14] Callwell, *op. cit.*, II, 23.
[15] Tasker H. Bliss, "The Evolution of the Unified Command," *Foreign Affairs*, I (December 15, 1922), p. 6.
[16] Georges Clemenceau, *Grandeur and Misery of Victory* (New York, 1930), p. 37. English translation. Hereafter cited as Clemenceau, *Grandeur and Misery*.
[17] Charles Seymour, ed., *The Intimate Papers of Colonel House* (New York, 1928), III, 213. Cf. Terrail, *Le commandement unique*, p. 169.
[18] Lloyd George, *op. cit.*, V, 2721.
[19] Clemenceau, *Grandeur and Misery*, p. 38.
[20] Quoted in Seymour, *op. cit.*, III, 214.
[21] *Ibid.*
[22] Jean Jules Mordacq, *Le commandement unique* (Paris, 1929), p. 34. Hereafter cited as Mordacq, *Le commandement unique*.
[23] Seymour, *op. cit.*, III, 252.
[24] *Ibid.*, p. 253.
[25] *Ibid.*, p. 253–254.
[26] *Ibid.*, pp. 259–260.
[27] *Ibid.*, p. 261.
[28] Callwell, *op. cit.*, II, 32.
[29] Seymour, *op. cit.*, III, 263.
[30] Poincaré, *op. cit.*, IX, 393.
[31] Clemenceau, *Grandeur and Misery*, p. 37.
[32] Mordacq, *Le ministère Clemenceau*, I, 125.
[33] Poincaré, *op. cit.*, IX, 413.
[34] *Ibid.*
[35] *Ibid.*
[36] *Ibid.*, X, 56.
[37] Painlevé, *op. cit.*, p. 220.
[38] Martet, *op. cit.*, p. 194.
[39] *Annales de la Chambre* ... Séance du 22 novembre 1917, III, 3098.
[40] Adam, *op. cit.*, p. 101. Cf. Marcellin, *op. cit.*, II, 269.
[41] Alfred Fabre-Luce, *Caillaux* (Paris, 1933), p. 127. See also Joseph Caillaux, *Devant l'histoire: mes prisons* (Paris, 1920), pp. 71–72, 149–154.
[42] Adam, *op. cit.*, p. 136.
[43] Cour de Justice, *Procès Caillaux* (Paris, 1920), p. 74. The Senate did find Caillaux guilty of maneuvers which furnished the enemy with useful information. For this offense he was sentenced to imprisonment, but the sentence was made retroactive and the deputy was released at once.
[44] Terrail, *Sarrail*, p. 144. Cf. Mordacq, *Le ministère Clemenceau*, I, 72.
[45] On Pétain's unpopularity with the Leftist deputies who suspected him of being a royalist and an authoritarian, see the diary of the British ambassador to Paris, Lord Bertie, *The Diary of Lord Bertie of Thame, 1914–1918* (London, 1924), II, 77. Cf. Repington, *op. cit.*, I, 549.

NOTES

[46] Poincaré, *op. cit.*, IX, 402.
[47] *Ibid.*, p. 403.
[48] Mordacq, *Le ministère Clemenceau*, I, 74, footnote.
[49] Bliss, *loc. cit.*, p. 10.
[50] Lloyd George, *op. cit.*, V, 2718. Cf. Peter E. Wright, *At the Supreme War Council* (New York, 1921), p. 88. Hereafter cited as Wright, *War Council*. See also Cooper, *op. cit.*, II, 218.
[51] *Ibid.*, V, 2738.
[52] Clemenceau, *Grandeur and Misery*, p. 35.
[53] *Ibid.*, p. 22.
[54] Lloyd George, *op. cit.*, V, 2739–2740.
[55] Mordacq, *Le commandement unique*, p. 46.
[56] André Tardieu, *The Truth about the Treaty* (Indianapolis, 1921), p. 37.
[57] Cooper, *op. cit.*, II, 222.
[58] Wright, *War Council*, p. 65.
[59] Robertson, *op. cit.*, I, 231. Cf. Cooper, *op. cit.*, II, 223–224.
[60] Bliss, *loc. cit.*, p. 17.
[61] *Ibid.*, pp. 18–19.
[62] Ferdinand Foch, *Mémoires pour servir à l'histoire de la guerre de 1914–1918* (Paris, 1931), II, iv.
[63] Bliss, *loc. cit.*, p. 19. Cf. Foch, *op. cit.*, II, iv.
[64] *Ibid.*, p. 22.
[65] Callwell, *op. cit.*, II, 65. Cf. Cooper, *op. cit.*, II, 234.
[66] *Ibid.*, p. 66. Cf. Cooper, *op. cit.*, II, 234.
[67] *Ibid.*, p. 67.
[68] *Ibid.*, p. 69.
[69] Lloyd George, *op. cit.*, V, 2871.
[70] Callwell, *op. cit.*, II, 66. Cf. Lloyd George, *op. cit.*, V, 2873.
[71] Cooper, *op. cit.*, II, 234. Cf. Lloyd George, *op. cit.*, V, 2863, 2874.
[72] *Ibid.*, p. 236.
[73] Foch, *op. cit.*, II, lvi.
[74] Lloyd George, *op. cit.*, V, 2875.
[75] Foch, *op. cit.*, II, lvi. Cf. Lloyd George, *op. cit.*, V, 2875.
[76] Bliss, *loc. cit.*, p. 24.
[77] Mordacq, *Le commandement unique*, pp. 54–55.
[78] Quoted in Edward Mead Earle, ed., *Makers of Modern Strategy* (Princeton, 1944), pp. 303–304, footnote. Cf. Lloyd George, *op. cit.*, V, 2871. See also Cooper, *op. cit.*, II, 240.
[79] Callwell, *op. cit.*, II, 70–71.
[80] Ludendorff, *op. cit.*, II, 594.
[81] Alphonse Grasset, *Le maréchal Foch* (Paris, 1919), p. 65.
[82] Ludendorff, *op. cit.*, II, 589.
[83] *Ibid.*, p. 590.
[84] *Ibid.*, p. 595.
[85] *Les armées françaises*, VI:1, 226.
[86] *Ibid.*, pp. 232–233.

NOTES

[87] *Ibid.*, p. 246.
[88] Lloyd George, *op. cit.*, V, 2900.
[89] Herbillon, *op. cit.*, II, 228.
[90] Poincaré, *op. cit.*, X, 83.
[91] Wright, *War Council*, p. 135. Cf. Foch, *op. cit.*, II, 18.
[92] Lloyd George, *op. cit.*, V, 2894.
[93] See Milner's memorandum on Doullens Conference, quoted *in extenso* as an appendix to Clemenceau's *Grandeur and Misery of Victory*, pp. 407–423. For above reference, see pp. 411–412.
[94] Bliss, *loc. cit.*, p. 27. Cf. Foch, *op. cit.*, II, 19.
[95] Clemenceau, *Grandeur and Misery*, p. 412. Cf. Foch, *op. cit.*, II, 19.
[96] *Ibid.*, p. 413.
[97] *Ibid.*, p. 414.
[98] Bliss, *loc. cit.*, p. 27.
[99] Poincaré, *op. cit.*, X, 58.
[100] Martet, *op. cit.*, p. 197, footnote.
[101] Raymond Recouly, "Foch and Clemenceau," *Scribner's Magazine*, LXXVI (October, 1929), p. 358.
[102] Mordacq, *Le commandement unique*, pp. 73–74. Cf. Foch, *op. cit.*, II, 20.
[103] Clemenceau, *Grandeur and Misery*, p. 416. See also Bliss, *loc. cit.*, p. 27. Cf. Foch, *op. cit.*, II, 20.
[104] Mordacq, *Le commandement unique*, pp. 74–75.
[105] Poincaré, *op. cit.*, X, 88. Cf. Lloyd George, *op. cit.*, V, 2908–2909. See also Ribot, *Journal*, p. 257.
[106] Clemenceau, *Grandeur and Misery*, p. 39. Cf. Mordacq, *Le commandement unique*, p. 80.
[107] Tardieu, *op. cit.*, p. 38. Cf. Mordacq, *Le commandement unique*, p. 81.
[108] Lloyd George, *op. cit.*, V, 2906.
[109] Clemenceau, *Grandeur and Misery*, p. 418.
[110] Terrail, *Le commandement unique*, p. 212.
[111] *Ibid.*, p. 213.
[112] Clemenceau, *Grandeur and Misery*, p. 421.
[113] Foch, *op. cit.*, II, 24.
[114] Wright, *War Council*, p. 143. Cf. Foch, *op. cit.*, II, 24.
[115] Bliss, *loc. cit.*, p. 28.
[116] Seymour, *op. cit.*, III, 437, footnote.
[117] Bliss, *loc. cit.*, p. 29.
[118] *Ibid.*, p. 30.

NOTES TO CHAPTER 10

[1] Clemenceau, *Grandeur and Misery*, p. 124.
[2] John J. Pershing, *My Experiences in the World War* (New York, 1931), I, 373–374.
[3] *Ibid.*, II, 30.
[4] Foch, *op. cit.*, II, 44.

NOTES

[5] Clemenceau, *Grandeur and Misery*, pp. 44–45.
[6] Raymond Recouly, *Foch: My Conversations with the Marshal* (New York, 1929), pp. 19–20. English translation. Hereafter cited as Recouly, *Foch*.
[7] Clemenceau, *Grandeur and Misery*, p. 64.
[8] *Ibid.*, p. 65. Cf. Mordacq, *Le ministère Clemenceau*, II, 89–91.
[9] Clemenceau, *Grandeur and Misery*, p. 74.
[10] Charles Bugnet, *Foch Speaks* (New York, 1929), pp. 250–252. Hereafter cited as Bugnet, *Foch Speaks*.
[11] Clemenceau, *Grandeur and Misery*, p. 84.
[12] *Ibid.*, p. 75.
[13] Recouly, *Foch*, pp. 22–23.
[14] T. Bentley Mott, *Twenty Years as Military Attaché* (New York, 1937), p. 242.
[15] Recouly, *Foch*, p. 28.
[16] Paul von Hindenburg, *Out of My Life* (New York, 1921), II, 172.
[17] Grasset, *op. cit.*, p. 76.
[18] Ferry, *op. cit.*, p. 305.
[19] *Ibid.*, pp. 316–317.
[20] Foch, *op. cit.*, II, 88. Cf. Basil Henry Liddell Hart, *Foch: The Man of Orleans* (London, 1931), p. 318.
[21] Liddell Hart, *Foch*, p. 319.
[22] Ludendorff, *op. cit.*, II, 627–628.
[23] Mordacq, *Le ministère Clemenceau*, II, 49. Cf. Clemenceau, *Grandeur and Misery*, p. 51.
[24] *Ibid.*, p. 43.
[25] *Ibid.*
[26] Clemenceau, *Grandeur and Misery*, p. 46.
[27] Hindenburg, *op. cit.*, II, 171–172.
[28] Quoted in Mordacq, *Le commandement unique*, p. 145, footnote.
[29] Clemenceau, *Grandeur and Misery*, p. 47.
[30] Foch, *op. cit.*, II, 91.
[31] *Ibid.*
[32] Clemenceau, *Grandeur and Misery*, p. 52, footnote. Cf. Mordacq, *Le ministère Clemenceau*, II, 73–75.
[33] Poincaré, *op. cit.*, X, 197.
[34] *Ibid.*, p. 198. Cf. Mordacq, *Le ministère Clemenceau*, II, 51.
[35] Herbillon, *op. cit.*, II, 260–261.
[36] Poincaré, *op. cit.*, X, 199.
[37] Mordacq, *Le ministère Clemenceau*, II, 50–51.
[38] Clemenceau, *Grandeur and Misery*, p. 49.
[39] Mordacq, *Le ministère Clemenceau*, II, 52.
[40] Poincaré, *op. cit.*, X, 203.
[41] Renouvin, *op. cit.*, p. 146.
[42] See, for example, Lloyd George, *op. cit.*, VI, 3083. Cf. Mordacq, *Le ministère Clemenceau*, II, 56–57.
[43] Pershing, *op. cit.*, II, 79–80.

NOTES

[44] Mordacq, *Le ministère Clemenceau*, II, 54–56.
[45] Clemenceau, *Grandeur and Misery*, pp. 45–46.
[46] *Ibid.*, pp. 54–55.
[47] Poincaré, *op. cit.*, X, 213.
[48] Pershing, *op. cit.*, II, 85.
[49] *Annales de la Chambre* ... Séance du 4 juin 1918, II, 1460.
[50] *Ibid.*, p. 1462.
[51] *Ibid.*
[52] *Ibid.*, p. 1463.
[53] *Ibid.*, p. 1469.
[54] Clemenceau, *Grandeur and Misery*, p. 55. Cf. Recouly, *Foch*, pp. 217–218.
[55] *Ibid.*, p. 61.
[56] *Ibid.*, p. 60.
[57] *Ibid.*, p. 62.
[58] Pershing, *op. cit.*, II, 172.
[59] Liddell Hart, *Foch*, p. 335.
[60] *Ibid.*, p. 336. Cf. Hindenburg, *op. cit.*, II, 195.
[61] Pershing, *op. cit.*, II, 157–158.
[62] Foch, *op. cit.*, II, 160.
[63] Hindenburg, *op. cit.*, II, 201–202.
[64] Pershing, *op. cit.*, II, 172.
[65] *Ibid.* Cf. Recouly, *Foch*, p. 59.
[66] *Ibid.*, p. 175.
[67] Hindenburg, *op. cit.*, II, 212–214.
[68] *Ibid.*, pp. 221–222.
[69] Pershing, *op. cit.*, II, 266.
[70] *Ibid.*, II, 291–292.
[71] Mott, *op. cit.*, pp. 256–257.
[72] Recouly, *Foch*, pp. 23–24.
[73] Mordacq, *Le ministère Clemenceau*, II, 267. Cf. Cooper, *op. cit.*, II, 389.
[74] *Ibid.*
[75] Clemenceau, *Grandeur and Misery*, p. 81.
[76] *Ibid.*
[77] *Ibid.*, pp. 82–83.
[78] *Ibid.*, p. 85.
[79] Mordacq, *Le ministère Clemenceau*, II, 268. See also Jean Jules Mordacq, *Pouvait-on signer l'armistice à Berlin?* (Paris, 1930), p. 13.
[80] Mott, *op. cit.*, pp. 254–256.
[81] Recouly, *Foch*, p. 26.
[82] *Ibid.*
[83] Foch, *op. cit.*, II, 250–251.
[84] *Ibid.*, p. 252.
[85] Italics Foch's.
[86] Foch, *op. cit.*, p. 253.
[87] Clemenceau, *Grandeur and Misery*, p. 114.
[88] Wright, *Poincaré*, p. 182.

NOTES

[89] Harry R. Rudin, *Armistice 1918* (New Haven, Conn., 1944), p. 186.
[90] *Ibid.*, p. 183.
[91] Jean Jules Mordacq, *La verité sur l'armistice* (Paris, 1929), p. 58. Hereafter cited as Mordacq, *La verité*.
[92] Recouly, *Foch*, pp. 39–40.
[93] Foch, *op. cit.*, II, 279.
[94] *Ibid.*, p. 278.
[95] Recouly, *Foch*, pp. 42–43.
[96] *Ibid.*, pp. 42–43.
[97] *Ibid.*, p. 44. Cf. Mordacq, *Le ministère Clemenceau*, II, 288–290.
[98] Foch, *op. cit.*, II, 279.
[99] Recouly, *Foch*, pp. 43–44.
[100] *Ibid.*, p. 44.
[101] Mordacq, *La verité*, p. 19.
[102] *Ibid.*
[103] *Ibid.*

BIBLIOGRAPHY

Bibliography

A TOPIC as controversial as the one treated in this book poses a difficult problem in documentation. It is notorious that memoirs, diaries, campaign journals, and the like are usually elaborate attempts at self-justification. Equally biased are many biographies. But in this particular subject, the official governmental publications are no less partisan. As a French scholar (to whom an early draft of this manuscript was submitted) observed: "All the authorities ... are suspicious because partisan.... The official publications, of course, are the worst: they are not satisfied with *suppressio veri et suggestio falsi."*

Such being the case, the task was to draw "reliable conclusions out of wholly unreliable material." At first blush, this would appear a well-nigh impossible undertaking, calling for powers of divination, at least. But in reality the problem is not insoluble. It is possible to weigh contradictory assertions and arrive at a fairly probable conclusion. Most statements contain at least half truths. Furthermore, military history is a relatively exoteric field, since the outcome of battle is usually an open secret, although opinions may differ as to the means employed and the degree of responsibility for success or failure. The same is true of political contests and of politico-military strife. One must set against one another conflicting accounts, one must look for some possible "area of agreement" and then exercise "common sense" in a judgment based upon "probabilities" which, in the last analysis, might turn out to be merely the author's "conceptual framework" or bias. But even so, the same problem exists for nearly all historical studies. When one knows the evidence to be manifestly biased, as in this case, one is at least on guard against being misled by either side.

BIBLIOGRAPHY

GOVERNMENT DOCUMENTS

France. Assemblée nationale. *Annales de la Chambre des Députés, débats parlementaires, sessions ordinaire et extraordinaires de 1914–1918*. Paris, 1918–1919.

France. Assemblée nationale, 1871–*Annales du Sénat, débats parlementaires, sessions ordinaire et extraordinaires de 1914–1918*. Paris, 1915–1919.

France. Ministère de la Guerre. Etat-Major de l'armée. Service historique. *Les armées françaises dans la grande guerre*. Paris, 1922–1938. 92 vols.

France. Assemblée nationale, 1871–*Journal officiel de la république française*. Paris, 1871–.

HANDBOOKS

Samuel, René and George Bonet-Maury. *Les parlementaires français: 1900–1914*. Paris, 1914.

NEWSPAPERS

La Guerre Sociale, 1915. Paris.
Le Journal, 1915. Paris.
Le Matin, 1916. Paris.
Le Petit Parisien, 1916. Paris.

COLLECTED LETTERS AND WORKS

Lyautey, Louis Hubert. *Paroles d'action*. Paris, 1927.
Ribot, Alexandre. *Lettres à un ami*. Paris, 1924.
Seymour, Charles, ed. *The Intimate Papers of Colonel House*. New York, 1926–1928. 4 vols.

DIARIES

Bertie, Lord. *The Diary of Lord Bertie of Thame, 1914–1918*. London, 1924. 2 vols.

Corday, Michel. *The Paris Front: An Unpublished Diary, 1914–1918*. London, 1933. English translation of *L'envers de la guerre: journal inédit*.

Gallieni, Joseph Simon. *Les carnets de Gallieni*. Paris, 1932.

Repington, Charles à Court. *The First World War, 1914–1918*. London, 1920. 2 vols.

Ribot, Alexandre. *Journal d'Alexandre Ribot et correspondances inédites, 1914–1922*. Paris, 1936.

BIBLIOGRAPHY

REMINISCENCES AND AUTOBIOGRAPHIES

Baquet, Louis Henry. *Souvenirs d'un directeur de l'artillerie.* Paris, 1921.

Bugnet, Charles. *Foch Speaks.* New York, 1929. English translation.

Caillaux, Joseph. *Devant l'histoire: mes prisons.* Paris, 1920.

Clemenceau, Georges. *Grandeur and Misery of Victory.* New York, 1930. English translation.

Dartige, Louis. *Souvenirs de guerre d'un amiral, 1914–1916.* Paris, 1920.

Dubail, Yvon Edmond. *Quatre années de commandement, 1914–1918.* Paris, 1921. 3 vols.

Falkenhayn, Erich von. *General Headquarters 1914–1916 and Its Critical Decisions.* London, 1919. English translation.

Ferry, Abel. *La guerre vue d'en bas et d'en haut.* Paris, 1920.

Foch, Ferdinand. *Mémoires pour servir à l'histoire de la guerre de 1914–1918.* Paris, 1931. 2 vols.

Frappa, Jean-José. *Makédonia: souvenirs d'un officier de liaison en Orient.* Paris, 1921.

Gallieni, Joseph-Simon. *Mémories du général Gallieni.* Paris, 1920.

Gheusi, Pierre Barthélemy. *Guerre et théâtre, 1914–1918.* Paris, 1919.

Herbillon, Emile E. *Souvenirs d'un officier de liaison pendant la guerre mondiale.* Paris, 1930. 2 vols.

Hindenburg, Paul von. *Out of My Life.* New York, 1921. 2 vols. English translation.

Humbert, Charles. *Chacun son tour.* Paris, 1925.

Joffre, Joseph Jacques Césaire. *Mémoires du maréchal Joffre.* Paris, 1932. 2 vols.

Klotz, Louis L. *De la guerre à la paix.* Paris, 1924.

Lloyd George, David. *War Memoirs of David Lloyd George.* London, 1933–1936. 6 vols.

Ludendorff, Erich. *My War Memories, 1914–1918.* London, 1919. 2 vols. English translation.

Malvy, Louis Jean. *Mon crime.* Paris, 1921.

Mangin, Charles M. *Comment finit la guerre.* Paris, 1920.

Messimy, Adolphe. *Mes souvenirs.* Paris, 1937.

Mordacq, Jean Jules. *Le ministère Clemenceau: journal d'un témoin.* Paris, 1930–1931. 4 vols.

Mott, T. Bentley. *Twenty Years as Military Attaché.* New York, 1937.

Painlevé, Paul. *Comment j'ai nommé Foch et Pétain.* Paris, 1923.

Pershing, John J. *My Experiences in the World War.* New York, 1931. 2 vols.

Pétain, Henri Joseph. *Verdun.* New York, 1930. English translation.

BIBLIOGRAPHY

Pierrefeu, Jean de. *G.Q.G. secteur I: trois ans au grand quartier général par le rédacteur du "communiqué."* Paris, 1920. 2 vols.

Poincaré, Raymond. *Au service de la France: neuf années de souvenirs.* Paris, 1926–1933. 10 vols.

Recouly, Raymond. *Foch: My Conversations with the Marshal.* New York, 1929. English translation of *Le Mémorial de Foch.*

Robertson, William. *Soldiers and Statesmen, 1914–1918.* London, 1926. 2 vols.

Sarrail, Maurice Paul Emmanuel. *Mon commandement en Orient.* Paris, 1920.

Spears, Edward L. *Liaison, 1914: A Narrative of the Great Retreat.* London, 1930.

Wilhelm, Kronprinz, *Mémoires du Kronprinz.* Paris, 1922. French translation.

Wright, Peter E. *At the Supreme War Council.* New York, 1921.

BIOGRAPHIES

Arthur, Sir George. *Life of Lord Kitchener.* New York, 1920. 3 vols.

Bréal, Auguste. *Philippe Berthelot.* Paris, 1937.

Bruun, Geoffrey. *Clemenceau.* Cambridge, Mass., 1943.

Callwell, Charles E. *Field-Marshal Sir Henry Wilson.* New York, 1927. 2 vols.

Coblentz, Paul. *The Silence of Sarrail.* London, 1930. English translation.

Cooper, Alfred Duff. *Haig.* London, 1935. 2 vols.

Daudet, Léon. *Clemenceau qui sauva la patrie.* Paris, 1930.

Ernest-Charles, Jean. *Painlevé.* Paris, 1925.

Fabre-Luce, Alfred. *Caillaux.* Paris, 1933.

Guedalla, Philip. *Two Marshals: Bazaine–Pétain.* New York, 1943.

Geraud, André [Pertinax, pseud.]. *Les fossoyeurs: Pétain.* New York, 1943. 2 vols.

Giraud, Victor. *Le général de Castelnau.* Paris, 1921.

Grasset, Alphonse. *Le maréchal Foch.* Paris, 1919.

Leblond, Marius-Ary. *Gallieni parle ...* Paris, 1920.

Liddell Hart, Basil Henry. *Foch: The Man of Orleans.* London, 1931.

———. *Reputations Ten Years After.* Boston, 1928.

Martel, Francis. *Pétain: Verdun to Vichy.* New York, 1943.

Martet, Jean. *Georges Clemenceau.* New York, 1930. English translation.

Maurois, André. *Marshal Lyautey.* London, 1931. English translation.

Mayer, Emile. *Nos chefs de 1914.* Paris, 1930.

Palmer, Frederick. *Bliss, Peacemaker: The Life and Letters of General Tasker Howard Bliss.* New York, 1934.

Recouly, Raymond. *Joffre.* New York, 1931. English translation.

Suarez, Georges. *Briand: sa vie–son oeuvre.* Paris, 1938–1941. 6 vols.

———. *Le vie orgueilleuse de Clemenceau.* Paris, 1920.

BIBLIOGRAPHY

MONOGRAPHS AND SPECIAL STUDIES

Adam, George. *Treason and Tragedy: An Account of French War Trials.* London, 1929.

Albert, François. *Le procès Malvy.* Paris, 1919.

Allard, Paul. *Les dessous de la guerre révélés par les comités secrets.* Paris, 1932.

Barthélemy, Joseph. "Le contrôle parlementaire en temps de guerre," *in* Gaston Jezé, Joseph Barthélemy, and Charles Rist, *Problèmes de politique et finances de guerre.* Paris, 1915.

———. *La démocratie et politique étrangère.* Paris, 1917.

Benoist, Charles. "Chronique de la quinzaine," *Revue des Deux Mondes* (août, 1916).

Bliss, Tasker H. "The Evolution of the Unified Command," *Foreign Affairs,* I (December 15, 1922).

Bourget, Jean Marie. *Gouvernement et commandement: les leçons de la guerre mondiale.* Paris, 1930.

Bugnet, Charles. *Rue St. Dominique et G.Q.G. ou les trois dictatures de la guerre.* Paris, 1937.

Civrieux, Commandant de. *L'offensive de 1917 et le commandement du général Nivelle.* Paris, 1919.

Clemenceau, Georges. *L'antipatriotisme devant le Sénat.* Paris, 1917.

Cour de Justice. *Affaire Caillaux, Loustalot et Comby.* Paris, 1919.

———. *Procès Caillaux.* Paris, 1920.

Daudet, Léon. *Le poignard dans le dos.* Paris, 1918.

Earle, Edward Mead, ed. *Makers of Modern Strategy.* Princeton, 1944.

Heuzé, Paul. *La voie sacrée.* Paris, 1919.

Laure, Auguste Marie. *Au 3éme bureau du troisième G.Q.G.* Pairs, 1921.

Maurice, Frederick. "Joffre, Gallieni and the Marne," *The Contemporary Review* (June, 1927).

Michon, Georges. *La préparation à la guerre.* Paris, 1935.

Millerand, Alexandre. *L'effort et le devoir français.* Paris, 1917.

Mordacq, Jean Jules. *Le commandement unique.* Paris, 1929.

———. *Pouvait-on signer l'armistice à Berlin?* Paris, 1930.

———. *La verité sur l'armistice.* Paris, 1929.

Paget, C., ed. *Revue des causes célèbres: Les procès de trahison.* Paris, 1918.

Pierrefeu, Jean de. *La deuxième bataille de la Marne.* Paris, 1919.

———. *Plutarque a menti.* Paris, 1923.

Pédoya, Jean Marie Gustav. *La commission de l'armée pendant la grande guerre.* Paris, 1921.

BIBLIOGRAPHY

Recouly, Raymond. "Foch and Clemenceau," *Scribner's Magazine*, LXXXVI (October, 1929).
Renouvin, Pierre. *Les formes du gouvernement de guerre.* New Haven, Conn., 1925.
Roux, Marie de. *Le défaitisme et les manoeuvres pro allemandes.* Paris, 1918.
Rudin, Harry R. *Armistice 1918.* New Haven, Conn., 1944.
Samuel, René. *Le parlement et la guerre 1914–1915.* Paris, 1918.
Tardieu, André. *France and America.* New York, 1927.
———. *The Truth about the Treaty.* Indianapolis, 1921.
Terrail, Gabriel [Mermeix, pseud.]. *Le commandement unique: Foch et les armées d'occident.* Paris, 1920.
———. *Joffre: première crise du commandement.* Paris, 1919.
———. *Nivelle et Painlevé: la deuxième crise du commandement.* Paris, 1919.
———. *Sarrail et les armées d'Orient.* Paris, 1920.
———. *Au sein des commissions.* Paris, 1924.
Vergnet, Paul. *L'affaire Caillaux.* Paris, 1920.
Weill, Georges. "Les gouvernements et la presse pendant la guerre," *Revue d'histoire de la guerre mondiale* (avril, 1933).
Wright, Gordon. *Raymond Poincaré and the French Presidency.* Stanford University, Calif., 1942.

GENERAL WORKS

Anonymous. *As They Are: French Political Portraits.* New York, 1923.
Aulard, A. E. Bouvier, and A. Ganem. *Histoire politique de la grande guerre.* Paris, 1924.
Bagger, Eugene. *Eminent Europeans.* New York, 1922.
Barthélemy, Joseph. *The Government of France.* New York, 1919.
Churchill, Winston S. *The World Crisis: 1915.* New York, 1923.
———. *The Unknown War.* New York, 1931.
Committee of Imperial Defence. *History of the Great War: Military Operations—Macedonia.* Cyril Falls and A. F. Becke, eds. London, 1933. 2 vols.
David, Robert. *Le drame ignoré de l'armée d'Orient.* Paris, 1927.
Driault, Edouard. *Histoire diplomatique de la Grèce de 1821 à nos jours.* Paris, 1925–1926. 5 vols.
Marcellin, Léopold. *Politique et politiciens pendant la guerre.* Paris, 1922–1924. 4 vols.
Pingaud, Albert. *Histoire diplomatique de la France pendant la grande guerre.* Paris, 1938. 2 vols.
Spears, Edward L. *Prelude to Victory.* London, 1939.
Zévaès, Alexandre. *Le parti socialiste de 1904 à 1923.* Paris, 1923.

INDEX

INDEX

Index

Accambray, Léon, 102, 116, 190
Almereyda, alias of Miguel Vigo, 182, 183, 202
Amade, General d', 75
André, Louis, 9, 68
Anthoine, General, 162, 185
Army commission of Chamber: function, 37; convened, 38, 39; commission president states intentions, 45; rejects Millerand's new pass formula, 60, 61; list of accomplishments, 64, 65; protests against promotion of Joffre to generalissimo, 86; warned of Verdun's danger, 90, 91, 92; demands explanations for press criticism of Joffre, 112, 113; assistance from Briand, 121; demands sanctions for mistakes in Chemin des Dames drive, 164; criticizes Mangin, 167; wants to "break" Nivelle and Mangin, 178; informed by Clemenceau of difficulty of unifying command, 200
Army commission of Senate, 37, 46, 47, 51, 121
Augagneur, Victor, 81, 83
Aurelle de Paladines, Louis d', 7

Bailloud, Maurice, 77, 78
Bapst, General, 122
Barrès, Maurice, 183
Barthélemy, Joesph, 2, 37, 109
Basch, Victor, 81
Battles of Chemin des Dames, First, 159, 161, 162, 182; Second, 224, 225, 226, 227
Battle of March 21, 1918, 211, 212, 213

Battle of the Marne, 29, 30, 31
Battle of the Somme, 125, 126
Bazaine, Marshal, 6
Bazelaire, General, 232
Beauvais, 141
Bel, Lieutenant Colonel, 113, 135
Benazet, Paul, 41, 81, 114, 117
Bepmale, Jean, 123
Berteaux, Maurice, 17
Berthelot, Henri, 15, 132, 232, 233
Berthelot, Philippe, 99
Besnard, René, 64
Bliss, Tasker H., 198, 199, 218, 238
Boehn, General von, 224, 225
Bolo Affair (Paul Bolo), 186, 202
Bonaparte, Napoleon, 6
Bonnet Rouge affair, 182, 183, 184, 186, 190
Bonneval, General, 122
Bordeaux, 28, 29, 35
Boudenoot, Louis Charles, 47
Boulanger, Georges, 8, 17
Bourgeois, Léon, 95, 164
Bratianu, Ioan, 131
Briand, Aristide: visits Gallieni, 32; supports "Eastern" strategy, 42; sees in Sarrail affair opportunity for Eastern campaign, 72; appointed president of council, 84; wants to promote Joffre to generalissimo, 85; defends promotion before army commission, 86; asks Gallieni to warn Joffre about Verdun, 93; persuades Gallieni to conciliate Joffre, 95; orders Joffre to hold Verdun, 98, 99, 100; rebukes Gallieni for note on High Command, 106; appoints Roques successor to Gallieni, 107;

INDEX

Briand, Aristide (cont.)
questioned on press criticism of Joffre, 112, 113; demands removal of certain Young Turks, 113; consents to secret committee, 114, 116; defends command, 117, 119; outlines conception of relations of government and command, 120, 121, 122; requests secret committee of Senate, 123; tries to conciliate Joffre over Roques letter, 130; hopeful over Rumania's entry into war, 130; decides to send Roques on inspection mission to Salonika, 134; defends policy before second secret committee, 135; announces Joffre technical adviser of government, 136; survives second secret committee, 137; reshuffles Cabinet, 137, 138; resigns over Lyautey speech, 148; alleged to be critic of Pétain, 227
Brugère, General, 182, 187
Buat, Edmond, 43, 44, 64, 113
Bülow, Karl von, 28, 30
Bugnet, Charles, 48, 222
Bulgaria, 80
Byng, General, 212

Caesarism, 3, 6, 8
Caillaux, Joseph, 202, 203
Calais Conference, 146
Carnot, Lazare, 5, 6
Cary, Langle de, 30, 97, 98, 109, 122
Castelnau, Edouard de, 26, 86, 96, 100, 111, 112, 126, 129, 133, 135, 141, 156
Chantilly, 35, 42, 43, 57, 71, 73, 77, 86, 87, 93, 98, 101, 117, 119, 129, 141, 143
Chaumet, Charles, 124
Churchill, Winston, 75, 109
Civrieux, Commandant de, 162
Claudel, Colonel, 97, 98
Clausewitz, Karl von, 1, 2, 3
Clemenceau, Georges, 6; concern over munition shortages, 38; member Senate's army commission, 47; urges Sarrail not to go to Salonika, 81, 82; attacks Malvy for leniency toward defeatists, 183; symbol of will to victory, 192; "combat" keynote to second ministry, 192; previous career, 193; indicates intention to outline strategy as well as policy, 195; relates difficulty of unifying command in west, 197; approves House-Bliss plan for president of Supreme War Council, 199; reviews negotiations for army commission, 200; informs *Comité de guerre* that he has last word in strategy, 200, 201; his attack on Malvy forces trial of former minister of interior, 202; brings Caillaux to trial, 202, 203; removes Sarrail, 203; equivocates toward Foch and General Reserve, 204; ambivalence toward Jesuit-trained Foch, 205; sides with Pétain and Haig in dispute over Reserve, 208, 209; tells Foch to "shut up" in conference with English, 210, 211; attends conference at Pétain's headquarters, 213; scoffs at British proposal to make him a generalissimo, 214, 215; accepts Milner's proposal to make Foch coördinator of western front strategy, 217; expects Foch to give orders to Allied subordinates, 220; wants Foch to incorporate American regiments into French ranks, 221, 222, 223; tries to learn facts about Second Battle of Chemin des Dames, 225; refrains from interfering with Foch's strategic plans, 226; prepares for interpellation, 227, 228; defends Foch before Allies, 228, 229; defends Foch before Parliament, 229, 230; demands that Foch change secondary commands, 231; disturbed over slowing down of American drive, 234; writes Foch

INDEX

rebuke which Poincaré thinks too severe, 235; convinced Foch and Poincaré are against him, 236; writes Foch to appeal to President Wilson to compel Pershing to obey, 237; agrees with Foch on armistice, 238, 239; puts Foch in his place over question of peace terms, 240, 241
Compiègne Conference, 156, 157, 158, 159, 164, 188
Constantine, King, 81, 131
Cordonnier, General, 132
Cornet, Lucien, 62, 63
Coutanceau, General, 90

Dalbiez, Victor, 180
Dardanelles, 71, 72, 73, 74, 75, 77, 78, 80
Daudet, Léon, 186, 202
Degoutte, General, 232
Delahaye, Dominique, 40
Delahaye, Jules, 148
Delcassé, Théophile, 27, 80, 81, 83
Deschanel, Paul, 20, 44, 65, 116, 148, 201
DeWeerd, H. A., 4
Diagne, M., 179, 180
Doullens Conference, 199, 216, 217, 218
Doumer, Paul, 17, 31, 69, 116, 184
Doumergue, Gaston, 29, 73, 133, 138
Dreyfus Affair, 8
Driant, Emile, 91, 92, 93, 97, 116
Dubail, Yvon, 70, 90, 107, 109, 122, 203
Dubois, General, 122
Dubost, Antonin, 167, 168, 200, 201
Duchêne, General, 162, 163, 188, 212, 225, 227, 232
Dumouriez, Charles, 5
Duval, M., 183

Etienne, Eugène, 17, 23, 24

Falkenhayn, Erich von, 84, 97, 132
Favre, Albert, 160, 179
Fayolle, Emile, 125
Ferry, Abel, 58, 59, 91, 102, 103, 114, 116, 117, 136, 180
Foch, Ferdinand: reports Sarrail's distrust of Joffre, 43; aids army commissioners, 125; in Battle of Somme, 126; passed by for Nivelle, 140; chief of staff for Pétain, 168; agrees with Pétain and Painlevé on defensive strategy, 171; supports Pétain's strategy, 184, 185; report on Chemin des Dames, 187; sent to Piave front, 188; cannot serve as inter-Allied chief of staff without first resigning as French chief of staff, 189; obstacles in directing Allied armies, 196; future authority outlined in House-Bliss memorandum, 199; viewed askance by Clemenceau for his clericalism, 205; indignant over attitude of Pétain and Haig toward General Reserve, 208, 209; protests against burking of General Reserve, 210; told to "shut up" by Clemenceau, 211; attends conference at Pétain's headquarters, 213; favors strong stand with heavy commitment of reserves, 214; opposes British plan to make Clemenceau generalissimo, 215; inspires Clemenceau with fighting spirit, 216; silences Clemenceau for his jibe, 217; adviser to Franco-British armies in France, 218; becomes commander in chief of Allied armies operating in France, 219, 220; conciliatory attitude toward Haig and Pershing, 221, 222, 223; recognizes German feint in Second Battle of Chemin des Dames, 225; moves available reserves to Marne, 226; refuses to denude Flanders of reserves, 227; defended in Parliament by Clemenceau, 229, 230; consents to

INDEX

Foch, Ferdinand (cont.)
changes in secondary commands, 231, 232; launches great counteroffensive, 232; instructs Americans to wipe out St. Mihiel salient, 233; wrangles with Clemenceau over slowing down of American drive, 234, 235; asked by British for several American divisions, 235; evades request, 235; Clemenceau demands that he appeal to President Wilson to order Pershing to renew drive, 237; instructs Americans to renew drive, 238; agrees with Clemenceau on armistice, 238, 239; is rebuffed by Clemenceau and Pichon over peace terms, 239, 240, 241
Franchet d'Esperey, Louis, 30, 81, 144, 153, 156, 158, 232
Freemasons, 9, 12, 68
French, John, 30
Freycinet, Charles de, 7, 47, 51, 107, 116, 142, 155

Gallifet, Gaston, 9
Gambetta, Léon, 7
Gallieni, Joseph Simon, 12, 22; recalled from retirement, 23; military governor of Paris, 27, 29; Battle of Marne, 30, 31; forbidden to write government, 32; "demoted" by Joffre, 33; replacement by Sarrail proposed, 81; appointed war minister, 83; promotes Joffre to generalissimo, 86; told to warn Joffre about Verdun, 93; sends historic letter, 94, 95; analyzes role of command in theory and practice, 103, 104, 105; offers resignation, 106, 107
Gallwitz, General, 211
General Reserve, 204, 205, 206, 207, 208, 209, 210, 211
Gérard, Augustin, 73, 74, 109
Gervais, Auguste, 141
Gillain, General, 220

Godart, Justin, 64, 187
Gourand, Henri Joseph, 74, 75, 182, 187
Gough, General, 212
Grandmaison, Colonel de, 13
Grévy, Jules, 8
Grodet, Albert, 148
Guesde, Jules, 27, 28
Guillaumat, Adolphe, 125, 185, 203
Guiraud, Jean Marie, 180

Haig, Douglas, 146, 161, 164, 197, 198, 204, 206, 207, 209, 210, 212, 213, 216, 217, 235
Hamilton, Ian, 75
Herbillon, Emile, 26; told government is to leave Paris, 28; reports on Poincaré's gloom, 33; told of shortages, 34; reports Joffre's suspicions of Pédoya, 56; reports Joffre's unwillingness to have Millerand enter combat zone, 57, 58; told to warn Joffre about Verdun sector, 109; protests dismissal of Young Turks, 113; reports on dispute between Roques and Joffre over artillery allocation, 126, 127, 128, 129; concerned over Roques' letter giving parliamentarians carte blanche in visiting front, 130; suspects Lyautey of returning to plan for a generalissimo, 143; disturbed by Lyautey's skepticism toward Nivelle, 145; told to ask Nivelle to postpone attack on Craonne, 162, 163; delivers Nivelle's protest, 166; reports criticism of Pétain's defensive strategy, 184; pleased with Verdun and Malmaison drives, 185; tells government Pétain fears effects of British retreat, 212
Herr, General, 90, 91
Hervé, Gustave, 19, 68
Hindenburg, Paul von, 224, 226
Hirschauer, Edouard, 47, 162, 163
House, Edward M., 198, 199

INDEX

Humbert, Charles, 37, 38, 47, 60, 116, 186
Humbert, General, 212

Jaurès, Jean, 16, 19
Jeanneney, Jules, 47, 235
Jesuits, 9
Jobert, Aristide, 179
Joffre, Joseph Jacques: early career 12, 13; orders general mobilization, 15; favors press censorship, 21; his Plan XVII, 22; administrative authority, 24; appoints liaison officers, 26; Battle of the Marne, 30, 31; censors battle reports to government, 32; brooks no rivals, 33; concerned over shortages, 34; threatens to resign over proposed "Eastern" diversion, 41, 42; protests against shuttle trips of mobilized deputies, 51; forbids Millerand to enter combat zone, 57, 58; disciplines Abel Ferry, 59; campaign to replace him with Sarrail, 69; selects Dubail as inspector general of Sarrail's army, 70; opposes sending French reinforcements to Dardanelles, 75; favors Gallieni as war minister, 83; resents Sarrail's taking orders from War Ministry, 85; overconfident about Verdun, 89; rebukes Gallieni for "meddling," 94, 95; reluctant to send reserves to Verdun, 97; suspects Roques of officiousness, 109; criticized in articles, 110, 111; disappointed in Battle of Somme, 126; angered by Roques' promise of guns to Pétain, 127; orders Roques to postpone trip to Verdun and Somme, 128, 129; threatens to resign over letter from Roques, 130; orders Sarrail to attack Bulgaria, 131; sends Berthelot to Rumania, 132; wants to send Castelnau to Salonika again, 133; technical adviser of government, 136;
charges Briand misled him about new assignment, 137; resigns, 138
Jugy, M., 148

Kitchener, Lord, 84
Klotz, Louis L., 17, 36, 181
Kluck, Alexander von, 23, 28, 30

Lacaze, Lucien, 106, 133, 137, 138, 154, 156
Lafayette, Marquis de, 5
Lanrezac, Charles, 22, 23, 26
Law, Bonar, 147
League of Patriots, 8
Le Matin, 111, 118
Le Petit Parisien, 110, 112, 113, 118
Lloyd George, David: favors Balkan campaign, 82; War Cabinet, 137; assists Painlevé in setting up Supreme War Council, 188, 189; understands English opposition to unity of command, 197; pretends to oppose an Allied generalissimo, 198; opposes House-Bliss plan, 199; nominates Foch as executive of General Reserve, 206; supports Haig in dispute over General Reserve, 210; asked by Haig to arrange for a supreme commander, 213; supports Foch during Second Battle of Chemin des Dames, 228
London Conference, 146
Loucheur, Louis, 213, 216
Ludendorff, Erich, 159, 176, 211, 225
Luxburg, Count, 202
Lyautey, Hubert, 138, 142, 143, 145, 147, 148

Mackensen, General, 132
MacMahon, Marshal, 6, 7, 18
Maginot, André, 113, 114, 116, 117, 154, 160, 164
Mahon, General, 82, 84

INDEX

Maistre, General, 175, 185
Malvy, Louis Jean, 19, 71, 73, 143, 164, 168, 182, 183, 186, 202
Mangin, Charles, 153, 160, 161, 162, 163, 167, 232
Marcellin, Léopold, 41, 49, 53, 61, 119
Maud'huy, General, 232
Maunoury, Michel, 30
Maurras, Charles, 41
Mayer, Emile, 70
Mazel, General, 153, 160, 161, 162, 166, 167
Merrheim, Adolphe, 201
Messimy, Adolph, 12, 13, 14, 16, 17, 23, 27, 154, 155
Micheler, General, 144, 153, 154, 155, 156, 158, 161, 165, 166, 167, 168, 200, 232
Millerand, Alexandre: appointed war minister, 27, 28; deference to command, 32; opposes government's return to Paris, 35; agrees to convening of army commission, 38; rebukes Poincaré, 47; restricts parliamentarians in visiting War Ministry, 48, 49; tries to exclude commissioners from war plants, 50; attitude toward army of maneuver, 52; rejects claims of army commission, 54; told by Joffre not to enter combat zone, 57; specifies forms for passes to front, 60, 61; insists on new form, 62; holds up Cornet mission to front, 63; unruffled by badgering, 66; orders Sarrail to make known his wishes, 76; assigns "busy work" to Sarrail, 77; refers to Sarrail in speech to Chamber, 79; reproved by fellow Cabinet members, 80; replaced by Gallieni in War Ministry, 83; allows commander to promote generals, 109; embarrasses Painlevé by questions about Supreme War Council, 189, 190
Milner, Lord, 188, 213, 214, 215, 216, 217

Moltke, Helmuth von, 30
Mordacq, Jean, 193, 194, 195, 206, 215, 216, 225, 227, 228, 235, 236, 241
Mutinies of 1917, 172, 173, 174, 176, 177, 178

Napoleon III, 6
National Defense, Government of, 6
Nivelle, Robert: appointed commander in chief of Armies of North and Northeast, 138; early career, 140; moves headquarters to Beauvais, 141, 142; inherits Franco-British offensive commitment, 144; ignorant of Painlevé's doubts about his plan, 152, 153; promises to break off offensive if no break-through, 154; defends strategy at Compiègne Conference, 157; threatens to resign, 158; orders continuation of Chemin des Dames drive, 160, 161; angered over Poincaré's intervention in Craonne drive, 163; to be removed by Painlevé, 164; yoked with Pétain, 165; told to call off attack upon Brimont, 165; protests to Painlevé, Ribot, and Poincaré, 166; asks removal of Mangin, 167; refuses to resign, 168; assigned to nonexistent army group, 169

Orlando, Vittorio E., 228

Painlevé, Paul: defends Sarrail, 133; appointed war minister, 149; early career, 169; misgivings over Nivelle offensive, 150; in quandary over course of action, 151, 152; summons conference at rue St. Dominique, 154; favors delay in Nivelle's offensive, 155; attends Compiègne Conference, 156; tries to mollify Nivelle,

INDEX

158; rumored to be threatening Nivelle, 160; decides to remove Nivelle, 163; moves indirectly to sack Nivelle, 164; denies he told Nivelle not to attack Brimont, 166; ready to resign if Nivelle is not dismissed, 168; agrees with Pétain and Foch on defensive strategy, 171; dissents from Pétain on cause of mutinies, 173, 174; favors retention of *conseils de guerre* but suspension of right of appeal, 176, 177; commutes all mutineer sentences but twenty-three, 177; agrees to secret committee, 178; defends government's policy and Pétain's strategy, 180; appoints board to investigate Chemin des Dames campaign, 182; appointed president of the council, 183; promises firm course, 184; criticized for not taking offensive, 184; pleased over small Verdun and Malmaison offensives, 185; smeared by *affaires,* 186; grants Socialists concession on parliamentary inspection, 187; worried over "erroneous" report on Chemin des Dames offensive, 187; handicapped in explaining intentions with regard to Supreme War Council, 189; overthrown, 190

Paris, 6, 19, 25, 26, 27, 28, 35, 141, 172, 173, 226

Parliament, 11, 12; convenes, 16; conception of its role during war, 17, 18; passes special legislation, 20; adjourns, 21; responsibility for war policy, 37; relation with commissions, 39; reconvenes, 40; objections to prolonged session, 41; promises rigorous "inspection," 44; members excluded from War Ministry, 48; supervision of War Ministry, 55; wants its rights respected, 55; circularized on Sarrail's merits, 68; parliamentarians' disingenuousness in secret committee, 119, 120;

shrinks from direct supervision of armies, 124, 125; appeased by Joffre's removal, 139; Nivelle widely known in Parliament, 141; Painlevé declares Parliament did not meddle in Chemin des Dames strategy, 162; eclipsed by executive power in Clemenceau's ministry, 192, 195, 196; no longer able to insist on secret committees after the scandalous *affaires,* 228; ready to sack the High Command, 229

Pédoya, Jean Marie, 18; convenes army commission of Chamber, 38; states intentions of commission, 45; desires to inspect army zone but recognizes difficulty, 46; attempts to visit Verdun, 48; protests against inaccessibility of War Ministry, 49; asserts right of commissioners to visit war plants, 49, 50; tries to enter army zone at Dunkirk, 53; asserts right of commissioners to go "wherever necessary," 54, 55; arouses opposition in Chamber, 61; protests Millerand's new pass form, 62; protests placing Near Eastern Command under Joffre, 86; warns of danger to Verdun, 91; tries to visit Nancy-Lunéville sector, 92; pleased with Chaumet proposal, 125

Pellé, General, 113, 135

Pénelon, Jean, 26, 93, 126

Pershing, John J., 219, 221, 222, 223, 229, 233, 235, 236, 237, 238

Pétain, Henri Philippe: account of attack on Verdun, 96; given command of Army of Verdun, 100; defense strategy, 101; promised guns by Roques, 127; passed over for Nivelle, 140; to command army group in Nivelle offensive, 144; considered as chief of staff, 152; doubtful about rupture in Nivelle offensive, 153; attends Compiègne Conference, 156; hopes to pierce line, 158; questioned

INDEX

Pétain, Henri Philippe (cont.)
about continuation of offensive, 161; Nivelle's chief of staff and successor designate, 165; defensive strategy, 170; dissents from Painlevé over cause of mutinies, 173, 174; orders defensive strategy, reliance upon artillery, and improves lot of troops, 175; allows Maistre to slacken drive along Chemin des Dames, 176; orders staff officers to visit front, 176; demands restoration of courts-martial, 176; commutes all mutineer sentences except twenty-three, 177; explains defensive strategy to *Comité de guerre*, 184; mounts offensives at Verdun and Malmaison, 185; eclipsed by Clemenceau, 195; offers to resign, 201; reluctant to dismiss Sarrail, 203; opposes General Reserve, 204; assists Haig in trying to by-pass president of General Reserve, 206, 207; anxious over English withdrawal in battle of March 21, 1918, 212; pessimistic at conference of March 25, 213; charged with defeatism by Clemenceau, 216; Socialists demand dismissal of, 228

Pichon, Stephen, 195, 240, 241
Pierre, Eugène, 17
Pierrefeu, Jean de, 42, 43
Poincaré, Raymond: war message, 11; visits Russia, 13; decrees siege, 20; opposes leaving Paris, 28; gloomy over stalemate, 33; has to postpone visit to front, 34; suggests "Eastern" strategy, 41; fears parliamentary "usurpation," 44, 45; rebuked for visiting War Ministry, 47; interested in proposed army of maneuver, 52; seeks solution to inspection problem, 57; appoints Briand president of council, 83; warns of Verdun's danger, 93; disturbed over press criticism of High Command, 113; opposes secret committee, 116; optimistic over defense of command, 118; concerned over direct parliamentary missions to armies, 123; angered by Joffre's request to postpone trip to Verdun and Somme, 127, 128, 129; refuses Briand's resignation, 137; names Joffre marshal, 138, 139; warned by Freycinet of Lyautey's ambition, 142; distressed over Nivelle's complaints about Lyautey's conduct, 145, 146; asks Ribot to form Cabinet, 148; concerned over Ribot's warning from Messimy, 155; attends Compiègne Conference, 156; tries to mollify Nivelle, 158; disgusted over parliamentary meddling in drive of Chemin des Dames, 160; warns of attacking Craonne too soon, 162; supports Painlevé in dispute over Brimont attack, 166; cedes to Pétain right of pardon in *conseils de guerre*, 177; accused of trying to block appointment of Pétain, 179; appoints Clemenceau president of council, 193; claims Clemenceau wanted to be a generalissimo, 214; told of Pétain's pessimism by Clemenceau, 216; accused of supporting Foch against Clemenceau, 222; upbraided by Clemenceau for receiving malcontents, 227; sides with Foch in dispute with Clemenceau over Pershing's actions, 235, 236; favors unconditional surrender, 238

Public Safety, Committee of, 5, 9
Pugliesi-Conti, 40
Putz, General, 232

Raffin-Dugens, 63, 148
Rapallo agreements, 189, 196, 197, 199, 200
Rawlinson, Henry, 208, 219
Recouly, Raymond, 221, 223, 237, 239, 240
Renaudel, Pierre, 47, 117, 136, 160

INDEX

Renouard, Georges, 144
Renoult, René, 181, 227, 228
Renouvin, Pierre, 123
Reynies, Colonel de, 175
Ribot, Alexandre, 72, 137, 139, 146; forms Cabinet, 148; defines war policy, 151, 152; attends rue St. Dominique conference, 154; disturbed over Messimy's warning, 155; attends Compiègne Conference, 156; tries to soothe Nivelle, 158; notes French losses in Chemin des Dames drive, 159; reports rumors of parliamentary meddling, 160; opposed to secret committee, 178; defends Poincaré over appointment of Pétain; forced to resign, 183; foreign minister in Painlevé Cabinet, 183
Robertson, William, 82, 189, 206, 207
Robespierre, Maximilien, 5
Roques, Pierre Auguste: appointed war minister, 107; spirit of "independence," 108; warns Joffre about Verdun sector, 109; rumored to have permitted press criticism of Joffre, 111, 112; defends High Command, 119; dispute with Joffre over artillery for Pétain, 127; angered by Joffre's demand that he forego a visit to Verdun and Somme sectors, 127, 128; agrees to visit Joffre at Chantilly, 129; writes Joffre that parliamentarians cannot be prevented from getting military information, 130; sent to inspect Salonika sector, 134; dismissed by Briand, 136, 137
Rousset, Léonce, 41
Rupprecht, Crown Prince, 211, 212

Saint-Just, Antoine de, 5
Salonika: Sarrail plans campaign, 79, 80; front to be opened against Bulgaria, 81; entrenched camp laid out, 84; British reluctant to support Salonika expedition, 122; Joffre proposes to send Castelnau on a mission to Salonika, 133
Sarrail, Maurice Paul, 22; suspects Joffre's loyalty to republic, 43; orders Charles Humbert to leave Verdun, 60; position in the French army, 67; early career, 67, 68; puffed as successor to Joffre, 69; dismissed and ordered to Paris, 71; receptive to a Near Eastern command if it is augmented, 74; ordered to make known his wishes, 76; named commander of the Army of the Orient, 76; sketches possible campaigns in the Levant, 78, 79; seeks clarification of his assignment at Salonika, 81; embarks for Greece, 82; retreats from Krivoloh and lays out entrenched camp at Salonika, 84; protests to Briand over being subjected to Joffre, 87; praised in secret committee, 123; contends could not attack Bulgarians as ordered, 131; accused of meddling in Greek politics, 133; Roques defends, 133; defended in secret committee, 135; restored to war minister's control, 136; removed by Clemenceau, 203
Sarraut, Albert, 73, 74
Schlieffen plan, 22, 26, 30
Schoen, von, 13, 15
Secret committee: first, 114, 115, 116, 117, 118, 119, 120; second, 135, 138; third, 147; fourth, 178, 179, 180, 181, 182
Sembat, Marcel, 27, 28
Sibille, Maurice, 122
Socialists, 19, 26, 27, 43, 47, 61, 67; suspicion in Sarrail affair, 70; protest Sarrail's treatment, 73; oppose Sarrail's retirement, 74, 77; angered by Millerand's reference to Sarrail affair, 79, 80; profit from Sarrail affair, 88; demand secret committee, 113, 114; Briand identifies dismissed generals, 122; feared in Sarrail af-

293

INDEX

Socialists (cont.)
 fair, 134, 135; indignant over Lyautey's insult in Parliament, 148; opposed to execution of mutineers, 177; passports refused to Stockholm Conference, 179; attack Ribot Cabinet's policy, 179; pleased by Painlevé's promised solicitude for troops, 181; refuse to serve in Cabinet with Ribot as foreign minister, 184; indignant over charge of Malvy's treason, 186; win concession on parliamentary inspection, 187; notify Clemenceau against reactionary policy, 196; demand dismissal of Pétain, 228; claim they belong to a chained assembly, 230
Spears, Edward L., 169
Supreme War Council, 188, 189, 190, 196, 197, 198, 199, 200, 204, 205, 210, 220

Tardieu, André, 112, 116, 123, 124, 206
Thierry, Joseph, 64
Thomas, Albert, 64, 149, 154, 155, 183
Turmel, Victor, 186

Urbal, General d', 122

Varenne, Alexandre, 183, 196
Venizelos, Eleutherios, 80, 81, 122

Verdun: state of preparedness, 89, 90, 91; Gallieni warns Joffre, 93, 94; beginning of February 21, 1916, drive, 96; Briand orders defense of city, 98, 99; Joffre's role in defense of city criticized, 110, 111; strategy attacked by Abel Ferry, 118
Villeboisnet, Espivent de la, 117
Viollette, Maurice, 47, 73, 116, 120
Viviani, René, 11; visit to Russia, 13; returns to Paris, 14; receives German war declaration, 15; complains of lack of military information, 26; visits G.Q.G., 34; proposes "Eastern" diversion, 41, 42; promises to respect parliamentary control, 62; harassed by questions of commissions, 65; tries to mollify Sarrail, 72; avoids deputies during height of Sarrail affair, 73; resigns, 83, 137

Weygand, Maxime, 200, 241
Wilhelm, Crown Prince, 211, 212, 226
Wilson, Henry, 207, 208, 209, 211, 214, 215, 216, 217

Ybarnegaray, Jean, 178, 179, 190
"Young Turks," 22, 43, 64, 90, 91, 98, 99, 113, 135

Zimbrakakis, Colonel, 133
Zola, Emile, 8

GENERALS & POLITICIANS

72125180   16—

7/9

WITHDRAWN